An OPUS book

What is Psychotherapy?

Sidney Bloch

What is Psychotherapy?

Oxford New York

OXFORD UNIVERSITY PRESS

1982

Oxford University Press, Walton Street, Oxford OX2 6DP

London Glasgow New York Toronto
Delhi Bombay Calcutta Madras Karachi
Kuala Lumpur Singapore Hong Kong Tokyo
Nairobi Dar es Salaam Cape Town
Melbourne Auckland

and associates in
Beirut Berlin Ibadan Mexico City Nicosia

First published 1982 as an Oxford University Press paperback
and simultaneously in a hardback edition

British Library Cataloguing in Publication Data

Bloch, Sidney
What is psychotherapy?
1. Psychotherapy
I. Title
616.89'14   RC480
ISBN 0-19-219154-3
ISBN 0-19-289142-1 Pbk

Composition in Plantin by
Filmtype Services Limited,
Scarborough, North Yorkshire.
Printed in Great Britain
by Richard Clay (The Chaucer Press) Ltd
Bungay, Suffolk

Contents

For my mother and
to the memory of my father

Preface

Psychotherapy is a complex subject, with a multitude of ramifications. The question of how to present it to the non-specialist general reader, in a book of about 60,000 words, led me to consider a number of possible options. I decided, finally, that the best course was to treat the subject selectively, that is, to cover the essentials of psychotherapy only, and to offer the interested reader further guidance through the bibliographical references for each chapter and through a general list of suggestions for further reading.

As a result, I have covered the subject in the following way. In the introductory chapter I address myself to the question of definition: What is psychotherapy, what are the basic factors that underlie its theory and practice, and what are the common ways in which it is conducted? The highly characteristic relationship between patient and therapist that emerges as most salient in this discussion paves the way for the material dealt with in the next two chapters. In Chapter 2 I first look at the features of the typical person seeking psychotherapy and then at the factors in him which are favourable and unfavourable to improvement. Chapter 3 is similar in that those qualities in the therapist relevant to the effects he produces are considered, in particular the relative weight of the clinician's personality and of the methods and techniques he uses. I also touch briefly on the personal effects of practising as a professional psychotherapist.

One reason for the complexity of psychotherapy is the vast array of theoretical 'schools' that fly its banner. The number well exceeds a hundred and a recent publication, containing almost a thousand pages, describes no less than sixty-four 'innovative' approaches.[1] Rather than whizz through this enormous field, I have taken what I hope is the more sensible course of comparing the three fundamental therapeutic theoretical models of which virtually all others are mere variations or derivatives: the psychodynamic, the humanist-existential and the behavioural. In each case I consider the model's theoretical underpinnings and its practical application in treatment. I also furnish references to its many variations, where appropriate, for the reader who wishes to delve into them.

The chapter on schools of psychotherapy is written only with treatment of the individual patient in mind. In Chapter 5 I turn to the group approach. Again, many contenders compete for our attention, but, in line with my selective approach, I have confined my account to three commonly used group therapies: long-term, small group therapy, family therapy and marital therapy. In addition, because of their contemporary social significance, I consider, somewhat more briefly, the encounter group and the self-help or mutual-help group, and comment on the implications of these new forms of 'group therapy' for traditional psychotherapy.

Since psychotherapy is both an art and a science, I have devoted a special chapter to the place of scientific research. The ground that could be covered here is enormous – the most outstanding handbook[2] of psychotherapy research, for example, is nearly one thousand pages long. My emphasis therefore is on the various approaches available to the researcher in psychotherapy and on the advantages and limitations of these approaches. I then examine what is known about such key issues as the effectiveness of psychotherapy, the comparative value of different schools and forms of treatment, and potential harmful effects. Elsewhere in the book, and especially in Chapters 2 and 3, I have unashamedly referred to the findings of systematic research. I am partly motivated here by the need to dispel the commonly held notion that there are no 'facts' in psychotherapy and that a scientific approach to the subject is incompatible with the 'art' dimension of treatment.

In the final chapter I focus on the ethical dimensions of the practice of psychotherapy. This aspect is often ignored, although it is widely conceded that values do permeate almost every facet of the therapist's work. Many important issues present themselves – among them are confidentiality, the therapist's imposition of his values on to his patient, respect for the patient's basic rights, and the principle of least harm. But I have opted to concern myself with the fundamental question of accountability, that is, the responsibilities and obligations that the psychotherapist has toward his patients, his colleagues and the public.

Two purposes are served by the references for the chapters: the first is the conventional one of indicating the source of a statement or quotation; the second is to guide the reader to books, chapters or articles on topics that, because of limitations of space, I can tackle only briefly or not at all. The general list of suggestions for further reading covers the chief areas of psychotherapy and should be consulted in conjunction with the end-of-chapter bibliographies.

In a book for the non-specialist reader there is always a risk of writing in too technical a style or even in a jargon-ridden way. I have tried not to use jargon. I hope I have also succeeded in avoiding unduly technical language. It seems to me that in writing about psychotherapy for any audience, the simpler the language the better. It can only help to lessen obfuscation, an unfortunately common feature of the psychotherapy literature, and demystify what is an unnecessarily mystique-laden subject.

There are several people I would like to thank most cordially for the help they gave me in writing this book. I am grateful to many of my colleagues with whom I discussed my ideas, particularly Dave Kennard. Liz Burrows was an excellent critic of one of the drafts and made several helpful suggestions. Judith Tuck and Mark Howard, the librarians at the Warneford and Littlemore Hospitals, were exceptionally conscientious at tracking down material, and I am very much in their debt. My sincere thanks to Marie Vickers and Beverly Haggis who typed the manuscript in most co-operative fashion. Adam Sisman originally conceived the idea of the book and I thank him sincerely for all the encouragement he gave me. Nicola Hunter has done a marvellous job as editor, especially in converting my customary technical language into ordinary English. Finally, I would like to thank my wife, Felicity, for her constant support and editorial suggestions.

1 What is psychotherapy?

I have always found it a rather daunting exercise to contemplate the question: 'What is psychotherapy?' There have been many attempts to define psychotherapy; considerable confusion has been the product. Elsewhere, I have written about my own introduction to the world of psychotherapy thus:

The most striking memory I have of my first few months in psychotherapy training was how bewildering it all seemed. No one could define it, controversy raged over the question of its effectiveness, different schools engaged in constant warfare with one another, and the training programme itself lacked goals and a coherent structure.[1]

Fifteen years later, the picture has changed, but, alas, only marginally. Psychotherapy remains a nebulous term with widely differing connotations. There are over a hundred schools of therapy, each with its own theoretical model of normal and abnormal behaviour and its particular set of practical methods. The debate about the clinical efficacy of psychotherapy persists: proponents of one school claim the superiority of its approach to that of its competitors, and there is little consensus about which forms of therapy are genuinely more useful. Unhappily, there is only a tenuous link between scientific research in psychotherapy and clinical practice, and most therapists seem to be only minimally influenced by the findings of research. This is a point which I shall return to later in the chapter but it does raise the question of whether psychotherapy is basically an art or a science. If the latter is the case, research findings should have some bearing on the practitioner's work.[2]

There is still no solid evidence as to what makes a good psychotherapist. Is it a set of personal qualities which no amount of training can engender or are techniques that can be imparted by training of greater relevance? This is an issue we shall have occasion to discuss in a later chapter, on the therapist.

Predictably, in the face of this state of confusion, psychotherapy (like its companion, general psychiatry) is a favourite topic for the humorist and cartoonist, and therapists commonly serve as the butt of unflattering jokes. The image is not only a result of the controversy that envelops psychotherapy but also, in part, a reaction to the psychotherapist's power – he may be ridiculed but he is also held in awe, feared, and even seen by some people as the possessor of the means to control and influence behaviour.

The vagueness of the idea of psychotherapy could be attributed to the uniqueness of each therapeutic encounter. Clearly, the practice of psychotherapy is unlike that of, say, surgery, in which a standard set of techniques is used repeatedly and predictably. We know more or less what a surgeon does in the case of a particular disorder even though there may be some variation in technique. The same cannot be said of psychotherapy. Freud, for example, considered psychoanalytic psychotherapy akin to a game of chess when he wrote:

Anyone who hopes to learn the noble game of chess from books will soon discover that only the openings and end-games admit of an exhaustive, systematic presentation, and that the infinite variety of moves which develop after the opening defy any such description. This gap in instruction can only be filled by a diligent study of games fought out by masters.[3]

He proposed that the practical applications of psychoanalysis in treatment were subject to the same limitations. Despite the use of techniques such as the couch or the therapist's interpretations, the entire middle chunk of treatment was inextricably bound up with the particular relationship established between therapist and patient.

Nearly seventy years later, Freud's position has been tackled head on by various groups of psychotherapists who have promoted the notion of 'manualised psychotherapies'. I offer apologies for such a nasty piece of jargon. The term does however indicate the essential thrust of such an approach. The foremost examples are 'interpersonal therapy',[4] as given in cases of depression at Yale University and 'cognitive-behaviour therapy',[5] also mainly used for depression, and pioneered at the University of Pennsylvania. The therapy is described in the most methodical detail. By contrast with the chess game, the aim is that, throughout the course of therapy, any practitioner of a manualised therapy will act more or less similarly. A parallel is an instruction manual for a technical expert. Psychotherapies of this more modern variety are therefore more preoccupied with the application of highly specific strategies and methods and less on the personality of the therapist.

The researcher's enthusiasm for therapy by manual has become obvious with the choice of treatments like interpersonal therapy and cognitive behaviour therapy in large-scale collaborative research on the effectiveness of psychotherapy. The researcher wishes to ensure that the therapy to be used is well defined so that it can be assumed with reasonable confidence that a highly specific programme of treatment was administered in a similar fashion to each patient.

Thus far I have no doubt merely bewildered the reader and I must now grapple with the question which provides the title of this chapter. Let me attempt to reduce the confusion by dealing with three issues:

1. I shall consider the ways in which psychotherapy has been defined by various experts; this may pave the way for a clearer approach to the question of what it is.

2. I shall focus on certain components of treatment which appear to be shared by all forms of psychotherapy, whatever the school or theory represented. In Chapter 4 I shall do just the opposite – discuss the chief theories of psychotherapy and note their distinctive features. But here our concern is with the factors common to all models. These therapeutic components are usually referred to as non-specific factors, but this may in fact be a misnomer. Probably a more accurate representation of these factors is embodied in the term 'basic common factors' in that they are probably as important as, if not more so than, features which distinguish different forms of treatment. As we shall see presently, basic common factors may well be the core of all psychotherapy.

3. I shall offer a scheme for classifying the major forms of psychotherapy. In a book I edited for trainee psychotherapists, I used the plural form of the subject by entitling the book *An Introduction to the Psychotherapies*.[1] I argued there that several forms of psychotherapeutic treatment can be differentiated according to their goals, techniques, and targets of intervention. A brief presentation of a classification of psychotherapies may, I hope, contribute to answering the question 'What is psychotherapy?'

Definitions of psychotherapy

Literally dozens of definitions are available for our scrutiny. I have selected a few at random in order to convey on the one hand how

divergent definitions can be and on the other hand to highlight features
which are repeatedly included (these features are in italics).

Professor Hans Strupp, a distinguished American psychotherapy
researcher, describes psychotherapy as 'an *interpersonal process* designed to bring about modifications of feelings, cognitions, attitudes,
and behaviour which have proven troublesome to the person seeking
help from a trained professional'.[6]

A popular American textbook of psychiatry defines psychotherapy
as 'the treatment of emotional and personality problems and disorders by psychological means. Although many different psychological techniques may be employed in an effort to relieve problems
and disorders and help the patient become a mature, satisfied and
independent person, an important therapeutic factor common to
them all is the *therapist-patient relationship, with its interpersonal
experiences*. Through this relationship, the patient comes to know that
he or she can share feelings, attitudes and experiences with the
therapist and that the latter, with warmth, understanding, empathy,
acceptance and support, will not deprecate, censure or judge no
matter what may be revealed but will respect the patient's dignity
and worth.'[7]

Anthony Storr, a noted British psychoanalyst, defines
psychotherapy as 'the art of alleviating personal difficulties through
the agency of words and a *personal, professional relationship*'.[8]

Contrasting with Storr's emphasis on a personal and professional
relationship, Thomas Szasz, the fiery critic of psychiatry, argues that
'psychotherapy refers to what two or more people do with, for and to
each other, by means of verbal and non-verbal messages. It is, in short,
a relationship comparable to friendship, marriage, religious obser-
vance, advertising or teaching.'[9] Szasz appears to be referring to a
more egalitarian form of relationship in which those involved act
reciprocally on each other. Here, he differs from most writers who, as
is reflected in the preceding definitions, differentiate between the
person giving the treatment and the person who seeks it.

Indeed, probably the most commonly emphasised characteristic in
almost all definitions of psychotherapy is the therapist – patient
relationship. Apart from Szasz, this relationship is generally viewed as
being different from other forms of relationship such as friendship or
marriage in important and fundamental ways. The person who makes
himself available as a therapist is in effect a socially sanctioned healer
who has been designated thus by virtue of his training and skills. The

therapist is a professional who makes a commitment to help others in need of his expertise.

The person who seeks out the therapist, whether directly or indirectly through, for example, his family doctor, does so invariably because of some overwhelming need. It may be to reduce suffering and distress or to find out how to cope more effectively with life's demands or to learn more about himself in order to live more creatively and fulfillingly or, as in the case of the trainee therapist, to uncover psychological blind spots which impair his effectiveness. Sometimes, the need is far from clear and may amount only to a general sense of dissatisfaction. But no matter how covert the problems, the essential point is that an individual designates himself as in need of help and chooses someone who has been socially sanctioned as able to provide that help.

I have perhaps laboured this centrality of the therapist – patient relationship and its composite parts but it is the one feature that is included in almost all definitions of psychotherapy and is at the heart of the subject. I should qualify these remarks by alluding to a development which I shall describe in a later chapter: the phenomenon of self-help. It has become increasingly commonplace for those who regard themselves as in need of help to approach others with similar difficulties so that through a process of mutual help and understanding, these common difficulties can be dealt with. In this context, the relationship remains all important but the professional healer is dispensed with. As this development is still in its infancy and is unlikely to make a take-over bid for psychotherapy as a whole, I defer my discussion of it until later.

Apart from self-help, observers can point out that psychotherapy has also been conducted by 'mechanical aids'. In a significant research study on encounter groups (for a definition see pp. 127 *et seq.*) at Stanford University, two of the student groups investigated were led by 'tape recorders'.[10] The participants were played tapes on which were recorded instructions on how the group should proceed. Similarly, there are reports of video-taped material being used. These developments do not however undermine the premiss that the therapist–patient relationship is supreme. After all, the tapes, whether they be audio or video, have been prepared by human beings, and their voices and in the case of video, their faces, are decidedly present. In this vein, would it be fanciful to envisage a computer-therapist? Some intriguing efforts have been made here. Kenneth Colby, a Californian psychoanalyst, has undertaken, in all seriousness, a project in which he attempts to programme a computer in order that the programmed 'therapist' can 'relate' to someone seeking its aid. Of course we still have the human hand at the controls; Colby devised the computer programme in the first place. Moreover, it is almost inconceivable that a person in real distress would opt for a computer-therapist in preference to a human one. What might be possible is the evolution of a computerised method to diagnose a patient's state and to assign the person to the form of psychotherapy which, according to the scientific evidence available, best suited him. The human therapist would then replace the computer-assessor.

In addition to the basic pattern we have established so far – the coming together of a person who seeks help with another person who is designated as a healer – it is obvious from the definitions I have cited that there is something intrinsically helpful and therapeutic about the interpersonal process that takes place. It is to a consideration of this process that we now turn our attention.

We have now entered the territory of the *common basic factors* which I mentioned earlier. The delineation of these common factors is somewhat arbitrary – the pie can be cut in different ways. Let us however consider the approach adopted by Jerome Frank, a doyen of American psychotherapy research and practice, and the person principally responsible for bringing the concept of common factors into prominence. What is especially impressive about Frank's contribution is its blend of cautiously formulated theory and the scientific testing of the validity of different facets of that theory. Rather unusually, Frank and his psychotherapy research colleagues at Johns Hopkins University, conducted a whole series of investigations to try to unravel the questions they had encountered in clinical practice. In psychotherapy, this is undoubtedly the most productive way to proceed. Ideas and problems stemming from the actual clinical practice of psychotherapy are translated into hypotheses which can be subjected to systematic investigation. The adoption of such an approach has been relatively uncommon in psychotherapy. More common is the generation and proliferation of theoretical concepts many of which are so esoteric as to preclude them from conversion into testable hypotheses.

Professor Frank[11] suggests that six factors are common to all forms of psychotherapy. He regards them as necessary although not sufficient in themselves for psychotherapy to operate. The factors are:

1. An intense, emotionally charged confiding relationship, with a helping person;

2. A rationale which contains an explanation of the patient's distress and of the methods for its relief;

3. The provision of new information about the nature and origins of the patient's problems and of ways of dealing with them;

4. Hope in the patient that he can expect help from the therapist;

5. An opportunity for experiences of success during the course of therapy and a consequent enhancement of the sense of mastery;

6. The facilitation of emotional arousal in the patient.

Frank's first factor is reflected in most of the definitions we considered earlier. The description of the type of relationship is revealing. Unlike an ordinary social interaction, it has an intense quality – patient and therapist are meeting on serious business; the patient is sufficiently distressed or disabled to have sought out a professional's help while the therapist has made a firm commitment to offer his personal resources in conjunction with his professional skills. The relationship could not be otherwise but emotionally charged. After all the patient is invariably upset or disturbed, and often quite desperate for help. The therapist for his part enters into the emotionally charged situation even though he may maintain a certain sense of detachment so as to be able to view the patient and his problems more objectively. A useful term in this context is participant observation – the therapist must, in order to reach an understanding of his patient, place himself in the patient's shoes and attempt to appreciate what the patient is experiencing. Yet, at the same time, the therapist remains a kind of observer and does not become so immersed in the patient's world that he thenceforth does little else but ward off the threat of being totally submerged.

The confiding nature of the relationship is intrinsic to psychotherapy. It goes without saying that the therapist can be of little use if the patient does not disclose his problems, feelings, fantasies and attitudes. Ostensibly therapeutic in itself is the process of self-disclosure. The patient makes public (in the sense that the therapist is initially a stranger to him) what has hitherto remained private or perhaps has only been divulged in part to intimates such as family members. This act of self-disclosure is associated with the sharing of what is typically painful, threatening, embarrassing, depressing or shameful. Often, the confiding quality is implicit. The mere occurrence of a meeting in a private room for example is an intimation to the patient that confidentiality is a priority. More often than not, the therapist highlights the prominent place of confidentiality and this enhances the sense of security the patient enjoys.

Note that Frank refers to the therapist as a 'helping' person. This is a reminder that a tape recorder or a computer are unlikely to match the helping qualities evinced by the human therapist. His decision in the first place to commit himself to a patient is testimony of his willingness to be helpful. (Motives may be otherwise on occasion. For example, some therapists may ostensibly take on a helping role but are primarily interested in using the relationship for research or other purposes.) Once therapy is in motion, a whole spectrum of communication from therapist to patient conveys his helpful stance. The use of gestures such as nodding the head or sitting forward in the chair; the discreet use of touch; encouraging the patient to make direct visual contact; demonstrating his ability to attend actively – these are some of the non-verbal means whereby the patient can come to trust in the helpfulness of his therapist. Then obviously there is communication by words. An encouraging comment, a remark which testifies to the therapist's understanding of the patient's dilemma, an explicit invitation to the patient to feel confident in sharing his difficulties, and to be trusting are only some of the messages a therapist conveys in an effort to act benevolently.

Many of the features mentioned also typify other helpful human relationships. A close friendship and a good marriage are obvious examples. The important distinguishing feature is that the psychotherapy relationship incorporates a helper who is socially sanctioned in that role and has been formally designated to act as the healing agency. To repeat Anthony Storr's phrase, the relationship is a 'personal professional' one. As we shall see in a moment, the professional basis of the therapeutic relationship is relevant to at least two of Frank's other common factors, factors which could not be incorporated into a non-professional helping relationship such as friendship or marriage. Before moving on to a consideration of these other factors, I should point out that various investigations into the patient as consumer of psychotherapy tend to point to his emphasis on the therapist as a form of friend who is understanding, accepting, respectful, encouraging, trustworthy, willing to help. Technical expertise is secondary to this image of the therapist as a benign, kind and helpful person. Indeed, so important is this emphasis that the Chicago psychoanalytic school have put forward the notion of the 'corrective emotional experience'. This implies that the patient comes to enjoy a new experience of relating closely to another person which can in turn, serve as a model for other intimate relationships. It constitutes some proof that the patient can enter into such a relationship, even if he has not had such opportunities previously, in particular with his own family.

The second common factor advanced by Frank is the shared belief by patient and therapist in a rationale which includes an explanation of the patient's problems and of the treatment methods used for their solution. A person who seeks relief from his distress through psychotherapy is commonly perplexed – his experience is baffling and seemingly irrational. The therapist's provision of the rationale contributes to a diminution in the patient's state of confusion; even giving a complaint a name is helpful.

Paradoxically, the exact content of the rationale does not seem crucial; more important is the confidently held belief by the therapist that his theoretical propositions and the related practical methods he uses in treatment are beneficial. Equally important is the patient's acceptance of the rationale as making sense and offering some order to his state of disarray. Generally, the rationale is compatible with the outlook of the world of both patient and therapist. We may compare this factor's relevance to the tribal witch-doctor–client relationship. The witch-doctor holds views which are intimately bound up with tribal custom and heritage. His client comes to share these views, finding it reasonably easy to do so because of their association with tribal tradition. In many ways there is a parallel between the witch-doctor–client relationship and the Western-based psycho-therapist–patient relationship with the factor of shared rationale prominent in both. The close link between the rationale and the world view of both healer and client in both cases is obvious if we consider the likely results were a witch-doctor to attempt to treat a woman born and bred in an English village and conversely were a Western psychoanalyst to try to analyse a member of a remote Tanzanian tribe! The discrepancies in world view would preclude any possibility of the sharing of a rationale or myth.

The need for a belief in a rationale is probably of equal importance for both therapist and patient. We have already commented on the patient's need to unravel the confusion which has enveloped him in the course of his distress. The vast majority of therapists require a rationale in order to pursue their task effectively. Imagine for a moment the therapist who is uncertain about the methods he uses. His ambivalence soon becomes transparent leading to disillusionment on the part of the patient. Most therapists, although tolerant of ambiguity and uncertainty, still require a framework within which to conduct their enterprise. Only the occasional therapist can dispense with a theoretical model and work exclusively on the basis of trial and error and reliance on personal experience. Experience is undoubtedly a great teacher to every therapist but only within the context of an adopted set of theoretical suppositions. A dangerous side-effect of the dependence on theory needs mention: the assumption of a rationale to help protect the therapist from his failures. If his patients do not benefit from his methods, it need not be the theory that is faulty but rather the unsuitability of the patients in the first place or their disinclination for whatever reason to exploit the therapist's theory.

Closely linked to the shared rationale is the therapist's provision of information, new to the patient, about the nature and, sometimes, origin of his problems and ways of grappling with them. Here we note a didactic role in psychotherapy – it is essentially an opportunity for learning. Again, as in the case of the shared rationale, the specific content of what is learnt may not be critical – so long as it is experienced as useful by the patient. It is not so much the discovery of the precisely accurate explanation of his problems that matters but an account which is perceived as coherent, logical and illuminating. The added significance of this factor above and beyond the shared rationale factor is that the patient experiences psychotherapy as a forum for learning about himself and for determining ways of overcoming his problems. In many schools of psychotherapy, the process is one of self-discovery with the therapist helping as facilitator. In other approaches, the therapist assumes a more strictly pedagogic role whereby he educates his patient about the nature and causes of his troubles and/or instructs him on how to go about their solution.

If the learning quality of psychotherapy is so central, could it be practised along educational lines? Can we envisage the use of a typical classroom situation in which mental-health experts enlighten their patient-audience? Or even more simply, could those who are in distress study psychotherapeutic 'guides for the perplexed'? These alternatives are not too fanciful and indeed in some psychotherapy practices, the patient's role is akin to that of a student. Reading tasks and homework of various kinds are in fact becoming more popular. One prominent psychotherapist in California has adopted a procedure in which the patient attends therapy sessions for two months and then has a third month on his own to do some independent learning about himself and his experience; moreover, a comprehensive reading list of texts is provided for this independent study.

These developments however can only be secondary to a unique learning experience that takes place in psychotherapy. The fact that people in psychological need usually find books on mental health and psychotherapy of only limited help testifies to the peculiar type of learning characteristic of psychotherapy. It is a form of learning rather difficult to depict in words. Probably the commonest term used for the lesson learned is insight and a focus on this term may help to understand the learning that takes place in therapy. Insight is defined in Webster's dictionary as 'the ability to see and understand clearly the inner nature of things' or as 'a clear understanding of the inner nature of some specific thing'. In therapy, the patient comes to understand the nature of various aspects of himself – he is the subject of his understanding. And because the process is inevitably intensely personal, the learning embraces the intellectual, perceptual, emotional and fantasy dimensions of the individual. The term commonly used in this context is 'experiential learning'. This is an apt term in that it conveys what is a central characteristic of learning in psychotherapy: that it involves the patient understanding all that he experiences in treatment.

A useful illustration is the place of dreams. The patient may have a particularly emotionally-charged dream which he then shares with his therapist. Invariably, the dream is far from straightforward and rational and includes all variety of the patient's psychic experience. Moreover, when a patient talks about the dream, it conjures up in him further fantasies, thoughts and feelings all of which are of potential significance and may require attention. Thus, in examining the dream in therapy, the process cannot possibly be limited to a detached intellectual appraisal for this will negate the many other elements that comprise the overall experiencing of the dream and its recall.

Another term useful in our discussion of the nature of learning in psychotherapy is the 'self-reflective loop'. The term has been coined to reflect the learning that occurs in group therapy but it is indeed applicable to all forms of psychotherapy. The patient undergoes some intense experience in the course of a session; he is encouraged to immerse himself thoroughly in it without inhibition or constraint, and, when the intensity of the experience has waned, the self-reflective loop comes into operation. The patient now attempts to stand back somewhat from what he has just gone through in order to try and make sense of the experience. A patient, for example, has reminisced about his adolescence and recalled a key event in which his older brother was prominently involved. Without warning, the patient has found himself harbouring intense envy for the brother followed by waves of shame. The experience becomes even more elaborate and endures for the entire session. In the following session the patient begins to reflect on the experience and tries to make sense of his feelings of envy and shame. He comes to appreciate that he has always felt inferior to his more successful brother, and tended to feel envious of his success, but he has strenuously buried those envious feelings when they have arisen in the past. He begins to sense that his feelings of shame are linked with his uncontrolled outburst of envy. Henceforth, the patient will proceed to unravel the component parts of the experience further but not necessarily on an analytic plane alone. In further exploration, additional feelings and fantasies may arise which may shed yet further light on the problems he has had in relation to his brother.

I have anticipated, and to a large extent dealt with, Frank's sixth factor – the need for emotional arousal in a patient to achieve learning and associated change in behaviour. It is a well-established observation that a psychotherapy encounter devoid of emotion is highly unlikely to prove profitable. A patient's cool, rational view of himself and his difficulties is rarely followed by substantial change. In ways which are not easily definable the patient must repeatedly enter a state of emotional arousal. We have already cited the example of the man with feelings of envy and shame. It is only with those feelings fully experienced that he can come to an appreciation of what they may represent. Similarly with a vast range of other feelings including anger, apprehension, grief, jealousy and guilt. Not uncommonly patients enter therapy with an array of confusing feelings about themselves and their relationships. By facilitating the expression of this constellation of feelings, the therapist helps the patient to discover the emotions that are at the core of his experience and to appreciate what relevance they have to his problems. Conversely, a patient entering therapy may be quite unable to get in touch with his feelings no matter how hard he tries. Here the therapist has an important role to help such a patient to overcome his inhibitions with the assurance that whatever feelings emerge will be tolerated and respected.

When a person consults a psychotherapist, he generally does so in the hope that his distress will be relieved or his difficulty in functioning improved. The arousal of hope that life will be better as a result of treatment is undoubtedly a cogent factor common to all forms of psychotherapy. Frank and his colleagues[12] have shown how crucial the factor of hope is in a variety of ingenious experiments. They took as a basis for their work the well-recognised placebo effect. This refers to the positive effects of a pharmacologically inert substance, such as a sugar pill. Since the pill has no active ingredient, its effectiveness must be attributable to other factors. The most obvious of these is the recipient's suggestibility; that whatever he is being administered by a person who is sanctioned as the healer will be beneficial. This suggestibility is reinforced by the healer's investment in the inert substance; it has been shown that the effectiveness of placebo administration is in part a function of the enthusiasm of the doctor. Even in the administration of pharmacologically active drugs, there seems to be a relationship between the level of enthusiasm the physician has for the drug and the response shown by his patient. Thus, as might be expected, the physician who has great faith in the drug he uses, will produce greater benefit in his patients compared to his colleague who is ambivalent about the drug's potency or about administering drugs in the first place. The placebo effect is so strong that even in circumstances where recipients of a placebo are informed at the time of administration that the substance is inert, benefits can still occur. Clearly the pill has immense symbolic significance and represents the considerable powers invested in the physician by the patient.

The same is true of the psychotherapist. He does not administer a pill but the level of enthusiasm and optimism he conveys to his patient represents his contribution to the placebo effect. The patient for his part has decided to seek help from a professional therapist in the hope that his situation can be altered for the better. His choice of a professional therapist is not accidental. He has ascertained through hearsay or via the media or from a family member or friend who has undergone psychotherapy that he stands a good chance of deriving benefit. He usually has some notion about the therapist's professional status – that he is a psychiatrist, social worker, clinical psychologist or other mental-health professional – who has undertaken a comprehensive training and must consequently know something about the business of helping people like himself. This appreciation of his status may be reinforced by a knowledge that a particular therapist has written scholarly articles or books or is a teacher of the subject or has had years of experience. The therapist's work setting is another factor influencing the arousal of hope. If a therapist works in a respected institution, the patient inevitably identifies his particular therapist with the whole institution. Indeed, some institutions are so well established and known that their mere mention conjures up in the prospective patient a sense of optimism: he is to receive help from the 'right hands'. Once in the institution, the therapist's office is yet a further factor in promoting hope for change. Customarily, the office contains a personal library of books and related files which demonstrate the therapist's professionalism and potential expertise. The therapist's receptionist or his answering service are further illustrations of his professional standing. The other obvious side of the placebo effect in psychotherapy, to which we alluded above, is the therapist's personal qualities. The therapist who demonstrates a sense of optimism will invariably transmit that optimism to his patient. The mere fact that the therapist is taking on the patient for treatment indicates that he has some confidence that improvement is possible. The patient also may assume, justifiably in part, that the therapist has treated others in the past like himself and that the results of those encounters were presumably favourable.

There has long been debate about the ethical questions surrounding the use of the placebo effect. Certainly when it comes to using an inert substance like a sugar pill, critics have argued that such practice is deceptive and demeaning. A counter-argument is based on pragmatism – if a placebo can produce improvement, is it not negligent to avoid its usage? Why prescribe a pharmacologically active substance with its attendant dangers and side-effects when a totally innocuous substance will do? In psychotherapy, the issue is perhaps less complicated. The arousal of hope undoubtedly occurs whatever the therapist's attitude to it. It could be maintained, again on grounds of pragmatism, that if this arousal of hope is a potent ingredient of change, then it should be exploited without hesitancy. The research evidence[13] on the question is somewhat equivocal. A number of experiments have been conducted to try to demonstrate whether the explicit promotion of positive expectations in the patient has a beneficial effect. Interestingly, those studies in which the therapists were familiar with the aim of the experiment and aware that they were comparing two groups – one in which the patient's hopes were intentionally aroused and the other in which they were not more aroused than in the usual practice – found that the level of improvement was greater when the placebo effect was maximised. But it may not have been the placebo effect at work but rather the zeal and eagerness of the therapist, motivated to see the experiment succeed. Notwithstanding, there does seem to be evidence that a patient's faith and trust in his therapist's powers to help is influential in all psychotherapies.

It will be clear from the above discussion that the placebo effect is particularly relevant before therapy is instituted and in the early phases of treatment. Thereafter, hope for improvement may be maintained or even strengthened if therapy progresses satisfactorily. Conversely, hopes may be dashed for one reason or another. In the former case, the reinforcement of initial positive expectations, Frank's fifth factor comes into play. This is the opportunity that psychotherapy provides for experiences of success. As a patient overcomes his difficulties, begins to comprehend the nature of his problems and enjoys new favourable experiences, so he develops a growing sense of self-confidence. More often than not, patients enter psychotherapy with a record of repeated failures be they in the sphere of social relationships, work, sex or generally an inability to cope with the ordinary demands and challenges of their lives. The actual record may not be as grim as the patient himself perceives it but whatever the case he enters therapy with the idea that his achievements are minimal and his chances of enjoying any success paltry. Not unusually, self-esteem is at an all-time low. A chief function of therapy is to reverse the image the patient has of himself and this can be achieved in no better way than by heightening his sense of mastery and ability to cope. Most schools of psychotherapy would recognise this as an essential ingredient although the degree of explicitness in which experiences of success are identified varies. The behavioural therapy school is probably most aware of the need for direct acknowledgement of a patient's achievements. Behaviour therapists, as we shall see in Chapter 5, emphasise two points in this regard – first, providing a chance for the patient to effect actual changes in his behaviour which can be readily observed and monitored; second, setting graded tasks so that the patient encounters relatively undemanding tasks to achieve at first and once having established mastery of those minor tasks proceeds to slightly more demanding tasks, and so on. With an experience of success at each level of task, self-confidence is reinforced and contributes to an optimistic tackling of the next task.

Whether the approach is explicit or not, the ultimate aim of all psychotherapies is to instil in a patient the sense that he is capable, can attain a substantial measure of self-control rather than be the victim of his environment, and that he can have a reasonable self-image.

Classifying the psychotherapies

In discussing the definition of the term psychotherapy, I used its singular form. Now, as we attempt to classify the various treatments that are conventionally regarded as examples of psychotherapy, the plural form of the term is more appropriate. As surgery can be further sub-divided into its various branches – neurosurgery, cardio-thoracic surgery and so forth, so can psychotherapy be categorised. But the picture is somewhat more complicated in psychotherapy because there are so many ways of doing this. One classification of the psychotherapies revolves around theory and thus we have classical psychoanalytic psychotherapy, Jungian therapy, Adlerian therapy, Kleinian therapy, and all the other derivatives of basic Freudian theory named after the schools' founders, Rogerian therapy, existential therapy, Gestalt therapy, transactional analysis, behaviour therapy, and many many more beside. We shall consider some of these schools in Chapter 5.

Another approach to classification is according to the target of treatment. Obvious examples here include family and marital therapy in which attention is focused on relationships between members of a family on the premiss that it is in the sphere of relationships that the trouble lies, and sex therapy where the obvious focus is a sexual relationship. Family, marital and sex therapies are in a sense group therapies since more than one patient is treated at the same time. But the groups are obviously naturally-occurring. Groups can also be composed of strangers who meet so that their individual problems can be dealt with chiefly by focusing on the way group members behave towards each other. We shall return to these group psychotherapies in Chapter 6.

A third way to classify the psychotherapies is in terms of the goals of treatment. Categorising the psychotherapies thus is revealing of their diverse nature. There is no standard classification in this context; let me present my own efforts for what they are worth. First, *crisis intervention* – as the name indicates, the therapist intervenes actively in the midst of some crisis that has befallen his patient with the goal of helping that patient to overcome the crisis. Second, *supportive psychotherapy* – the term describes the objective of treatment which is the provision of support to the patient who cannot cope without it, either in the short or long-term. There is an obvious overlap between crisis intervention and supportive therapy in that support is basic to both but supportive therapy is the term generally applied to treatment of those with a need for prolonged support, often life-long. Third, *symptom-oriented psychotherapy* – it is hard to find a better term than this to describe those psychotherapies in which the goal is limited to the relief of symptoms presented by the patient (the behavioural psychotherapy approach is most applicable here). No substantial change in personality is sought and there is no requirement for the patient to acquire insight into, or understanding about, the nature of his symptoms. Fourth, and contrasting with all these categories, is *insight-oriented psychotherapy*. Here, the aim, as the term suggests, is insight on the part of the patient into the nature of his problems and their origin. One leading American psychotherapist has labelled this last category 'reconstructive therapy', but I must declare my prejudice against this term in so far as it is rather mechanistic in quality. Although the focus is on the acquisition of insight, the assumption is usually made that changes in behaviour and personality will follow. Let us now consider the four categories in more detail.

Crisis intervention[14] – fortunate and exceptional is the person who is spared major stress during his life. We are all prone to crises of various kinds at different stages in the life cycle. That most crises do not require professional attention can be attributed to a mixture of three factors – a person's capacity to adjust to the stress involved by using his personal resources, help commonly obtained from key people such as family and friends, and the fact that the crisis may be of only moderate intensity. But, even a person with a well integrated personality can be engulfed and overwhelmed by a major crisis. Erik Erikson[15] has differentiated between developmental and accidental crises. The former are those potentially traumatic transitional periods at particular points in the life cycle, such as early adolescence, the menopause and the onset of old age; these periods are commonly marked by psychological distress. Accidental crises, as the name suggests, occur as a result of some specific incident – bereavement, loss of job, physical illness, divorce, among others.

Whatever form a crisis takes, the person's usual methods of coping become ineffective. The result is acute distress – expressed variously as anxiety, depression, guilt, irritability, sense of helplessness and sense of hopelessness – which rises to an uncomfortable level, and the associated failure to function adequately in customary social roles.

The person, now quite unable to cope in his state of crisis, attempts to gain relief by seeking the assistance of a professional psychotherapist with the appeal: 'Please help me deal with the problem which seems to have got the better of me.' The therapist responds by providing a supportive framework within which his transiently disabled patient can acquire a breathing-space, feel hopeful about obtaining help and receive reassurance and guidance. Invariably, a contract is established, either explicit or implicit, in which therapist and patient agree on a collaborative endeavour whose objectives are relief from distress and better adaptive coping with the stress. In most cases the treatment programme lasts a period of weeks, frequency of contact is weekly or twice weekly, the length of each session is between half and one hour, and there is possible involvement of others such as the family, employer or schoolteacher. Ideally, both patient and therapist are aware of the objectives and methods of treatment and recognise and accept their proper roles and tasks. It is emphasised that the patient's need to forego some measure of independence is temporary and that as he comes to feel and function better he will resume his former responsibility for himself.

The goal of relief from the effects of the crisis may be supplemented by a form of new learning. Gerald Caplan,[16] in his elaborate account of crisis theory, asserts that the experience of a crisis can bring benefits by facilitating the development of new effective methods of coping and solving problems. The patient can thus not only emerge from what was an overwhelming crisis but also acquire in the process a wider and richer psychological repertoire to call upon in the event of future stress.

Supportive psychotherapy[17] – this term is usually reserved to describe the psychological care of the chronically handicapped patient. Such a patient is typically disabled by an enduring condition that is not amenable to fundamental change; patients with chronic schizophrenia, chronic neurosis and severe disorders of personality fall into this category. These patients are often impaired socially and either lack intimate relationships or are unable to maintain them; their record of work is often erratic and poor; commonly they have been hospitalised on one or more occasion, and they are prone to break down even under relatively mild stress.

Supportive therapy is probably the most commonly applied psychological treatment in mental-health practice and yet it is the most difficult to define. The word support is derived from *sub* – under, and *portare* – to carry. The therapist 'carries' the patient by helping to prop him up and to sustain him. The obvious implication is that the patient is so handicapped by his condition that he requires from the therapist a form of psychological aid which enables him to 'survive'. The objectives of supportive therapy are: to promote the patient's best possible emotional and social functioning by restoring and reinforcing his personal resources; to boost his self-esteem; to make him appreciative of his own limitations and those of treatment, of what can and cannot be achieved; to try and avoid a relapse of his condition and thus deterioration or rehospitalisation; to enable the patient to require only that measure of professional support which results in his optimal adjustment (and so prevents undue dependency); and to transfer some of the support from professional to family or friends if they are available and competent.

Because of the chronic nature of his condition, the patient often requires help for several years, if not for life. A medical parallel is the chronic diabetic patient who, because of the incurability of the condition and its association with severe complications, requires medical supervision throughout his life.

The therapist–patient relationship in supportive psychotherapy is characterised by the active and directive role which the therapist plays. He assumes a level of responsibility, which is not seen in other forms of psychotherapy, on the premiss that his patient's chronic handicap precludes him from caring for himself independently. The relationship resembles that between parent and child. The chief components of therapy include reassurance and simple explanation about such matters as the nature of the symptoms, the reasons for a relapse and the rationale for medication. Guidance is a core component of supportive therapy, mainly by means of direct advice. The focus is on practical issues including such fundamental matters as budgeting, personal hygiene and nutrition. Sometimes advice is ineffective or inadequate and persuasion is then necessary with the therapist moving from a gently directive posture to a more controlling one in an effort to convince his patient to act in a particular way. Suggestion is similar to guidance but the patient is offered less choice in deciding whether to comply or not. Here the therapist attempts to induce a change by influencing the patient implicitly or explicitly. A mainstay of supportive therapy is encouragement, the objective behind which is to combat feelings of inferiority, to promote self-esteem, and to urge the patient to adopt some behaviour of which he is frightened. The therapist can also effect changes in the patient's environment. Any stress factors can be suitably modified. Environmental changes of a more positive kind, by adding something to the world of the patient, are as important as the removal of stress. Thus, participation in appropriate social activities and hobbies is actively encouraged.

Typically the provision of supportive psychotherapy is on a regular continuing basis (although the therapist may change periodically because the treatment lasts many years). The frequency of contact varies according to the patient's circumstances, from monthly to three monthly. The duration of each session is usually no longer than a half hour. Participation of a family member is common, so that he can be guided by the therapist in how to offer helpful 'natural' support.

Symptom-oriented psychotherapy – as I have already mentioned, symptom-oriented psychotherapy is a rather poor term and I only use it in the absence of a better alternative. The idea however is conveyed that the goal of this category of psychotherapy is the relief of complaints that the patient has. The therapist sets out specifically to help the patient gain relief from his distressing symptoms. Nothing more is aimed for although there are potential spin-offs in terms of understanding the patient may acquire about the underlying basis for his symptoms. Symptomatic treatment is often associated with the prescribing of medication – a tranquilliser to reduce anxiety, a hypnotic to promote better sleep, an antidepressant to relieve depression, and so forth. Symptomatic psychotherapy may indeed be given in tandem with one of these drugs but a general aim is the substitution of the drug by the psychologically-based treatment and thus the avoidance of possible problems like drug dependency.

An illustration of symptom-oriented psychotherapy is the various psychological procedures to reduce anxiety. Anxiety-management training is a commonly applied term in this regard. A wide spectrum of techniques is available ranging from Eastern approaches like transcendental meditation and yoga to muscular relaxation. Some relaxation methods have also been used in the treatment of insomnia. Training in social skills[18] is another example of a symptom-oriented psychotherapy but in this case the therapist aims to improve and amplify a patient's repertoire of social skills. Here there is a slight shift from the attempt to remove or reduce a distressing symptom or troublesome behaviour to introducing some new form of behaviour or effecting an improvement in one that is inadequate. Typically, a person who enters a training programme in social skills describes his inability to initiate contact with others, his apprehension about relating in a social group, his inability to eat with others in a canteen, and so forth. In therapy, the question of why these difficulties exist or how they came about is not examined. Instead, a number of patients with similar social difficulties are brought together and directed by the therapist to participate in a series of structured exercises. These include the practice of direct visual contact with others, a focus on how the patient speaks, and taking part in various role-plays. An example of the last might be a patient acting out his entry into a staff canteen and eating with his colleagues.

I have already mentioned that the behavioural school of psychotherapy tends, by and large, to adopt a symptom-oriented approach but since behaviour therapy is discussed in detail in Chapter 4, let us now proceed to consider the fourth category of psychotherapy.

Insight-oriented psychotherapy – Freud once commented that the aim of psychoanalysis was to 'secure the best possible psychological condition for the functions of the ego'.[19] The conditions he had in mind were freedom from symptoms, a reduction in anxiety and inhibition, and an understanding of what was formerly unintelligible and baffling. Although Freud himself did not define the aim of psychoanalysis as the acquisition of insight, the concept has become popular among both classical analysts and practitioners of psychodynamic therapies whose propositions stem from his theories. Freud's own notion was that therapy should aim to make what was previously unconscious conscious, particularly through the interpretation of dreams. Whether we consider insight in Freudian terms or in a wider sense, three chief strands are involved. The first is the recognition and understanding of the unconsciously determined type of relationship that evolves between patient and therapist during the course of treatment (the so-called transference, which is dealt with in Chapter 4). The second is the identification of the mechanisms of defence[20] customarily used by the patient. These are unconsciously determined strategies which a person utilises to ward off unpalatable or threatening feelings and thoughts. They include repression – a process of active forgetting of threatening material which is kept in the unconscious; denial – a self-deception whereby the reality of a situation is minimised or avoided; rationalisation – some plausible explanation is given to account for a threat but the explanation is patently ill-founded; projection – placing unacceptable feelings outside oneself and attributing them to others;

and regression – reverting to earlier modes of behaviour, usually child-like or even infant-like. These mechanisms, and others like them, are used by any person as an essential part of his psychological function. It is when the use of one or more of them becomes exaggerated and extreme that normal personality development and functioning is interfered with. The third aspect of insight entails exploring, discovering and comprehending the relationship between current personality traits and modes of behaviour, and key events of the past, usually from childhood.

Lest this all sounds too technical let me offer a case illustration. A student in her twenties became excessively dependent on her therapist, hanging on his every word and apparently completely unable to take any decisions on her own or indeed act independently in any way. Her dependency on the therapist was highlighted in her requests for extra appointments, acute distress when holiday breaks occurred, and frequent attempts to make contact by telephone. This then was the pattern of her relationship with her therapist. Or to put it in other words, her transference to him was similar to that of a young child on a parent. She had come to therapy in the first place because of the series of disastrous relationships with men. Invariably, her boyfriends had retreated in the face of her ever growing and exceptional demands on them. She was inclined to cling to each of them almost as if she were a babe and in no way could a normal adult heterosexual relationship evolve. When challenged by her most recent boyfriend to stand on her own two feet and stop clinging to him, her retort was to deny that she was relating in the way he described and to concede, that even if this were partially true, she had every reason to depend on him for some things. After all, wasn't he older and more experienced than herself, and a man to boot! Surely, it was one of his functions to protect her.

Here we see at least three defence mechanisms in operation, namely, regression, partial denial and rationalisation. In the course of therapy it became obvious that her clinging dependency, both to her therapist and to her boyfriends, was intimately bound up with a most insecure early childhood. A daughter of a military family, her father was frequently away from home, sometimes for periods of several months. Moreover the family moved on several occasions during the patient's first five years, following which she went to a boarding-school for her primary and secondary school education. She had never felt a member of a family and in particular had little idea of what her father was like and what feelings he had towards her. He was a remote figure, often geographically and always psychologically. Her insight-oriented therapy succeeded in unearthing all these threads so that she came to make sense of her transference, her typical defences and the connections between her early family life and contemporary difficulties in relating to men.

Little purpose would be served by the acquisition of insight alone. In the case of the student, for example, even her full understanding of her problems and their origin would be of little point unless this was accompanied or followed by some enduring changes in her personality. In her case the appropriate change presumably would be the ability to relate in an adult fashion to a man, without recourse to dependent-like behaviour. Most therapists who practise insight-oriented therapy hold the notion that fully-fledged insight is a prerequisite to behavioural change (in contrast to behaviour therapists who argue that changes in behaviour can be tackled directly without the intermediary of insight). The issue of whether behavioural change must actually occur during the course of treatment is more debatable, with some therapists arguing that 'the proof of the pudding is in the eating', and others claiming that the patient is liberated from neurotic inhibition through the acquisition of insight with consequent behavioural change inevitable. This latter position is also conceptualised in terms of 'un-blocking' – the patient has been trapped in his neurosis, often for many years, quite unable to experience normal psychological growth. Insight-oriented psychotherapy helps to extract him from this trap: he is thus no longer blocked and can develop freely. This notion of growth is closely linked with insight. Terms such as self-realisation, self-actualisation and increased awareness all point to a major aim of insight-oriented psychotherapy – to enable the patient to express himself creatively and fulfillingly. Goals of this kind are particularly associated with the humanist-existential school of psychotherapy which I discuss in Chapter 5. Here, it is sufficient to mention that these sorts of goals are more vague and amorphous than those formulated by the more traditional psychoanalytic schools.

Summary

In this chapter we have tried to define the nature of psychotherapy. It must be obvious that this is no easy matter. Notwithstanding, we can conclude, at the least, that psychotherapy is an interpersonal process in which a socially sanctioned professional healer meets with a person who seeks out help because of incapacitating distress or an inability to function adequately. More than one healer and more than one patient may be involved at the same time. What occurs between healer and patient varies tremendously. Common to all psychotherapy however is a relationship which is emotionally charged and confidential and in which both therapist and patient agree on a rationale which serves as an explanation of the patient's problems and of the methods to deal with them.

Psychotherapy is probably better conceptualised as the 'psychotherapies' since there are many different forms. These can be classified in several ways, according to their theoretical basis, targets of treatment and objectives sought. In terms of objectives, the psychotherapies can be reduced to four main categories: crisis intervention, supportive psychotherapy, symptomatic psychotherapy and insight-oriented psychotherapy.

In the next two chapters, we turn to the two protagonists involved in therapy, beginning with the patient and then moving on to the therapist.

2 The patient

Who seeks psychotherapy? What sort of patient, with what kind of problems benefits from the experience? In this chapter we consider characteristics of the typical person undergoing psychotherapy, and then look at factors in the patient that appear to be linked to effective outcome.

The typical patient receiving treatment has changed radically over the decades. At the time of Freud's first foray into the world of the neurotic his classical patients were women, who had physical symptoms not attributable to any organic cause. These women, usually young adults and from middle-class families, were unable to express their conflicts in psychological terms, and therefore resorted to the language of the body. Dramatic loss of power in a limb, fainting attacks, or unaccounted for bodily pain, for example, constituted the indirect message that they were emotionally distressed. Soon other forms of emotional disorder were brought under the rubric of the neuroses – anxiety, phobias, obsessions, hypochondriasis, compulsions, among them – and treated by pioneering therapists who applied newly described psychoanalytic principles and strategies. By contrast, the major psychiatric disorders – schizophrenia and severe depression – were viewed as beyond the capabilities of the psychotherapist, as were extreme forms of disordered personality. The neuroses soon came to be regarded as treatable conditions *par excellence*, a view held widely until recent years. Sufferers in early adulthood and from an educated and literate background were thought to be the most suitable patients. The middle-aged and beyond, and the relatively uneducated, were regarded as unlikely to benefit. Freud and his colleagues were by and large medically trained and saw their therapist role as closely aligned to that of the physician. The person with neurotic symptoms was identified as suffering from a specific diagnosis for which a specific form of treatment was indicated; a view akin to the 'medical model' typical of general medical practice.

Progressively, and particularly during the 1960s and 1970s, this model has been bursting at the seams. The notion of providing psychotherapy for a patient suffering from a named illness has become entirely blurred as a result of the mental-health professional's growing appreciation of the limitations and the constraints of this approach. Enormously influential in this change of attitude has been the Human Potential Movement, with its emphasis on 'mind expansion' and the fulfilment of the person's potential. This view is quite contrary to the more circumscribed approach inherent in traditional clinical psychiatry, in which the physician tries to relieve a patient of his symptoms in order to re-establish some form of psychological equilibrium. Moreover, the definition of a symptom has steadily advanced into virtually every sphere of life: to the original and classical group of phobic, obsessional, hypochondriacal, hysterical and depressive symptoms must now be added a variegated batch of what Thomas Szasz has termed 'problems of living'. Included among these are a lack of clear identity, doubts about self-worth, a feeling of purposelessness, a lack of direction, procrastination, unawareness of one's feelings, inability to express feelings like love or anger, lack of intimate relationships, and discomfort in groups. Indeed, the boundlessness and diffuseness of these problems of living have led some critics to aver that the psychotherapist has assumed a fraudulent role – claiming an expertise far in excess of what he can realistically offer. Whatever the merit of this argument, the growing dimension of the therapist's role is no doubt contributed to by the ever increasing demands on his services by the community: people seek out his help in the belief, possibly ill-conceived in some cases, that he is the most appropriate figure.

This choice of a psychotherapist to help sort out problems in living provokes the question of what prompts one person to summon therapeutic aid and another to manage independently. Or, to pose the question in another way: do people who seek and receive treatment have something fundamentally in common? A convincing hypothesis formulated by Jerome Frank suggests that 'The chief problem of all patients who come to psychotherapy is demoralisation' [1] and that their most frequent symptoms – anxiety and depression – are expressions of this loss of morale. Characteristically, the demoralised patient shows one or more of the following – feelings of impotence, isolation, despair, poor self-regard and rejection by others because of failure to meet their expectations. Demoralisation intersects with other symptoms in two ways: the more demoralised the person is the more severe his symptoms; and the same symptoms impair his capacity to cope, with a consequent accentuation of his sense of failure. For Frank the potency of the non-specific factors in psychotherapy, discussed in Chapter 1, buttresses his argument that many different schools of psychotherapy are equally effective because they all serve to restore morale. Whether loss of morale is the key feature that precipitates a person to seek help, he usually does so when his degree of distress has reached a level too uncomfortable to tolerate, or his ability to function in family, work and other social spheres is impaired. Obviously, feelings of distress and poor social functioning are often linked.

The duration of the person's disordered emotional state may vary from lifelong to a matter of hours or days. Thus, for example, a usually content and well-integrated man may undergo a severe stress reaction after his involvement in a car accident in which his wife has been killed. He may seek help soon thereafter to cope with his intense feelings of loss. Crisis intervention of this kind is usually short-term and designed to support the patient in his 'hour of need' and to help him regain his previous personal integrity. By contrast, a young adult may seek therapy for problems which have endured for many years, not infrequently lifelong. Consider the following example: June, a twenty-six-year-old, single secretary sought treatment in the hope that she would overcome three interlocking problems: confusion about her femininity, a disastrous record in relating intimately to men, and uncontrollable outbursts of rage. Since early adolescence she had felt puzzled about her identity as a woman – she tended to down-play her femininity by wearing male-type clothing and had never experienced satisfying sexual relationships with men. Her occasional homosexual explorations had left her all the more confused. A series of friendships with men had ended unhappily. Often June chose the 'unattainable' married or much older man, and when the relationship began to achieve a more intimate quality she would promptly sabotage it by various devious strategies. Since early childhood she had been prone to explosive outbursts of anger, quite out of proportion to what the occasion warranted, or directed to an unfortunate innocent bystander, who happened to move into her target range. Underlying this pattern was her chronic resentment towards her parents for the shabby way she felt they had treated her. June's three problems had contributed to a continuing state of misery and gross lack of satisfaction with her life, as well as interfering with her capacity to function socially or in her work.

June and our bereaved man represent two ends of a continuum, between which a varied range of people, with a wide assortment of difficulties, seek help from the therapist. Many of them have a relatively circumscribed problem and require help of a duration and intensiveness midway between short-term, crisis intervention and long-term, insight-oriented psychotherapy. A middle-aged man with a ten-month history of sexual impotence; a young married woman with diffuse, irrational fears of travelling by public transport or shopping; an adolescent struggling to come to terms with his developing sexuality; a mother of two young children feeling stifled in her marriage; an executive shattered by sudden redundancy; a student confused about the direction his life should take; a young woman with eating binges; a retired man with a prolonged grief reaction following his wife's death – are illustrative of cases I myself have treated in recent years.

Who benefits from psychotherapy?

Despite almost a century of the systematic practice of psychotherapy, the question of what sort of patient benefits from treatment has not yet been adequately answered. Although there are factors on which many psychotherapists would agree, assessment for suitability remains an unsatisfactory and sometimes even arbitrary process. Research findings on the topic – notwithstanding the immense effort involved – are inconsistent and at times contradictory. The clinician is thus left with the problem of not being able to predict with any great measure of certainty which patients among those he evaluates for psychotherapy will benefit or remain unchanged or, indeed, be made worse.

In assessment the therapist poses the question: 'Is this particular patient suitable for psychotherapy?' But the patient cannot be viewed as independent of the many other variables involved in treatment such as the therapist, patient–therapist relationship, and the type of therapy given. A more appropriate question therefore is: 'Which characteristics and problems of patients are most amenable to which techniques conducted by which type of therapist in what type of setting?' In this chapter the focus is limited to characteristics and problems of patients but, as we shall see later, the four components of the question are to some extent interdependent.

Factors in the patient that clinicians have traditionally used in assessment

The psychotherapist has judged suitability for treatment on a variety of different factors in the patient. Indeed, their number and range has mushroomed since Freud's original caveats about psychoanalytic psychotherapy at the turn of the century: psychotically disturbed patients (that is those with no contact with reality) were poor candidates as were those aged over fifty. Later he added unfavourable circumstances under which the patient lives as another poor prognostic feature. The emphasis among the earlier psychoanalysts was on diagnosis; for example, five diagnostic entities were listed as suitable by one author in 1920: hysteria, phobia, obsessive–compulsive neurosis, hypochondria and psychosomatic disorder. Later some analysts argued that diagnosis *per se* was an inadequate basis for selection and that certain conditions were associated with greater 'accessibility' to treatment. This led to the development of the concept of 'analysability', and with it less attention to diagnosis.

Some of the features I have mentioned are concerned with the patient's illness (for example, psychosis as an indication of unsuitability), some with the process of treatment (for example, analysability), others with the patient's personal attributes (for example, his age), and others with his current life circumstances. These four categories, although arbitrary and overlapping – especially between illness and personal characteristics – are convenient when trying to catalogue the many variables in patients that have been considered as pertinent to outcome:

1. *Factors related to the illness* – diagnosis, severity of symptom, course of illness, emotional state particularly anxiety and depression, and response to previous therapy.

2. *Personal factors related to the treatment* – motivation, expectation of improvement and of the therapeutic process.

3. *Personal factors not directly associated with the illness* – age, sex, marital status, socio-economic status, educational attainment, intelligence, habitual patterns of coping with stress, previous sexual adjustment, previous social adjustment and nature of interpersonal relationships. This category includes ego strength – the patient's overall level of personality functioning – which is frequently mentioned as relevant to outcome.

4. *Current life circumstances* – financial state, marital and/or family

situation, and accidental crisis such as an acute physical illness.

Since it is beyond the scope of this chapter to consider all these factors in detail, only those which have a close bearing on clinical practice will be considered.

1. *Factors related to the illness*

Inherent in the medical model is the determination of a *diagnosis* and with it an associated prediction of outcome and plan of treatment. As I have already said the early psychoanalysts adhered to such a model and attempted to distinguish those conditions for which treatment was suitable. Through subsequent clinical observation therapists have tended to identify *indications of unsuitability* to psychotherapy rather than indications to suitability and have regarded patients with such diagnoses as acute psychotic states and severe disorders of personality as unsuitable; these patients are either too disorganised mentally, too distrustful or too intolerant of frustration. These guide-lines stem mainly from the experience of therapeutic failures although some therapists would contend, without however providing objective evidence, that progress can be achieved with such disorders as the acute schizophrenic and the severely depressed patient.

Research studies which have compared the outcome of different diagnostic groups – they are few in number and tend to approach the concept of diagnosis in broad terms – indicate that patients with more severe diagnoses, particularly the various psychoses, are resistant to psychotherapy. There is no evidence for a different response between the broad groups of neurotics and personality disorders. In one survey[2] of 127 patients, no significant differences were found in levels of improvement as judged by their performance at work, quality of interpersonal relationship and the capacity to experience pleasure, between varying diagnostic groups. The study however was limited in that therapists made the diagnosis and also assessed outcome, and the criteria for both were not clearly specified. Moreover the judgements were made in the midst of treatment and patients had been seen for varying periods.

A methodologically sounder study[3] examined the response of eighty-two patients to an average of nine months of psycho-analytically-oriented psychotherapy. Patients were allocated to either a severe group, consisting of personality disorders plus a few schizophrenics, or to a milder group composed of neurotics. No difference was found between their levels of outcome using a check-list of symptoms administered by the researchers before therapy and nine months later. The authors suggested that their findings were in keeping with previous work – that for patients not psychotically disturbed, the bulk of the out-patient psychotherapy population, there was no consistent research evidence showing that diagnostic syndromes have any predictive value.

Many therapists would probably agree with this and not use traditional diagnostic categories in their selection process other than as criteria for exclusion. They would argue that a diagnosis offers too constricted a view of the patient, that a diagnosis is not static, and that severity of disorder within a particular diagnosis can vary considerably. Thus, severity and the course of the illness may also be relevant. Some therapists for instance believe that a chronic illness, of more than five years' duration, will prove resistant to treatment while others suggest that a long-standing condition which has shown fluctuations in severity will have a better response than one that has become entrenched. Research is scanty in this area and available findings are not particularly convincing. But some evidence[2,3] supports the latter observation: greater improvement has been noted in patients who experienced new symptoms in the months preceding the onset of treatment, whereas those without fresh symptoms showed a uniformly low improvement rate. Also, the presence of stress as a precipitating factor in the illness has been found to be significantly related to good outcome.[4] Furthermore, several studies have shown that patients with high anxiety or other strong emotions such as depression and anger at the time of assessment are more likely to profit from psychotherapy. Possibly patients who are emotionally aroused when they enter therapy are manifesting a response to stress and their overall level of adjustment is not severely impaired. They may also be more motivated to work at lessening their distress.

The type of symptoms a patient complains of, whatever his diagnosis, may therefore be important in assessment. The presence of strong emotion is probably a favourable feature for outcome. A patient's preoccupation with physical symptoms by contrast tends to indicate a relatively poor prognosis. Although there has been little research in this area, one team found in a five-year follow-up study[5] of thirty patients diagnosed as neurotic or with personality disorders that the least improved complained of physical symptoms both before therapy and at the time of follow-up. The authors suggested that preoccupation with physical complaints implied a 'more deep seated and ingrained maladjustment'. It is commonly assumed by therapists that the hypochondriacal personality is unsuited to treatment and that patients who present their psychological problems in terms of physical complaints usually lack 'psychological-mindedness' and therefore cannot adjust to the customary verbal and conceptual processes characteristic of psychotherapy.

In this context we need to differentiate between the patient who presents his emotional problems in bodily terms and the patient who suffers from a typical psychosomatic illness[6] such as asthma, peptic ulcer, hypertension, migraine or ulcerative colitis. The findings of controlled studies of various forms of psychotherapy for these types of patients suggest that those with the same psychosomatic disorder show substantial differences in response to the same treatment and that psychotherapy is more effective in some conditions (for example, peptic ulcer, asthma and migraine) than in others (for example, hypertension and ulcerative colitis).[7]

The relationship of *previous psychotherapy* to assessment needs brief comment. Treatment in the past is probably of little significance in predicting outcome, since patients with a record of previous therapy are all different and factors like the nature of the condition originally treated, the appropriateness, quality and duration of the treatment offered, and the response to that treatment, all came into play.

2. Factors related to treatment

There has always been broad consensus among psychotherapists that a patient's motivation is a critical factor for therapeutic success. For some it is the most important factor. For example, one group of analysts[8] suggests that 'a person's wish to change himself and to come to terms with internal conflicts may be the ultimate factor determining whether or not a psychoanalysis will succeed or fail'. There is ample evidence that therapists prefer highly motivated patients and tend to select them if possible, and several investigators have found a positive relationship between motivation and outcome. But the opposite has also been shown.

These inconsistent findings no doubt result partly from the differing ways in which motivation has been conceptualised, defined and measured. Motivation reflects a range of differing, although related concepts: the patient's preparedness to take an active part in the therapy process, the wish to change, willingness to make sacrifices in terms of time and money, and so forth.

Furthermore, therapists are apt to regard motivation as a static concept, whereas clinical observation shows clearly that motivation is influenced by such factors as the therapist's behaviour and the progress of therapy. Motivation has been usefully viewed in dialectical terms: the product of a continuing battle between a patient's conscious willingness to work at therapy and to understand the basic nature of his underlying conflicts and then to resolve them, and his unconscious resistance to face painful, repressed memories and frustrations of treatment. Again, clinical experience demonstrates that a patient may waver in his initial motivation but become more motivated following an early success in the treatment itself. Conversely, high initial motivation may dissipate with failure or disappointment experienced during treatment. It would seem that motivation at the outset of psychotherapy is not necessary for good outcome but its development during treatment is important.

As with motivation, the study of a patient's expectations before entering treatment has been confounded by inadequate or differing definition. The term expectation has several connotations and may be readily confused with such feelings as hope, faith and confidence. In recent years the two chief strands of the concept have been more clearly delineated: the expectation of improvement or therapeutic gain and the expectation of participating in a particular therapeutic process.

Two approaches have been applied to the study of the influence of expectation of improvement on outcome: correlational – in which the patient's expectation is correlated with his outcome; and experimental – in which procedures are designed to increase or decrease expectation and their effects on outcome are noted. Studies conducted in the 1950s led one notable researcher[9] to state that 'a patient's expectation of benefit from treatment in itself may have enduring and profound effects on his physical and mental state. It seems plausible, furthermore, that the successful effects of all forms of psychotherapy depend in part on their ability to foster such attitudes in the patient.' The correlational studies have usually supported this point but the outcome measure used has invariably been the patient's own testimony. By contrast, a study using ratings by therapists of improvement found no relationship with expectation. With some colleagues I[10] attempted to overcome these deficiencies by examining the relationship between expectation of improvement and outcome in patients receiving long-term group therapy. Improvement was rated eight and twelve months after the beginning of treatments by patients, their therapists and by independent judges. Only in the case of self-ratings by patients was a positive correlation found. We concluded that evidence for an association between expectation of improvement and actual improvement was unfounded, and speculated that the positive finding in the case of the patient's own testimony reflected an entrenched expectational set of ideas about therapy which remained constant whatever its course in reality. The result from ratings of independent judges was perhaps more dependable than either of the other two sources.

The experimental approach has been applied in more than a dozen studies. These shared the hypothesis that a procedure designed to increase a patient's expectation of improvement would be more effective than the same therapeutic approach without such manipulation. A positive association between expectation and outcome was found in a third of these studies but not in the rest. Although some of the discrepancy could be explained by differences in samples of patients and in the types of treatment given, the most striking distinguishing feature was the knowledge by the therapists, in the studies with a positive finding, of which patients had received the high expectation instructions. In all studies with negative findings therapists were uninformed in this respect. The obvious implication is that the awareness of therapists and not the expectation of patients was the critical variable contributing to outcome. These therapists may unwittingly have behaved differently towards patients given high expectation instructions because of their vested interest in the experiment.

Expectation has also been studied in relation to the patient's notions about the actual *process* of therapy: what he envisages will be his role and tasks, the role and function of his therapist, the nature of his relationship with the therapist, the duration of therapy and so on. Therapists perhaps assume implicitly that their patients have similar expectations to their own but several studies show the fallacy of this assumption. They do not even necessarily agree about the time at which change will begin. Of one sample[11] of patients with no previous experience of therapy, seventy per cent expected improvement by the fifth session and the same proportion that the complete course would not exceed ten sessions. In another study[12] comparing those who stopped therapy at an early stage with those who completed their programme the drop-outs expected specific advice in the first interview and assumed that they would occupy a passive role in the therapist–patient relationship, an expectation not shared by their therapists.

These findings have paved the way for a number of studies of the value of preparing the patient for treatment, and thus inducing expectations which are realistic and appropriate. The first of these[13] – a well-designed and executed investigation from Johns Hopkins University – hypothesised that a 'role induction interview' (RII) should improve 'therapy behaviour', attendance and outcome in patients with only limited knowledge of psychotherapy. They were randomly assigned to an experimental or control condition and all received four months of weekly treatment by therapists who were ignorant of the aim of the experiment. They were then assessed on a number of outcome measures by independent judges. The results confirmed the hypothesis and the authors reasonably concluded that the RII – in which the therapist's future behaviour and the patient's required role were explained carefully – was a valuable therapeutic tool. A similar experiment[14] was conducted at Temple University, with the addition of another independent factor – inducing the expectation that improvement would be obtained within four months. Again, patients receiving an RII showed significantly greater improvement than a control group. However, the 'time' expectation on its own or coupled with the RII had no beneficial effect. Generally, the advantage of an RII was less convincing than that in the Johns Hopkins study; this was attributed to the fact that the patients were more sophisticated and many had previously received therapy – that is their expectations were already congruent with those of the therapists. The value of role induction has also been noted in intensive group therapy:[15] group members who are prepared prior to treatment show a higher level of interaction with fellow patients, an important component of the group process, than unprepared members.

Appropriate, realistic expectations are probably related to psychological-mindedness, a concept often mentioned by clinicians as a favourable characteristic in a patient, and implying his ability to be introspective, self-reflective and realistic. However, the concept still awaits clearer definition and more systematic study.

3. Personal factors not directly associated with the illness

'The better the individual's overall level of adaptation and function

prior to the onset of his disturbance, the better will be the prognosis.'
A patient showing evidence of past failure at adaptation and with
'inadequate, overall ego capacity' by contrast is a poor candidate for
psychotherapy. These rather bold statements emerge from a widely
used text on psychotherapy[16] and reflect the thinking of a large number of therapists. The concept of ego strength was developed in the
1950s to reflect this phenomenon of previous adaptation and function
and has since become a commonly agreed criterion of selection. Ego
strength can be conceptualised as an integrating force which allows a
person to use his adaptive resources; and is assessed by considering
such areas as heredity, constitution, early environmental experience,
developmental history, customary methods of handling stress, and
general level of social maturity – an inquiry not dissimilar to the
psychiatrist's conventional family and personal history taking. Important indicators of ego strength are pattern of relationships, tolerance
of anxiety and frustration, coping with stress, type of defences used,
and sexual adjustment.

Are clinicians justified in placing so much confidence in the concept
of ego strength in the assessment of suitability? An examination of the
origins of the concept is useful in trying to answer this question. The
term ego strength developed out of two measures that were first reported in the early 1950s: Barron's Ego Strength Scale and the Rorschach
Prognostic Rating Scale (RPRS). Barron's scale[17] was derived from a
popular personality questionnaire, and purported to measure the level
of maturity of the patient's personality. He originally devised it as a
predictor of outcome and found that scores correlated significantly
with improvement – as measured by two judges not involved in the
patient's treatment – in thirty-three neurotic out-patients. Among the
characteristics the improved patients showed were good contact with
reality, feelings of personal adequacy and vitality, and spontaneity
with the ability to share emotional experiences. Conversely, unim-
proved patients were, among other features, inhibited, chronically
fatigued and submissive. Barron attempted to test his scale in three
different settings and obtained reasonable correlations between ego
strength and outcome in each patient group. His findings of a positive
association were confirmed by two other research groups but unsup-
ported in several other studies.

The RPRS became a popular research instrument after its introduction by Klopfer and his colleagues in 1951.[18] This scale, derived from
the Rorschach Ink Blot Test, was developed as a predictor of the

response to treatment. Patients' responses to a series of ambiguous patterns are rated and, via a special procedure, converted into a score predicting level of outcome. The RPRS was used in a number of projects on assessment but with rather inconsistent results. In a review of the research on the use of the RPRS an almost equal number of positive and negative reports have been found; this is not a surprise in view of the different samples of patient, measures of outcome and perhaps the treatments used. A similar observation could be made regarding the mixed findings with Barron's scale.

Apart from this explanation it could well be that the two scales are only empirical extracts of two established personality assessment procedures, and neither has been designed or validated as a measure of ego strength. Indeed, the entire construct of ego strength was not sufficiently well-defined in the first place, and has remained prone to many different connotations. Despite the varied results of studies examining ego strength commentators on the psychotherapy research literature have tentatively concluded that 'relatively better integrated clients improve, with the most integrated improving rather quickly' or that 'the more adequate his general personality functioning the better his future course in psychotherapy'. It is not surprising therefore that some critics of psychotherapy have concluded that individuals who are least in need of psychotherapy tend to be those who receive it!

A widely held belief among psychotherapists that the young adult patient is the most suitable for treatment probably springs from Freud's notion that the upper age limit for a successful psychoanalysis was fifty. It has since been perpetuated in psychotherapy texts that a person above the age of about forty-five is an unsuitable candidate for psychotherapy. Freud specified his limit on the grounds that analysis needed an extended period and that the ability of the treatment to reverse psychopathology diminished after about fifty.

Although other therapists including Jung have extended the limit to sixty and beyond most therapists would still regard the young adult as best suited because of his greater flexibility and capacity to learn and experiment with new modes of behaviour. Further, he has a longer period to make use of his newly achieved insights. The older patient by contrast has less scope for readjustment and may become depressed by new insights because he now senses lost opportunities in his earlier life.

Research on age as an assessment factor has not resulted in guidelines for the clinician. No association between age and outcome has been found in about half the studies which examine the issue. In the remainder younger patients tended to show greater improvement. Two main obstacles have hampered this work. Because of the traditional bias against selecting older patients, studies have probably been influenced by the fact that of those older patients who have entered therapy many have had some particularly striking attributes while, conversely, younger patients may have been accepted for treatment primarily because of their age with minimal consideration given to other assessment factors. The only satisfactory way to test for the effect of age is through a fully controlled study – that is two groups, differing in age alone, are compared on outcome – not an easy task. The second difficulty is that age is not simply a chronological fact but is intimately linked to features such as flexibility and opportunity for readjustment.

As assessment factor that has attracted the attention of both clinicians and researchers is *socio-economic class*. Although some authorities have concluded that its relationship to outcome appears to have more consistent supporting evidence than other factors, the pattern that emerges from the research literature is rather blurred. This is not unexpected when one considers the complexity of socio-economic class. Like motivation and ego strength it reflects a cluster of inter-related factors, among them, income, occupation and educational attainment.

A broad range of measures of socio-economic class (for instance, level of income, occupational status, educational level) is used in the research literature which shows a tendency – one could not claim more than this – for patients of low socio-economic status to do less well in treatment. The results of these studies are complicated however by other findings (which in fact tend to be more consistent): lower-class patients are more likely not to enter treatment after selection or to drop out prematurely; they tend to be allocated to less experienced therapists; and they tend to receive less intensive forms of therapy. The difference in outcome between lower- and middle-class patients is also likely to be a function of therapist/patient interaction, a thoroughly neglected area of study: therapists are themselves usually middle-class and may consequently harbour a prejudice that the lower-class patient will not profit from therapy. Furthermore, they may not be able to identify and empathise with him because of differing values and life-styles.

They may also fail to appreciate the patient's verbal limitations and use terms and concepts that he cannot understand. This last possibility is supported by the finding, in a number of studies, of a positive relationship between improvement and educational attainment. But as is so common in assessment research, the chief criterion of outcome in most of these investigations has been therapist ratings. These ratings could well have suffered from a lack of objectivity because of therapists' possible preference for middle-class patients. The evidence is not wholly convincing: educational level is in all likelihood not a potent factor in determining improvement.

Educational level is obviously closely linked to *intelligence* and much work examining the latter as a predictor has found it to relate positively to outcome. This supports a commonly held belief among therapists that intelligence is a desirable feature since intensive psychotherapy is a learning process in which the patient aims to acquire insight, and which involves introspective, conceptual and verbal communicative skills. But, again, like educational level, the patient's actual IQ may not be decisive. Although a high level of intelligence may be advantageous for insight-oriented psychotherapy the question arises as to whether one can reasonably determine a necessary minimum level. Interestingly, some analysts have suggested that in the case of psychoanalysis the required intellectual level may have been set too high by therapists because of their own preference for working with bright, and therefore usually interesting, patients.

As discussed earlier recent work on preparing the patient for psychotherapy through a role induction interview suggests that intelligence and education level may be less significant than considered hitherto. It may be more crucial to give the patient specific knowledge about the process of psychotherapy and his required participation than to try to establish the basic levels of intelligence and education needed. This seems to obtain for many different forms of psychotherapy. Although preparation of the patient implies that a decision regarding selection has already been made one can profitably use the patient's ability to grasp the essentials of psychotherapy provided by the therapist as a guide to whether he has the intellectual wherewithal to participate in, and benefit from, treatment.

Other personal factors − sex and marital status have also been examined for their prognostic significance. Most investigations have shown no association between sex and outcome. The same is true of marital status although its effects have only been looked at occasionally. The effect on outcome of patient−therapist match in terms of marital status is an interesting issue. In a recent study[19] greater improvement was seen in cases where neither patient nor therapist had ever been married or where patient and therapist were both married; this result was attributed to the sharing of an important personal similarity. Studies that have been done to examine patient–therapist similarities in terms of, among others, personality questionnaire responses, social class and values, generally support the advantage of a close match.

4. *Current life circumstances*

The fourth group of factors influencing response to psychotherapy concerns the patient's current circumstances. Most therapists have assumed that a person in the midst of a crisis of any kind (but who otherwise would be regarded as a prospective candidate) is unlikely to prove suitable for a treatment which requires systematic, concentrated work over an extended period. Thus someone engulfed in the emotional tide of an intense conflict with a spouse, parent or other family member, or pressed by severe financial difficulties, or suffering from an acute physical illness, or trapped in a complicated job situation will probably be unable to face up to the demands of insight-oriented psychotherapy. These patients are more likely to benefit from a crisis-intervention approach with subsequent transfer to the definitive treatment after the crisis has resolved or at least diminished. The patient trapped in an unresolvable, difficult situation is commonly viewed as a poor candidate for therapy, and in this case, a long-term supportive approach is more apt.

Methods of assessment

Although the therapist is handicapped by not being able to depend completely on specific factors to predict who will benefit from treatment, the question still arises as to whether one type of selection *procedure* is more helpful than another. Ideally, a systematic and reliable procedure would be a valuable tool. Efforts to fashion one must have been in progress for some thirty years – unfortunately to little avail. This period has been noteworthy for diligent attempts to apply derivatives of commonly-used personality tests to predict outcome. We discussed earlier the development of the Klopfer Rorschach Prognostic Rating Scale and Barron's Ego Strength Scale as important examples of this endeavour. Their popularity for assessment waned within a decade as it emerged that they were not as valuable as had been originally envisaged. Similarly many other tests have been of limited value.

By and large the scales, originally designed for other purposes, have been employed as assessment devices without logical justification. Recognising this basic deficiency and the lack of a convenient instrument for assessing the patient's assets for psychotherapy one American group of workers[20] devised an entirely new instrument, the Prognostic Index (PI). Information is elicited from a prospective candidate for treatment through a semi-structured interview on thirty-one variables presumed to be predictive and derived from clinical observation and research findings. A set of guide-lines is available for the interviewer and scores on each variable are placed on a five-point scale. Four categories comprise the PI: *descriptive* for example diagnosis, duration and onset of illness, anxiety, depression, benefit from past treatment; *psychodynamic* for example tolerance of anxiety, coping ability, motivation, psychological-mindedness; *demographic* for example IQ, education, occupation; and *global* that is overall suitability for psychotherapy. In one study of forty-seven patients using the PI, outcome was predicted by scores on the level of depression at the time of assessment, general emotional health (consisting of items such as diagnosis, coping ability, quality of relationships and social maturity), and intellectual achievement. But another factor, the overall prediction of outcome, was as useful as these three factors. Two possible implications follow: overall prediction is improved when made in the context of a comprehensive and systematic interview (the authors' impression) or overall assessment is itself sufficient and the rest of the procedure can be dispensed with – perhaps replaceable by a customary clinical interview.

A similar approach has been adopted by a group of psychoanalysts in the assessment of patients for psychoanalysis. Their method consists of the administration of several intelligence and personality tests. The test protocols are examined and ratings then made on four criteria: reality testing – the level of perception of the world as it actually is; level and quality of interpersonal relationships; availability and tolerance of emotion (the authors point out that this area is poorly delineated and requires more work); and motivation to work at one's conflicts and hence for change. The ratings are made on scales with defined points of suitability. The relationship of these criteria to outcome was not however examined.

The PI is probably the more promising of the two methods in that its premisses and content are more directly pertinent to psychotherapy and a specific set of guidelines is available to the interviewer (and thus to any therapist who wishes to train himself in its use). However to make it workable, its thirty-one variables must be reduced to a more manageable number of factors. The second method harks back to the 1950s in using derivatives of other tests which were never devised as assessment measures for psychotherapy, and which must be given by a trained person. Ideally the therapist needs an instrument which is valid and reliable and which he himself can administer efficiently within the context of his own practice. Such an instrument has not yet been devised.

In its absence most therapists continue to use an ordinary clinical interview but the focus varies. Some emphasise gathering of information in order to generate a list of problems which will be tackled in therapy (a problem-oriented approach); others take a traditional psychiatric history with the goal of reaching a diagnosis; yet others concentrate their interviews so as to identify the psychological origins of the patient's problems. Without further research we can only conclude that any of the above interview approaches may be as useful as the other with the therapist's choice at present perhaps influenced by his own preference and style of working.

Whatever form of assessment interview is done, some therapists suggest that there is room for a 'trial of therapy' as an additional evaluative step. Indeed Freud advocated such a procedure as routine prior to accepting a patient for psychoanalytic therapy. This stemmed from his fear that supposed neurotic symptoms might perhaps foreshadow a psychotic condition. With Freud, one to two weeks were adequate. Later analysts suggested a trial of several weeks. There are obvious snags with a therapeutic trial: the patient eager to 'pass' the test may present himself as more disturbed than he actually is or express 'optimal' motivation. Development of the therapist–patient relationship may be affected by the procedure with a possible deleterious influence on therapy if the patient is accepted. On balance however the question of suitability is probably made clearer by a trial of therapy in a case where the assessment interviews have failed to yield a definitive decision.

A final question on selection procedure: should relatives or other significant persons in the patient's life be involved? The obvious advantage is that new information may be obtained to enhance the objectivity of the therapist's evaluation, but at the possible cost that the patient's confidence in treatment may be jeopardised. Both clinical and ethical issues are involved: relatives should be active participants in assessment as they will be affected by the therapist's subsequent interventions with the patient and their involvement can also reduce any possible sabotage of treatment. The research literature on this question, as on the trial of therapy issue, provides no help and for the moment the therapist can only weigh up the usefulness of both procedures in any particular case and arrive at his best possible clinical judgement.

Conclusion

After nearly a hundred years of systematic psychotherapy practice, the basic question: 'Who benefits from such treatment?' remains incompletely answered. The immense volume of research in the area of selection has yielded little of practical value and the impact of research on clinical work has been minimal. Therapists, it would appear, are more reliant on clinical lore – that body of information which has accumulated through careful observation by the clinician. What accounts for the rather dismal contribution of research?

Methodological snares abound in psychotherapy research generally (see Chapter 6) and the investigation of suitability is no exception. Many of the studies suffer from one or more of the following defects:

1. *patient* – poorly defined, small and heterogeneous samples of patients;

2. *therapy* – inadequate specification of the therapy given; the therapy usually short-term (rarely more than four months) although in clinical practice it is of longer duration; the treatment provided by inexperienced therapists and its quality therefore in doubt;

3. *outcome* – inappropriate measurement of outcome with the most common source of assessment being the therapist, who has an obviously biased viewpoint, and the application of questionnaires which are too general to reflect the intricate changes in personality that occur as a result of psychotherapy; only a minority of studies incorporate a reasonable follow-up period;

4. *predicting outcome* – commonly only one predictive factor is examined at a time; the effect of therapist–patient interaction tends to be ignored with factors in the therapist and in the patient studied independently. This last area suggests an important conceptual issue.

Theoretically it is likely that in a complex enterprise like psychotherapy, the matter of who will benefit is affected by a large number of factors which contribute in varying measure and in interaction with one another. The contribution of any single factor in the patient is probably quite small. Much research in the past has examined a single factor only, and ignored its possible interaction with other factors. For example, and as commented on earlier, a patient's marital status may be relevant to outcome but only in relation to the marital status of his therapist.

In summary, what features in the patient can we identify as favourable for psychotherapy? The combined product of the results of systematic research and cumulative clinical observation would suggest the following: (1) a reasonable level of personality integration and general functioning, that is patients who can face their disturbing feelings and still manage to live their lives independent of therapy; (2) motivation for change; (3) realistic expectations of the therapeutic process involved, reflecting 'psychological-mindedness'; (4) at least average intelligence; (5) non-psychotic conditions, namely the neuroses and the milder personality disorders, particularly if their clinical course has shown fluctuations in the months preceding therapy; (6) the presence of strong emotion like anxiety and depression at the time of assessment; and (7) life circumstances free of any unresolvable crises. Other features that we have looked at – age, sex, marital status, educational attainment, socio-economic status, expectation of improvement and previous therapy – seem of less relevance to outcome.

3 The therapist

In Chapter 1 we posed the question: 'What is psychotherapy?' After that discussion it should be straightforward to define a psychotherapist. Not so! Psychotherapy is such a boundless field that to talk about a profession of psychotherapists is almost impossible. Consider for the moment that those who claim to practise psychotherapy in one form or another include, and this is only a partial list, psychiatrists, psychologists, social workers, psychiatric nurses, marriage guidance counsellors, school and university counsellors, lay psychoanalysts, human relations consultants and pastoral counsellors.

There are three features that typify each of these professions: their members work with people who experience some form of distress; they help them psychologically; and they are perceived by their clients as experts in the management of human problems. Apart from these features, those who work as psychotherapists differ substantially from one another. Take the psychiatrist – therapist. First, he has to qualify as a medical doctor, then complete an internship, then specialise in psychiatry, and within and beyond that specialist training receive special instruction in the theory and practice of psychotherapy – a process taking an average of about a dozen years! By contrast, the marriage guidance counsellor is a volunteer, has not qualified as a mental health professional, and undergoes a circumscribed basic training over two years conducted by his peers, who in turn are aided by professionals.

Historically, psychotherapy began as a medical speciality. Although Freud was a physician and disseminated his early ideas among medical colleagues, he was not opposed to the concept of the 'lay analyst'. Indeed, he argued forcefully in *The Question of Lay Analysis*[1] that psychoanalysis was a branch of psychology and not of medicine, and that a medical training was not only unnecessary but also not particularly desirable. Psychoanalysis for Freud was a science, with the potential to contribute to the understanding of human nature as well as a method of treatment. It should therefore not be confined to the psychiatrist's office. This position was more or less supported by European analysts, but adamantly resisted by their American counterparts who to this day admit only the occasional non-doctor to their psychoanalytic institutes, and then not for a full training. The issue continues to bristle with controversy: who is entitled to enter psychoanalytic ranks? The question also applies to psychotherapy generally: should it be the exclusive province of medicine or psychology or social work or some other 'caring' profession or, indeed, an autonomous profession?

The actual picture of psychotherapy in practice provides one answer. Various professional disciplines have unhesitatingly embraced the role of psychotherapist and made claims that their own particular brand of education best suits the role. So, if you sought help for an emotional problem in Britain, with its National Health Service, you could well find yourself in the office of a psychiatrist, clinical psychologist or social worker. In the United States, you might be recommended to any one of these professions, all of whom have the right to offer their services on a contractual basis. In either country, and in many other Western countries, you would also be able to opt for 'treatment' in a so-called 'growth centre', where a team of professional and/or lay therapists would be available. (I deal with this more fully in Chapter 6.)

We shall turn later in this chapter to the issue of training and licensure but for the moment it is sufficient to summarise the situation as follows: anyone, it seems, can declare himself a psychotherapist and offer his services to clients, whatever his credentials, and whether he belongs to a mental-health profession or not. To dispute his claim would be difficult, if not impossible. As there is no evidence that one professional group is more effective than another in producing improvement it is probably futile to enter into an argument over who is best suited to the psychotherapist's job. More relevant, in all likelihood, are the desiderata for an effective therapist and it is to these that we now turn our attention.

Desiderata for the effective therapist

What makes for a good therapist? The answer depends in part on whom one asks: the patient, the therapist's colleagues, or the researcher who measures the degree of improvement achieved. The last could well argue that the appraisal by either patient or colleague is less important than the final product – is the therapist an effective agent in bringing about change? Comparison could be made with a surgeon. I may prefer one surgeon to another because he is sympathetic or gentle or caring; but I will want to be certain that he is effective with his scalpel and that I stand a good chance of losing, say, my gall-bladder, but not my life! His technique is infinitely more relevant to me than his personality. Psychotherapy is of course not like surgery. The therapist is his own chief resource – no scalpel, no drugs exist in his therapeutic arsenal. This difference throws up one of the foremost questions that psychotherapy has faced continuously over the past forty years or so. Is it features of the therapist's personality or the techniques he employs or some combination of both, which leads to change in the patient?

Again, Freud is a good starting-point. The birth of the psychoanalytic approach (and of systematic psychotherapy) was preceded by experimentation by Freud with hypnosis. With his experience of the great French neurologist Charcot behind him, Freud saw hypnosis, clearly a technical procedure in the main, as a therapeutic tool. On his discovery of free association – the encouragement of the patient to disclose anything and everything that comes into his mind – he abandoned hypnosis but still held on to the idea that technique was central. Progressively, a technical procedure was elaborated: the patient associates freely and, in so doing, develops a particular way of relating to the analyst, known as transference. The therapist, while adopting a neutral stance (this is not to deny that he also acts in a sympathetic and understanding way) and serving as a blank screen, comes to represent important figures in the patient's past, and so encourages the transference to unfold. The therapist's task is then to interpret the nature of this transference, with the goal of expanding the patient's self-awareness – unconscious is made conscious and the patient achieves insight into the origins of his neurosis. This is necessarily a schematic account of a complex and lengthy process (I return to the topic in Chapter 4), but we can readily recognise the relative values of the therapist's personality and of his technique. In 1912 Freud[2] noted the intrusion of the therapist's personality into this process. The therapist's unconscious attitudes and feelings towards his patient, referred to as counter-transference, were inevitable. Counter-transference constituted a hindrance to successful analysis. To become aware of 'blind-spots in his analytic perception' and thus abolish counter-transference, Freud recommended that the therapist undergo 'psychoanalytic purification'. Again, we note the emphasis on technique: a personal analysis for the therapist is designed for a specific purpose – to promote his objectivity and in turn his clear grasp of the patient's disclosures. Interestingly, later analysts, while not repudiating the value of a personal analysis, have seen counter-transference as a useful therapeutic tool and as a bridge to the unconscious. The therapist learns much about his patients through awareness of his own feelings and attitudes to them.

Beginning in the 1930s a prominent group of psychoanalysts in the United States – notable among them were Rollo May, Harry Stack Sullivan and Erich Fromm – began to suggest that personal attributes of the therapist were more relevant in treatment than Freud had postulated. The movement was the forerunner of an important school of psychotherapy that emerged in the 1950s – the humanist-existential. We shall consider this school in detail in Chapter 4. For the moment we can confine our discussion to the question of whether the therapist's personality and his relationship with the patient are key ingredients for effective therapy compared to the techniques he uses.

A wide range of personality traits have been suggested as desirable in the therapist. They include honesty, compassion, empathy, a caring attitude, flexibility, self-confidence, intelligence, integrity, imaginativeness, intuitiveness and genuineness. If psychotherapists possessed all these qualities they would be exceptional human beings! Clearly, the vast majority do not. Arrogant would be the therapist who claimed to be such an ideal person. Ironically, the typical psychotherapist has in some quarters been viewed as notably lacking the qualities listed and, indeed, as a bearer of neurotic traits, which he is keen to dislodge; hence his motivation to enter the psychotherapy profession in the first place. Generally, the therapist is neither an exceptional individual nor a disabled neurotic. Rather, he is pretty much the average person, with a mixed bag of positive attributes, weaknesses and vulnerabilities. To map out the ideal qualities of the therapist is probably a futile exercise. Opinions vary considerably over what features are important, and agreement is unlikely.

Carl Rogers,[3] the founder of client-centered psychotherapy (an example of the humanist-existential school) has in his prolific writings and research led the opposition to a technique-based treatment. Perhaps more than any other figure he has argued that specific personality features in the therapist are not only necessary but also *sufficient* to produce positive effects. Rogers's views have enjoyed widespread popularity among therapists, particularly psychologists and social workers, and have had a distinct impact on the practice of psychotherapy.

Rogers's approach is to designate certain specific *attitudinal* qualities as pertinent to treatment. In his view we can distinguish between the therapist's basic personality features which are independent of therapy, and specified attitudes that he incorporates into his relationship with his patient. Therapists come in all shapes and sizes: what differentiates the competent and effective from their less able colleagues is the capacity to master and show in their encounter with their patients, three qualities:

1. *warmth* – the non-possessive acceptance of, and unconditional positive regard for the patient; in essence, a genuine caring attitude.

2. *empathy* – the sensitive and accurate appreciation of what the patient is experiencing, by 'getting into his shoes'.

3. *genuineness* – the therapist's words match his feelings; he is 'transparently real'.

The vast majority of therapists, if not all, would support the notion that warmth, empathy and genuineness contribute to effective therapy. A substantially lesser proportion would accept Rogers's contention that these qualities are sufficient in themselves. But Rogers avers that if someone had these qualities he would be an adequate therapist independent of qualifications or training. A large body of research has accumulated over some twenty years to test the validity of Rogers's position. There are snags however in reaching firm conclusions about this work. The research has been of uneven quality and the results of the studies are inconsistent. The usual procedure has been to measure levels of warmth, empathy and genuineness in the therapist – irrespective of his theoretical school and level of training – and then to correlate these with the degree of improvement of his patients. Earlier studies pointed to a significant relationship between personal qualities and outcome, and it became widely accepted that the case was proven. Later studies, which tended to be superior in design and execution, found a less marked association. Yes, warmth, empathy and genuineness were important and probably contributed to the effectiveness of treatment, but the hypothesis that they were also sufficient could not be sustained.

The progressive decline in support of Rogers's position is reflected in a series of reviews of the pertinent research literature. The first major review, in 1970, concluded that the three personality features when measured in a wide range of therapists, were definitely central for a wide range of patients. A review three years later indicated that the results were more equivocal, and the most recent, in 1977, found the evidence conflicting.[4] Potency of the three factors was not as great as had previously been thought. A regular finding in many studies is the close relationship between warmth, empathy and genuineness. They are quite possibly not independent qualities at all, but point to the 'good guy'. Certainly, when they have been measured by the patient it is not unlikely that he is simply rating his therapist on how 'nice' a person he finds him. Rogers has argued that the patient is the appropriate source for rating the therapist, but others have pointed out the need for a more objective assessor such as an independent judge, who observes the therapist is action or listens to tapes of his therapy sessions. Another research difficulty is how to distinguish between therapists who are warm, empathic and genuine from those who are not. How can one determine a minimum amount of the three qualities on rating scales? The earlier studies failed to indicate how therapists had been classified. With these methodological complications and inconsistent research results the most reasonable conclusion we can reach is that warmth, empathy and genuineness are important qualities in a therapist, but that other complex factors have an effect as well.

Let us now examine some of these qualities and, in particular, level of experience, style of therapist – the way in which he predominantly relates to the patient, and training.

Experience

Common sense suggests that the experienced therapist should be more effective than his inexperienced counterpart. Experience presumably permits the therapist to build up knowledge about the sort of patient who profits from treatment and what variations in his own techniques produce beneficial effects; the therapist develops greater self-confidence in his approach, which is readily perceived by the patient; and the therapist can draw on his own experience of life and on that of his friends, family and colleagues, and relate them to his clinical work. The problem with a concept like experience is how to define and measure it. Is experience a question of the number of years in practice, or working with a wide range of patients, or working intensively with a few patients? Can experience be separated from training? If we wish to compare therapists of high and low experience, what criteria can we use to differentiate the two groups? The cut-off point must inevitably be arbitrary.

To note specific effects of experience on outcome we need to study therapists who are similar in most respects, especially with regard to quality and amount of training, some of whom have had no experience and others who have worked for several years. Another variant would be to compare two groups of therapists – one with a few years of experience and the other with many years more. Bearing in mind the problems of definition and measurement, what do research data show? Two surveys have examined the relationship between experience and outcome. In one[5] a significant positive association was found in eight out of thirteen studies. In the other[6] the proportion was five out of twelve. The latter survey was the more thorough and only included studies in which two or more levels of experience were directly compared by the researchers. So, in over fifty per cent of investigations experience has not been shown to be a significant factor. Perhaps we should reconsider the Rogerian idea that there is some personal or attitudinal quality in the therapist which is more relevant for effective therapy. Alternatively, experience may be of no consequence in terms of the number of years of practice – the usual way of measuring it – but rather in terms of its quality and, of course, a judgement about quality is bound to be arbitrary and prone to error. I have come across experienced therapists who have become rigid in their clinical approach during years of practice. This is a result, in some cases, of an unswerving allegiance to a particular theoretical framework or of an unwillingness to consider new ideas. For these therapists experience probably counts for little – they gain only minimally because they are entirely constrained in their approach. The converse is also known. Some therapists chop and change techniques, allowing no opportunity to evaluate what they do and obtaining no feedback on what facets of their therapy help their patients. The quality of experience of these two types of therapists is obviously different to that of an open-minded, but yet thoughtful, therapist who monitors carefully the product of his work and learns accordingly.

For the moment it remains unclear how important experience is. Like many other questions in psychotherapy, what appears at first sight as a reasonable proposition, and one that was supported by early (but less rigorous) research studies, still awaits a definitive answer. That answer can only emerge from investigations in which two or more levels of experience are demarcated as accurately as possible, with no overlap between the groups; and the therapists in each group treat similar types of patients who are randomly allocated to them. All the therapists studied would need to have a similar amount of training.

The therapist's style

The therapist's style is the way in which he predominantly relates to his patient, both verbally and non-verbally. For example, a therapist may be challenging or supportive, authoritarian or permissive, active or passive, opaque or self-disclosing, detached or involved, and so forth. The eventual pattern that typifies a therapist's style may bear little or no relationship to his professional school. Two Jungian therapists for example may claim to use a similar theoretical approach but exhibit radically different styles. Moreover, one of them may be closer in style to a therapist belonging to another school than to his own colleague. As we shall see in Chapter 6, inter-school differences in terms of outcome are minimal,[7] and one of the responsible factors could well be the substantial variation in therapist style across schools rather than between them. Interestingly, in a study comparing the effectiveness of behaviour therapy and psychoanalytically oriented therapy[8] therapists of these two schools shared many features in terms of their style. Both, for example, used interpretation to a similar degree.

A particularly valuable insight into the relevance of style is provided by the impressive project conducted at Stanford University on encounter groups.[9] Although these groups were composed of volunteer students, not patients, the results can be reasonably extrapolated to psychotherapy. Among the several schools of psychotherapy represented in the study were psychodrama, Synanon, psychoanalysis, transactional analysis and Gestalt. Through careful and systematic observation of the therapist at work, four categories of behaviour in leaders emerged: emotional stimulaton, caring, meaning-attribution (interpreting the group members' behaviour), and executive function (a sort of managerial role). By noting the outcome of the students in terms of personal awareness and other variables, the most effective leadership pattern was found to consist of moderate levels of emotional stimulation and executive function and high levels of caring and meaning-attribution. Conversely, high or low stimulation, low caring, low attribution and high or low executive function proved less effective leadership styles. These findings are important because for the most part style varied more as a function of the individual leader than as a function of his theoretical model. Customarily, therapists are much more aware of their theoretical position than of their actual behaviour with patients. The encounter group study, and others like it, contain a convincing message to therapists – that they need to pay more attention to the way in which they actually work with their patients.

Training

There is intense debate among therapists about what constitutes an optimal training. The different views no doubt reflect the basic confusion about the nature of psychotherapy. If, as we have already noted, the relative importance for effective treatment of the therapist's personality, his technique, or some combination of these two factors has not been firmly established, it follows that priorities in training must remain obscure. Clearly, with the emphasis on therapeutic technique, a training is required not dissimilar from, say, that of a car mechanic. The mechanic first learns about a car's components and their normal and abnormal function. Then, with the aid of a manual, and some experience of course, he is in a position to diagnose the car's defects and remedy them. The technically-minded therapist could presumably follow these sorts of steps – simply substitute 'mind' for 'car'. On the other hand, if the therapist's personality is the core ingredient for successful therapy, a formal training may be considered unnecessary. Selection then becomes all important; simply identify people who already bear those personality features deemed necessary. Alternatively, the position may be taken that these personal qualities can be inculcated and promoted through a specific process of training in all prospective therapists.

These positions are of more than theoretical interest. In most approaches to the education of a psychotherapist the recipe comprises the same ingredients, albeit in varying measure. Most teachers agree that the key component is clinical practice under the supervision of an experienced therapist. The obvious premiss is that only with actual participation in the treatment of patients can a therapist begin to appreciate the intricacies of the process. Typically, the neophyte is assigned a small number of patients, with whom he will work for a period of several months, and sometimes, as in the case of the insight-oriented therapies, for up to one, two or three years. Concurrent with the therapy sessions are regular meetings with a supervisor. His role is to help the student to recognise and understand the nature of the patient's problems and the changes that the patient exhibits in the course of treatment. The supervisor also encourages the student to monitor and evaluate his reactions to the patient, and to examine his role as therapist. The supervised clinical experience can assume different forms. For example, the supervisor observes the novice at work with a patient through a one-way screen, or he listens to audio-tapes of the sessions. More recently, with the advent of inexpensive video-recording equipment, sessions can be taped, thereby allowing all aspects of the therapist's behaviour to be noted. These technical aids also serve another training purpose. A student can observe his experienced colleagues. In marital, sex, family and group therapy there is the additional possibility of the trainee acting as the junior co-therapist of an experienced practitioner.

Theoretical instruction is another component of training about which therapists are in general agreement. The newcomer, it is assumed, needs to obtain knowledge about the range and nature of the clinical problems he will encounter in his patients, as well as the theoretical basis upon which treatment is practised. The teaching content depends very much on the particular school in which the student receives his training. One of the difficulties he faces is the sheer multiplicity and diversity of theoretical positions. How can he possibly master them all? How can he select a particular position without sufficient knowledge about rival schools? Can he afford to try out various schools? Will the process not prove too demanding? These are difficult questions to answer. The common solution is one of expediency, the student adopting the views of therapists to whom he has access. More unusually, a trainee will opt for a particular school and use his initiative to secure the corresponding programme of training (this requires a major investment of time and, frequently, money).

In recent years the notion of learning by personal experience has become popular. Instead of trying to imagine what it is like to be a patient in therapy a situation is created wherein the trainee assumes the patient's role. Let us look at the use of this technique in the education of group therapists. Trainees join a group comparable in most respects to a group of patients, and meet regularly over a period of months, or longer, with a leader, to explore both the way the group works and their own participation in it (this is known as the 'sensitivity training-group). They soon have the opportunity to experience, first hand, such group phenomena as scapegoating, dependency, sub-grouping, and competitiveness. A variant on this theme, in the training of family therapists, is the 'family sculpt'. This is a relatively simple technique, but extremely potent in its effect at revealing to the trainee the sort of family from which he himself originates. The protagonist selects co-trainees to play the roles of his family members. After cueing in his colleagues, he places them, as if they were clay, into positions which reflect the personalities and the relationships of his family. Mother may for instance be placed prone on the floor, with father towering above her and looking sternly down. The protagonist may tuck himself tightly at mother's side, together with his siblings, with whom he competes for protection. The sculpture, when finally positioned, invariably evokes intense feelings, not only in the protagonist but also in other trainees for whom it may also have special meaning. The exercise enables the trainee to tap deeply-held feelings about his own family and this, in turn, offers him insight into the dynamics of patients and their families.

The most controversial aspect of a therapist's training is whether he should have a personal analysis. In contemporary psychoanalysis it is universally held that the trainee should undergo extensive psychotherapy by a training analyst. This amounts to three to four sessions a week over two or more years. Recently, the number of sessions devoted to such personal therapy has increased dramatically, up to one thousand to two thousand stretching over anything up to a decade. The origins of analysis for trainees have already been mentioned. Freud's observation that psychological blind-spots in a therapist could reduce his effectiveness with patients led him to recommend a short period of analysis by a colleague, with possible repeated boosters every five years or so.[8] Freud's relatively limited objective, it appears, has been replaced, through the policies of psychoanalytic institutes of training, by a vastly more ambitious goal – the attainment of ideal, mature psychological health. Since it is the training analyst's decision when this ideal state has been attained, and he is not necessarily the most unbiased of judges, therapy may proceed indefinitely. Some trainee analysts have uttered rebellious groans about the present 'inflationary' scheme (inflationary in more than one sense, because the cost of analysis is invariably born by the trainee and can amount to a very large bill).

Critics argue that a psychoanalysis can never be complete and that the therapist, after a reasonable period in treatment, should 'graduate' and then use his newly won insights to practise self-analysis throughout his remaining professional life. This form of argument is also applied by some therapists to determine when it is most appropriate to terminate a patient's treatment. The critics buttress their position by pointing out, not perhaps unfairly, that some analysts, despite their hundreds of hours of therapeutic endeavour, remain as narcissistic, obsessive, envious, insecure, competitive, or whatever, as they were before they began treatment. Analysis, even of the most comprehensive sort, does not guarantee the ideal psychological state.

The voice of rebellion is isolated, since most analysts still abide by the norms laid down by their training institutes – a rather unsatisfactory situation in many ways. The inevitable result is the reign of dogma and doctrine, with the free interchange of ideas barely encouraged, as it should be, in a field of social science. Instead, psychoanalysis becomes tantamount to religion. The entrenchment of dogma has sometimes reached absurd lengths. A particularly notorious example is that of the French analyst, Jacques Lacan, who stubbornly professed that he alone remained completely faithful to the word of Freud, whilst other French analytic schools were tainted with the evil of dissent. As if Freud delivered the eternal word about human nature!

The question of personal analysis must be viewed in the above context. My own experience suggests that a period in therapy is of intrinsic value (I hope I may be immodest enough to conclude that in my own case there have been some useful results both personally and professionally!), but value linked chiefly to subsequent professional concerns: an increased capacity to behave empathically and a reduction, certainly not an abolition, in psychological blind-spots. Obviously a welcome spin-off is some improvement in psychological functioning, even some basic change in personality. Freud mentioned that the therapist brought a certain expertise to his patients, but this did not mean offering himself as a perfect person; on the contrary, he was obliged to admit to himself the existence of his weaknesses and vulnerabilities.[10] Surveys suggest that most therapists do undergo some form of personal therapeutic experience and that the vast majority of them recognise its relevance and benefit in terms of the less ambitious goals mentioned above. The frequency and duration of personal therapy must, inevitably, be tailored to the particular needs of the trainee and it is foolhardy to lay down inflexible requirements.

The mention of requirements leads us to consider the thorny issue of whether therapists should be formally accredited in some way, and if so, how this is to be done. The licence problem has been about for a long while, stubbornly resistant to easy solution. The consumer has every right to enjoy protection from unscrupulous or incompetent therapists, but how is this to be achieved? The right to practise medicine rests in the hands of a statutory body, which can deprive a doctor of registration if he is found to have acted unethically or ineptly. Is the creation of a similar body for psychotherapists feasible? Not readily, since most therapists, as we have mentioned, belong to other professional groups anyway – psychiatry, nursing, occupational therapy, psychology and social work, for example, and are already bound by a statutory authority and associated code of practice. Some psychiatric groups in the United States have developed an 'internal audit' scheme whereby therapists are subject to appraisal by a panel of colleagues when their capacity to practise adequately is suspect. But this is a voluntary process and the powers of the panel are limited. It would seem that it is not entirely satisfactory or desirable for professionals to police one another. Some form of statutory accreditation seems necessary and will, in all likelihood come about before long, but its shape and form remain obscure. The maintenance of professional standards by an elected, impartial and judicious committee, composed of representatives of the various caring professions, which is legally granted the power to impose sanctions on a therapist found guilty of malpractice (much along the lines, say, of the General Medical Council in Britain) may be workable.

But the determination of who is entitled to practise as a therapist in the first place will remain the big bugbear. What about the enterprising entrepreneur who develops a psychotherapy 'product' such as an intensive week-end group activity, euphemistically labelled as 'human relations training', and offers this to willing and paying customers? Should he be recognised as a therapist?

The question acquires a special importance in the light of an ingenious study[11] reported from Vanderbilt University in the United States. Let me outline the project and its results and it will then be seen that the specification of minimal training requirements is quite tricky. Highly experienced professional therapists treated fifteen male college students, selected mainly on the basis of elevated anxiety, depression and introversion scores on a questionnaire, with brief individual psychotherapy. This lasted up to twenty-five hours, over a period of three to four months. A comparable group of students was treated under similar conditions by professors at the college, who were asked to volunteer as therapists because they were widely respected for their interest in students, as well as for their warmth and trustworthiness. The major difference between the two groups of therapists concerned their training. In the case of the professional therapists, three were psychiatrists and two clinical psychologists. None of the professors had received any formal training or had any practical experience of psychotherapy. Multiple measures of improvement were used before therapy, at its completion, and at a one-year follow-up. Patients, therapists, and independent judges were all used as sources of this measurement. The results are illuminating. Students treated by the professors achieved on average the same level of improvement as students treated by the trained therapists.

There was however considerable variation in the results accomplished by particular therapists among both the professional and professor groups, some patients deriving great benefit and others remaining unchanged, or even deteriorating. Additional analysis suggested that improvement in patients from both groups could be ascribed to 'the healing effects of a benign human relationship'. Furthermore, change seemed to be associated with a therapist – patient relationship in which the patient was motivated, and saw his therapist as caring and genuinely interested in his welfare. Before any reader dashes off and beckons an unsuspecting client to receive his benevolent ministration, a few crucial qualifications need to be noted. In the Vanderbilt study, both professors and patients were carefully chosen – professors on the basis of particular personality traits well suited to psychotherapy, and patients who were suffering from relatively mild neurotic states. Moreover, the professors worked under the supervision of research staff who could be consulted in case of emergency. One other crucial point concerns commitment to the task. Unlike the professional therapists, there was a turnover of therapists among the professors, some of whom (the numbers were unspecified in the original report) had difficulty in completing their assignment. They could not work towards specific goals, for instance, and only a minority would have been inclined to work with patients over an extended period.

This last finding suggests that training either facilitates a greater preparedness to practise psychotherapy consistently, or that a process of self-selection exists in that people who opt to become therapists are temperamentally suited to the job. Whichever the explanation, a broader issue is involved here: the effects of psychotherapy on the personal life of its practitioners. Obviously a job which entails active involvement, day in day out, with troubled and distressed people is bound to have repercussions on the therapist as a human-being and also on his family.

There is no doubt that the practice of psychotherapy is tough and demanding. Therapists elect to work with people, many of whom feel devastated, desperate, demoralised, guilt-ridden or despondent. Not unusually the patient's life history is one of repeated failure and rejection. In order to appreciate his patient's problems and needs the therapist must accept him unconditionally and also exercise a great measure of empathy. This sharing of the patient's world inevitably causes the therapist to feel such emotions as anguish and depression, a wearisome and sometimes gruelling experience. No matter how well the therapist trains himself to act in a reasonably detached manner, and seeks to protect himself from becoming overwhelmed by the patient's feelings, the inherent nature of the therapeutic relationship calls for a substantial degree of emotional involvement. This may be even more pronounced in a case where the therapist faces problems similar to those of his patient and is constantly reminded of them. With such self-preoccupation he may fail to identify objectively with the patient and unwittingly use the sessions for self-therapy.

In addition to the intense emotions the patient brings to therapy he also develops a transference, that is, a set of feelings and attitudes unconsciously directed to the therapist who represents one or more key figures from the patient's past or current life. Examples of transference include anger, disappointment, reverence, dependency, jealousy and seductiveness. Although the transference 'belongs' to the patient this does not necessarily prevent the therapist feeling its impact and also, perhaps, confusing it with other processes. For instance, the patient who unconsciously sets out to undermine the therapist's authority by challenging and criticising his interventions may instil a sense of doubt in the therapist, especially a novice, about his competence and aptitude. In the case of one trainee, a patient under her care insisted that she was callous and hostile towards him. She had indeed felt impatience in the face of his 'stubborn refusal' to co-operate in therapy. The result was a period of confusion and concern lest her hostility was as prominent as the patient insisted and pervaded all her other therapeutic relationships. A colleague was needed to disentangle transference from reality.

Often a colleague is not readily available for this purpose and the therapist has no choice but to grapple with the confusion on his own. Many therapists, particularly those in private practice, work in isolation and have little idea of how they compare with fellow professionals in style and effectiveness at work. Patients are an obvious source of feedback but their reports are prone to bias. The actual results of therapy are generally ill-defined and long in coming. Support for the therapist when he is not 'up to scratch', or feeling discouraged for whatever reason, is not readily available. And yet, this same person feels obliged and is expected to offer support to his patients at all times. Every relationship with each of his patients is of this asymmetrical, non-reciprocated type. One would imagine that a therapist's obvious source of support is his family. But the picture is not straightforward because of the vital importance of confidentiality: the therapist is unable to disclose anything about his work and patients except in the most general terms. To complicate the problem further, the therapist, having spent his day intensely aroused, may well be emotionally fatigued and spent by the time he arrives home. As a result he has little emotional reserve left for the family and conversely feels bad about expecting any more in return.

The picture I have portrayed seems utterly forlorn, and you may well conclude that psychotherapy is ideally suited to masochistic personalities and no one else! Nothing could be further from the truth. To complete the picture I should highlight the rewards inherent in the practice of psychotherapy and also mention some of the strategies adopted by the therapist to cope with the range of personal problems he may encounter. There cannot be many other professions, and certainly none come readily to mind, in which the opportunity exists to get to know a wide range of people so intimately. An agricultural science student, a distinguished academic in the humanities, a housewife, a trade-unionist, a pest controller, a high-school teacher, a computer specialist, a lawyer, a graphic artist, a technical editor – these are but a few of the patients I have come to know closely during my years of clinical practice. And all of them have held a special interest for me whether it be because of their remarkable life history, their intriguing psychopathology, their fascinating cultural background – the list is endless. Rather than regard patients as constituting a 'clinical load' – a constant danger in a busy clinic with a rapid turnover – the therapist is apt, because of his long-term and close relationships, to recognise something 'precious' (to use Martin Buber's term) in each of the people he works with. I must not convey too mawkish a picture. These same patients can also be a cause of frustration and difficulty for the therapist at the same time. Therapy can rarely be described with a single epithet. It is typically a *melange* of the following: exhilarating, tiring, frustrating, amusing, inspiring, dispiriting, and much more beside.

The therapist is in a position to relieve himself of some of the emotional pressures to which he is vulnerable and he can do so in a variety of ways. Probably the most important measure is for him to acknowledge the intrinsic nature of his job: the mixture of rewards and stresses that it brings. A realistic appraisal of his limitations – that he cannot possibly treat everyone who seeks his help, that he may need to set quite limited goals with some patients who are incapable of more substantial change, and that he may come to dislike the occasional patient he treats – will spare the therapist much anguish and despair. The seasoned therapist has commonly attained this posture of 'realism' whereas his novice counterpart is full of eager zeal and ready to 'take on the world'. More practically the therapist can balance his clientele so that he treats at any one time a mixed group, from the relatively straightforward to the more complex, demanding case. He may also have to face the prospect of terminating his contract with a patient who proves resistant to change or is unsuited to psychotherapy, without feelings of shame, guilt or failure.

The novice, and even the experienced practitioner, can confer with a trusted colleague when he is in difficulty. An essential component of the trainee's programme is his regular supervision by an experienced therapist and the confidential nature of this forum enables the disclosure of both technical and personal problems. Less systematic is the colleagueship among trained therapists. The loss of face in consulting a colleague can constitute a real barrier to the receipt of help; the barrier needs to be removed by the troubled therapist so that he can benefit from the mere act of sharing, as well as from obtaining any subsequent support and guidance. This type of help is perhaps best provided by a fellow clinician who is well placed to recognise and appreciate the nature of the problems involved. Obviously, a spouse or other family member may feel inclined to take on this role but the result is bound to be less satisfactory. Family members should instead understand the often demanding quality of the therapist's task and help to facilitate the creation of a supportive and comforting family atmosphere.

The therapist can also serve himself well by respecting his need for diversion and relaxation: taking holidays, pursuit of hobbies and participation in physical recreation. Diversity within his work also has a salubrious effect. I have gained the impression over several years – and it is only an impression – that the therapist who is not totally absorbed in the practice of psychotherapy is more effective, or at least derives greater satisfaction from his work, than his colleague who spends eight hours a day, every day, seeing patients. Teaching, supervision, writing, conducting research, even administration, are common alternative activities which result in a more balanced professional life. Similarly, regular contact with fellow therapists at professional meetings and conferences takes the clinician outside his office, where he may feel quite isolated, into a different environment from which he can return recharged with new ideas and warm feelings of colleagueship.

4 Schools of psychotherapy

I referred briefly to the notion of 'schools of psychotherapy' in Chapter 3. Let us now look at these schools in order to identify what is distinctive about each of them. In considering the factors specific to each, it would be well to remind ourselves of the general factors that appear to be common to all psychotherapies – a subject we covered in the first chapter. In considering the various schools, a problem immediately arises. There are literally dozens of them – the current figure well exceeds 100 – and we could not possibly work our way through bio-feedback, Freudian psychoanalysis, several variants of dynamic psychotherapy linked to figures such as Jung, Adler, Horney, Sullivan, Klein and Fairbairn, primal-scream therapy, transcendental meditation, cognitive therapy, reality therapy, rational-emotive therapy, behaviour therapy, transactional analysis, Gestalt therapy, Rogerian therapy, hypnosis, existential therapy, and a host of others, without compiling an encyclopaedic volume and thoroughly exhausting ourselves in the process! In any event, by the time we had finished a few new therapies would bound to have come into being.

Fortunately, there is a way of obviating this problem. Although most schools appear unique on first examination, they are based on certain core concepts which stem from a limited number of theoretical sources. Moreover, several schools are too peripheral to the type of psychotherapy we discuss in this book to warrant attention. We can therefore conveniently focus on three basic theoretical models. These are usefully labelled: psychodynamic, humanist-existential and behavioural. Almost all psychotherapy schools belong to one of these three theoretical frameworks. I hope that it will be clear, by the end of the chapter, what distinguishes the 'big three' from one another. Their definition involves looking both at *theory* – of human behaviour and mental ill health, and *practice* – the application of this theory, the methods and techniques that constitute the therapeutic process. We begin with the psychodynamic model as it was the first to evolve and embraces the largest number of psychotherapy schools.

THE PSYCHODYNAMIC SCHOOL

Theory

All psychodynamic schools spring from the work of Sigmund Freud and are, in essence, variations of the psychoanalytic treatment he discovered. This is not the place to discuss Freud's ideas in general – these are conveniently collected together in the *Standard Edition*[1] of his writings. Let me rather consider those ideas that are especially relevant to the practice of psychoanalysis. Psychoanalysis is an exceedingly comprehensive set of theories about human behaviour, both normal and abnormal, and they include a vast range of concepts. For our purposes the following are worthy of mention: psychic determinism, early determinants of personality and behaviour, and the structure of the mind. A discussion of these concepts will pave the way for a schematic view of neurosis and of the practical methods used to treat it.

Freud set out initially to explain the origin of certain neurotic symptoms but ultimately evolved a general theory of human behaviour. A central tenet of this theory is that 'there is nothing trivial, nothing arbitrary or haphazard . . . in the determination of mental life'.[2] This notion, commonly known as psychic determinism, is intimately linked with the teasing out of three discrete levels of the mind – conscious, pre-conscious and unconscious. Mental phenomena, even the most mundane, are, according to Freud, meaningful, and their origins can be traced to the unconscious layer. He substantiated his thesis about the unconscious in two classical texts, *The Interpretation of Dreams*,[3] which was published in 1900, and *The Psychopathology of Everyday Life*,[4] published four years later.

Freud's concepts of dreams are absolutely central to psychoanalytic thought and, indeed, he regarded his book on them as his most original contribution. Briefly, he postulated that the dream as we are able to recall it – the memories that reach consciousness – is only its manifest part. Those parts which are hidden from the person and remain unconscious, the latent content, constitute the true dream. The latent parts are distorted by an internal censor, whose function is to prevent threatening impulses, thoughts and feelings from being expressed in their original form. Thus, the recalled dream, which may on first inspection appear trivial or even ridiculous, is nothing of the sort. Detection of its unconscious roots soon demonstrates its significance. Freud extended the concept of psychic determinism and of the omnipresence of the unconscious in *The Psychopathology of Everyday Life*, in which he referred to the many instances of forgetting we all show in our daily lives. Forgetting a name or missing an appointment are common examples. Another related class of behaviour covers errors and mistakes, such as misplacing an important object, and slips of the tongue, for example, mis-introducing one person to another in a way which proves embarrassing. Freud argued that these errors and instances of forgetting were motivated by unconsciously determined factors which could be identified through psychoanalysis and explained.

A further concept, associated with psychic determinism and the unconscious, concerns the causal links between current behaviour and preceding psychological events, especially those taking place in infancy and early childhood. Freud highlighted the potent influence of two basic instinctual drives on all subsequent behaviour – aggressive and sexual. In 1905 his *Three Essays on Sexual Theory*[5] appeared. The middle essay deals with infantile sexuality and examines the evolution of the sexual drive through a number of specific phases. The first three phases, which are auto-erotic in nature, are characterised by particular parts of the body being sensed by the infant or child as gratifying. The mouth is the first of these erogenous zones: the child derives pleasure in the form of sucking and biting. This oral phase is followed, at about eighteen months, by the anal phase, during which the anus takes over as the new erogenous zone and retention or defecation become the main sources of sensuous gratification. The genital or phallic phase follows, at about three years, during which the genitalia become the chief erogenous zone. During this time the Oedipal situation unfolds: the child forms in fantasy an intense love relationship with his parent of the opposite sex and regards the other parent as a rival. How does the child come to terms with this dilemma? He ultimately recognises that his Oedipal wishes cannot be met and that he is powerless to banish the rival parent. The conflict is resolved through a process of identification with the parent of similar sex, and repression – the active forgetting and pushing back of threatening thoughts and impulses into the unconscious. Repression of the conflict is considered as an explanation of our poor memory of these Oedipal experiences.

Repression is an example of a manoeuvre available to the personality to defend itself from the threats that unconsciously-based aggressive and sexual drives bring. A detailed formulation of how this process operates emerged much later, in 1923, in one of Freud's most notable works *The Ego and the Id*.[6] In the belief that his former conceptual framework was inadequate to explain all psychological phenomena, he now hypothesised that mental life was a product of the interaction of three psychic forces – the ego, the id and the super-ego. He defined the ego as the 'co-ordinated organisation of mental processes in a person', that part of the personality which perceives and makes sense of the environment, both the internal psychological environment and the external world. Part of the ego is unconscious and functions as the dream censor and the agent of repression, by keeping threatening material locked in the unconscious. As the executive part of the personality, it has the capacity for establishing what can and cannot be achieved and what sorts of wishes can be satisfied. The ego also serves to cope with danger, from whatever source. Anxiety is the warning signal to the ego that danger looms.

The id is not very different from what Freud originally described as the unconscious – the seat of repressed feelings, fantasies and drives. The id is the dominant psychic force in early childhood but gradually becomes subordinate to the developing, and ultimately more powerful ego. The id is totally unconscious and governed by an inborn pleasure principle – the psyche's wish for immediate gratification and for the avoidance of pain. As the ego gains ascendancy, so the pleasure principle is supplanted by the reality principle, whereby tolerance of frustration is managed and a person is freed from his primitive, instinctual drives and so enabled to act rationally.

The super-ego is the moral agency in the psyche. It is the conscience, or the ego ideal, the type of person the ego strives to become. The super-ego develops mainly as a result of the child assimilating the moral precepts held and taught by his parents.

All three forces – ego, id and super-ego – are in constant dynamic interaction with one another. In a normally functioning person the result is a state of balance and the psyche is in equilibrium. The ego's task is to restore the equilibrium whenever it is disturbed. In a well-integrated individual this is readily achieved. By contrast, the ego's failure to cope satisfactorily leads to the development of neurotic symptoms.

The psychoanalytic view of neurosis

Freud was an important contributor to the task of distinguishing between different forms of neurotic illness and he also pioneered their classification. In his view, there are certain basic features which underlie all neuroses. A neurosis can be regarded as the result of the following sequence: an unconsciously derived conflict disrupts the equilibrium of the three psychic forces: the id, ego and super-ego. One or more factors may be operating to cause this disruption: strong id drives which seek expression, or intense super-ego forces especially of a punitive kind, or a weak, vulnerable ego, the result of stressful external circumstances. The unconscious drives actively seek discharge. Anxiety ensues and serves as a warning signal to the ego that something is awry. Sensing danger, the ego tries to restore equilibrium and so re-establish its authority. But the result is failure: the ego, despite its resort to various defensive strategies such as repression (which we have already mentioned), denial and rationalisation, can no longer manage to fulfil its executive role. The symptom that emerges is a form of compromise and the product of the battle between the unconscious drives and the faltering ego. The neurotic symptom is the ego's way of adapting to the conflict and of re-establishing some, albeit far from durable, form of equilibrium. It is obviously an imperfect solution since the person is now faced with one or more neurotic symptoms and the underlying conflict that led to the emergence of these symptoms in the first place remains unresolved.

There are a number of different neurotic symptoms which may be experienced as a result of the above breakdown of equilibrium. Anxiety, phobias, depression, obsessions, compulsions, hysterical conversion reactions (physical symptoms without organic cause), are just some of them. The specific form of neurosis in a particular person is, according to psychoanalytic theory, dependent on the phenomenon known as fixation. We mentioned earlier the phases of infantile sexual development. Normally there is an orderly sequence in this development, with any problem arising during the phases or at transitional points being overcome, thus enabling subsequent development. Basically, the id drives within each phase are kept under firm control. But a developmental conflict may not be completely resolved and the child's psycho-sexual development, as a consequence, may get stuck. In other words, there is a fixation at either the oral, anal or genital phase. For example, a person in whom conflict at the anal phase has not been adequately managed is likely to display a neurosis in which obsessive and compulsive symptoms predominate.

Psychoanalysis in practice

Let us first consider the goals of psychoanalytic psychotherapy and then its main methods. Although there is some debate about what constitutes a cure, most analysts would agree that the primary objective of treatment is the patient's greater self-knowledge. Ideally, the patient achieves a clear understanding of the underlying conflicts within him and of their causal relationship to the symptoms he suffers from. What was formerly unintelligible, confusing and even weird, now becomes intelligible and clear. This gaining of self-knowledge or insight, as it is commonly called, is not only an intellectual pursuit, but also involves the emotional experiencing in therapy of the material that is brought up by the patient and subsequently analysed. Insight which combines intellectual and emotional aspects facilitates resolution of the neurotic process, both of its symptoms and of its underlying basis. The expression 'Where id was, let ego be' is apposite in reflecting the treatment's objective. The ego reasserts its executive status and control over primitive instinctual id drives. The person can now enjoy the freedom to act in a mature and rational way.

Conventionally, in psychoanalytic forms of psychotherapy, patient and therapist meet regularly, between one and five times a week. The patient lies on a couch with the therapist placed out of his vision. This physical arrangement fulfils two purposes: firstly, the therapist can better serve as a blank screen on to which the patient projects his feelings and attitudes; secondly, the patient can regress or revert more easily to earlier stages of psychological development, which allows him, together with his therapist, to examine closely the patterns of conflict associated with these stages.

From the outset, and thereafter throughout the entire course of therapy, there is one cardinal rule. The patient must speak openly, frankly and without any inhibition whatsoever. This notion of free association today seems far from revolutionary but in the 1890s it was tantamount to a fundamental discovery. If we bear in mind that Freud in the preceding decade had regarded hypnosis as the optimal mode of treating neurosis in which the patient was directed by the therapist to focus on particular thoughts, memories and feelings, free association amounted to a volte-face. The route into the unconscious was through the disclosure of everything and anything that entered the patient's mind, however shameful, embarrassing, distressing, confusing or irrational.

Following the notion of psychic determinism – that there is nothing trivial in mental life – the analyst views all the patient's emerging thoughts as significant in one or another way, and regards the process of free association as essential in leading to the discovery of the unconscious central conflict which underlies the neurosis.

Of particular importance in this regard are the patient's dreams. They constitute a rich and endless source of unconscious material; as Freud put it: 'The interpretation of dreams is in fact the royal road to a knowledge of the unconscious; it is the securest foundation of psychoanalysis'.[7] The patient is thus encouraged to recall his dreams and these are then unravelled collaboratively with the therapist. This process also serves as a spur to further free association. The purpose of the unravelling is to get beyond the dream's obvious, manifest content into the underlying, latent content; that is, to undo the effects of the dream censor and so identify the true nature of the dream.

Dream analysis is comparable to a translation of one language into another. The language of the original dream is of a quality labelled by Freud as primary process – time and place are not appreciated and contradictions are not tolerated. The ego's censor further disguises the themes which are unacceptable to it. The interpretation of the dream requires translation from primary process into secondary process language, the latter characterised by being reality-bound, responsible and socially aware.

Interpretation is the therapist's basic tool, and is closely associated with his active listening and keen observation of the patient's behaviour, both verbal and non-verbal. An interpretation is better conceptualised as a provisional hypothesis than as a dogmatic statement. Typical suggestions by the therapist might be: 'Perhaps all the frenzied activity over the last couple of years meant that you did not have to cope with your mother's death'; 'I wonder if your unpunctuality over recent sessions is related to your concern about becoming dependent on me'; and 'It sounds as if you are talking about a case you came across in a text-book rather than about yourself.' The therapist typically arrives at formulations about, *inter alia*, the unconscious roots of neurotic symptoms, the type of unconscious defences on which the patient customarily relies to keep unpalatable feelings and thoughts at bay, and specific aspects of the relationship between the patient and therapist.

Alas, the magic interpretation does not exist. There is no single formulation uttered by the therapist which will lead to the patient's cry of 'Eureka' and his complete acquisition of insight. On the contrary, the themes that crop up in therapy – via free association and corresponding interpretations – are explored and studied time and time again using a variety of approaches. What is so baffling and obscure to the patient (and often to the therapist as well) requires elaborate and painstaking work until clarification is reached. The patient is not always in a position to participate in this work or able to engage at a particular level of exploration. The therapist must intervene with his interpretations gradually and in accordance with his patient's stage of development in treatment. For example, to declare that a patient is using a particular set of defences to cope with his anxiety long before he has any inkling of what the therapist is even referring to, is bound to fail. Similarly, making an important interpretation when a patient is in the midst of a swirl of disturbing and puzzling feelings from which he can barely see the wood for the trees, is most unlikely to be heeded. From his stance of relative detachment and objectivity the therapist may well recognise underlying patterns of behaviour in his patient early on in therapy, but he needs to discipline himself to express his interpretations only when the patient is likely to appreciate them.

In psychoanalytic psychotherapy the therapist acts in a fairly neutral and detached way in order that the patient will disclose his feelings as if he were projecting them on to a blank screen. The subsequent study of these projections sheds light on the nature and causes of the patient's current problems and symptoms. The interpretation of these feelings is exceedingly pertinent to the therapeutic process, and for most analysts, the nub of their operations. The feelings chiefly involved are those that stem from infancy and childhood and which were originally experienced (and usually still are in the present) towards key figures such as a parent or a sibling. These feelings – they include love, admiration, possessiveness, envy, anger, hate, rivalry and dependence – are transferred to the therapist as if he were the original key relative. This phenomenon in psychoanalytic therapy, known as the transference, can become quite convoluted and involved and come to dominate the therapeutic relationship. The therapist's function is then to interpret the resultant 'transference neurosis' which is a transitional state between the original neurotic condition with which the patient presented and normal psychological functioning. The transference neurosis is in a sense an artificial state, the product of the relationship that evolves between the freely associating patient and the relatively detached therapist. The advantage of its formation is that it develops in the consulting room and is therefore immediately accessible to study; the roots of the basic neurosis are then clarified through the interpretation of the transference neurosis.

The evolution of the transference was initially not regarded by Freud as an essential component of the therapeutic relationship. Only later did he come to note it as the most cogent process in treatment and inherently necessary for improvement. He also pointed out the obstacles to its exploration, particularly those erected by the patient. Patients who ostensibly were in a position to accept interpretations about transference in a therapeutic relationship, appeared to resist such understanding. There seemed to be a force in the patient, both conscious and unconscious, which blocked out obvious revelations about himself that emerged in treatment; a sort of injunction: 'Do not allow the unconscious to become conscious.' The phenomenon of resistance is today well known and invariably insinuates itself into therapy in greater or lesser measure. Freud was the first to highlight the importance of this phenomenon when he wrote 'The struggle against all these resistances is our main work during an analytic treatment; the task of making interpretations is nothing compared to it'.[8] Resistance is one of the factors that account for prolonged therapy: the insights are there for the taking but the patient declines. 'Rather bear those ills we have, than fly to others we know not of'. The human psyche is a conservative place. A person may be severely disabled by neurotic symptoms yet they do constitute a compromise solution, a form of truce between conflicting forces within him; better that compromise than an alternative which is completely unpredictable and unknown.

Efforts to rush psychoanalysis almost always fail. An appreciation of the potency of resistance enables us to understand why. It is not a question of how long the therapeutic route is but to what degree that route is cluttered with hurdles – placed there by the patient, and for the most part unwittingly. I should point out that this does not negate the possibility of conducting brief therapy[9] based on psychoanalytic principles in highly motivated patients whose problems are reasonably well circumscribed and amenable to a clear focus.

It might be thought that mere exhortation of the patient to refrain from resisting would be appropriate, but indeed this is not the case – such exhortation is likely to prove futile. Instead, the therapist's role encompasses that of a scout. He looks out for evidence of resistance whenever it rears its head. On discerning a particular pattern, he notifies the patient of his observations whereupon both jointly seek to understand what thoughts, feelings, memories and fantasies are being avoided.

In summary then, psychoanalytic psychotherapy involves the following processes: the patient's unbridled disclosure of whatever enters his mind – free association; the transference of infantile and childlike feelings and attitudes to the therapist which were previously directed to key figures in the patient's earlier life – the development of a transference neurosis; the interpretation by the therapist of the nature of the transference as well as of customary defences the patient applies to protect himself and the resistances he manifests to self-exploration; and finally, the repeated working through of the discoveries made in the course of treatment. The ultimate aim is comprehensive insight with translation into corresponding changes in behaviour and personality.

Variations on a theme

Freud's theories about human behaviour and psychoanalytic treatment underwent numerous and sometimes radical revisions over the course of his long professional life. In addition, many of his close collaborators extended the boundaries of psychoanalytic thinking. But before long, differences of opinion surfaced, some of major proportion. The nature of the psychoanalytic movement in its pioneering phase, especially Freud's rather intolerant attitude to dissent, led some notable figures to leave the fold and to evolve their own theoretical models upon which corresponding schools of therapy were established. Carl Jung and Alfred Adler were two of the foremost European dissidents who founded their own schools; Karen Horney and H. S. Sullivan[10] were pioneering neo-Freudians (a convenient label for those who, while developing an emphasis on social factors in behaviour, still retained a basic psychoanalytic approach) in the United States; and W. R. D. Fairbairn[11] and Melanie Klein[12] were prominent in Britain. Let me now focus on three of these figures in order to illustrate how these analysts became disaffected with the classical Freudian position and developed their own approach.

Carl Gustav Jung was perhaps the most celebrated of all the Freudian dissenters for he was clearly being groomed by the master himself to take over the mantle of leadership of the psychoanalytic movement. But he was also celebrated because of his original contributions. Specifically with regard to psychotherapy, he advanced the notion of 'individuation' – the aim of therapy was to discover all parts of oneself and one's creative potential. Jung was less concerned than Freud with the biological roots of behaviour, especially infantile sexual development, but rather emphasised social and cultural factors. In psychotherapy itself, the relationship is akin to that of an encounter in which therapist and patient sit face to face rather than the latter using a couch. The role of transference is not given prominence and is replaced by a more adult type of collaboration.

The major work in therapy revolves around the patient's dreams. Here Jung differs sharply from Freud. The recalled dream in Jung's view is not merely the manifest dream serving as a disguise for the latent content which has then to be unravelled; instead, all aspects of the dream are rich with meaning and symbolism. The dream is the chief vehicle for the exploration of the vastly creative forces that constitute the unconscious. Moreover the unconscious is not merely the repository of the individual's personal history but also embraces a wider social history, a phenomenon Jung labelled the collective unconscious. He arrived at this notion through a study of myths, legends and symbols in different cultures, in different epochs. That many of these myths, legends and symbols are shared by a whole variety of cultures is not fortuitous but reflects cosmic mythical themes or archetypes, a salient feature of man's collective history. A chief aspect of Jungian therapy is amplification, a process which in Jung's view goes far beyond Freud's rather reductive free association. In particular the patient's dreams are explored in all their rich complexity. For example, the patient may be asked to pursue a dream by entering a state of active imagination; this might involve diverse methods of expression such as poetry, painting, sculpting or even dancing. In this way the patient reaches the deepest level of his unconscious and via this journey works towards the state of individuation.

Many clinicians have found this therapeutic process vague and tending to the spiritual. The question of where the patient's psychiatric state fits in is questionable. The vagueness is not altogether helped by the quality and content of Jung's writings: his rather unclear accounts of transcendental themes. Therapists who belong to the Jungian school have been apt to claim that their approach is particularly well suited to a more or less normal person who on reaching middle age is motivated to know more about his true self, more about what is ultimately of value to him in his life. This sounds more like a spiritual journey than the formal treatment of a neurotic condition. Notwithstanding, some Jungian therapists have applied his principles to the treatment of psychotic conditions including schizophrenia. With what degree of success is however debatable.

Alfred Adler, a Viennese physician, was like Jung a prominent dissenter from the early psychoanalytic movement. Adler joined Freud's circle in 1902 but only remained a member for some nine years. He then broke away to form his own school of 'individual psychology'. An important tenet in Adlerian theory concerns the development of the individual. We begin life in a state of inferiority, weak and defenceless, for which we compensate as we grow by striving for power and by evolving a life-style to make our lives understandable and purposeful. The pattern that eventually emerges varies and may include such goals as the acquisition of money, procreation, high ambition or creativity. The drive for power and the choice of life-style may however go awry in which case a neurosis results. Ideally, an individual should move towards the goal of self-realisation which necessarily entails the need to take risks. In contrast, a path may be followed which leads to ineffective efforts to cope with the basic feeling of inferiority, the assumption of a façade or false self, and a withdrawal into neurotic behaviour. Neurosis is defined by the Adlerians as a failure to learn how to overcome the initial inferiority state.

Adler regarded therapy as a re-educative process in which the therapist, who serves as a model and as a source of encouragement, engages in a warm and close relationship with the patient and enables him to discover and understand the life-style he has assumed. The therapist's role is that of a 'helping friend'. The patient is regarded as discouraged in terms of facing the demands of life and not as suffering from a diagnosable illness.

Other notable facets of Adlerian therapy include the following: clear goals are explicitly discussed by therapist and patient at the outset; therapy remains goal-directed throughout its course; the focus is on the present and the future; seeking to identify factors in the patient's past which may account for his current sense of discouragement is regarded as relatively unimportant; unconscious determinants of behaviour are much less crucial than the conscious ones and the term 'unconscious' is not regarded as a construct, as by Freud and Jung, but rather used descriptively to refer to those aspects of the person that are not understood by him.

With the achievement of insight, the patient can dispense with his previous patterns of behaviour and seek an alternative life-style, particularly one which involves other people. This goal reflects a fundamental feature of Adler's thinking, namely, that all behaviour occurs in a social context – an individual needs to feel some sense of belonging and enjoy engagement with his fellows. This social focus is reflected in Adler's idealistic view of society as potentially egalitarian, caring and co-operative. Adler was in fact a socialist. A concrete representation of this idealism was his founding of family education centres, an obvious example of a community mental-health service. The rise of the community mental-health centres in the 1960s was regarded by their developers as radical but the credit should in fact go to Adler. Indeed, a number of his innovations, in terms of both theory and practice, have been utilised subsequently without due recognition. As we shall see in a moment, Adler could also be regarded as a pioneer in another area – as the first exponent of the humanist-existential movement in psychiatry. It is only the occasional writer however who has acknowledged this particular contribution. Today the Adlerian psychotherapy school *per se* is small and relatively insignificant compared to the Freudian one but Adlerian ideas are everywhere.

Adler's break with Freud was very much related to the former's emphasis on social forces in the origin and maintenance of neurotic behaviour. This focus on the individual's social and cultural world became a prominent feature of an inter-related group of neo-Freudian approaches in the United States. In the case of neo-Freudians such as Karen Horney and Erich Fromm,[13] their initial home was in orthodox analysis. They practised in this way in their native Germany until their flight to the United States from Hitler's Fascism. The foremost American born analyst with an 'interpersonalist' stamp was Harry Stack Sullivan. His influence has probably been the most enduring for contemporary psychotherapy although limited in the main to North America.

We can consider the chief features in the approach of the neo-Freudians by looking briefly at Karen Horney; her stablemates differ more in the use of terminology than in substance.

Horney developed her views after settling in the United States in the early 1930s. In Berlin she practised as an orthodox analyst but became disenchanted with Freud's rigid focus on instinctual biological factors as determinants of behaviour. She argued that cultural factors were more salient than biological ones, as reflected in the major differences in psychological development and behaviour among different social cultural groups. Sexual differences in particular were attributed to social rather than biological factors. There was, in her view, no universal 'normal' pattern of behaviour. Indeed, behaviour regarded as normal in one culture could be viewed as quite neurotic in another culture. Two qualities however characterise all neurotics – they are inflexible in their attitudes and behaviour, and they fail to fulfil their potential because of inner conflicts.

In line with her emphasis on culture as a potent influence on behaviour, Horney advanced the concept of the vital role of parental love in the life of a young child. Children typically suffer basic anxiety, a consequence of feeling small and helpless in a threatening world. The child fortunate enough to be reared in an atmosphere of love and protection succeeds in overcoming his basic anxiety. By contrast, the deprived child comes to view his world as unfair, cruel and hazardous. The inevitable result is his experience of low self-esteem.

The significance of the interpersonal approach is further illustrated by the three basic options available to contend with the anxiety associated with the original state of helplessness. A person can move towards, against, or away from others. Moving towards others, he accepts a helpless submissive position striving to win affection by depending on them for protection – 'If I submit to the will of others they will look after me and I will avoid being hurt.' A move against others involves the supposition that the world is hostile; the need is to fight and to win: 'If I am stronger than you, I can't be harmed.' The third attitude is to move away from others – neither to approach nor to engage in battle. The safest solution is withdrawal – to avoid involvement and to strive for security in one's solitude. Horney also argued that the neurotic might use more than one of these solutions.

The task of therapy according to Horney is to recognise and analyse the patient's defective patterns in relating to others. In part this is achieved through the study of what takes place in the actual relationship between patient and therapist. There is however no emphasis on transference as occurs in Freudian analysis. Therapy aims to enable the patient to move *with* others, by engaging in relationships which are reciprocal and mutual. Another goal is a greater level of self-realisation in the patient, that he may be freed of rigid determined modes of thought and action.

As was the case with Adler, it is apparent that many of Horney's ideas and those of her fellow neo-Freudians, have infiltrated into the practical procedures of many contemporary psychotherapists, although this 'osmosis' has not generally been acknowledged.

Only in the case of Sullivan has there developed a more organised assembly of adherents, albeit limited to certain parts of the United States. The reason for the implicit absorption of neo-Freudian concepts rather than their formal recognition by practitioners is probably related to the inherent limitations of the theories. This can be seen from our brief account of Horney's views. She fails to offer a comprehensive model of neurosis. What we get is a rather diffuse and global approach without any systematic consideration about the diversity of neurotic states. How is it that one person becomes grossly at odds with society, manifests antisocial behaviour and fails to learn from experience whereas another individual develops a crippling state of anxiety with panic attacks, whilst a third suffers from obsessive thoughts about being contaminated and indulges in compulsive cleansing rituals? Freud may have been too dogmatic about the exclusive relevance of instinctual forces but he did seek to explain the specific origins of particular neurotic patterns of behaviour. Whatever the limitations of the neo-Freudian models, thinkers such as Horney, Sullivan and Fromm must be credited with having made significant contributions to both the theory and practice of psychotherapy, in particular through their emphasis on the interpersonal sphere in the evolution of normal personality, and in neurosis. They have been instrumental in widening the boundaries of Freud's unduly constricted framework.

THE HUMANIST-EXISTENTIAL SCHOOL

The roots of the humanist-existential school of psychotherapy were initially planted in the soil of Western Europe but here they remained rather fragile and tender. A small number of European analysts,[14] mainly German and Swiss, and foremost among them Ludwig Binswanger, Medard Boss, Roland Kuhn and Viktor Frankl, began to react against what they regarded as the unduly reductive and materialistic approach to the study of man's behaviour by Freud and to his insistence on instinct-based, unconscious determinism. Instead, each in his own way championed the basic idea, derived from existentialist philosophy, that every human being is (a) the author of his own world and (b) that his knowledge of the world can only be achieved through the experiencing of it by his consciousness – 'Man constitutes his own world.'

Perhaps because their work remained untranslated for many years, the new insights of this group of European therapists failed to attract the attention of psychotherapists in Britain and North America. It is true that in Britain a minuscule group – Ronald Laing[15] is its most distinguished representative – became influenced by European existentialism in the 1960s but the vast majority of British psychotherapists have not been so. Laing has become something of a cult figure especially among the ranks of anti-psychiatrists, a group who deride the use of psychiatric diagnosis with the argument that this objectifies and dehumanises the patient. The reaction of most psychiatrists in Britain has been to dismiss Laing in his entirety, an unfortunate development since it has robbed British psychotherapy of a potentially valuable contribution. Psychiatric resistance can be ascribed in part to his becoming a cult figure but no doubt has other sources. Perhaps it should not come as a surprise that the European existentialist movement has not found a haven across the channel. Strongly positivist and rationalist bodies of opinion in philosophy and psychology have held sway, looking askance at rivals which threaten them, particularly anything which has a taint of anti-rationalism.

The picture in the United States is somewhat different. When Rollo May, the humanist psychologist, introduced existential psychotherapy in the form of an edited volume entitled *Existence*[16] to an American readership in 1958, the reception while not effusive was reasonable. May himself has been a mainstay of the New World variation of existential psychology and psychotherapy together with other well-known figures[17] such as Abraham Maslow, Carl Rogers and Gordon Allport. Coincident with the European import, an indigenous force in American psychology evolved, more of an ideology than a school. It is usually called humanistic psychology. Maslow referred to it as the 'third force', complementing the psychoanalytic and behavioural approaches. Although the humanist-existential school has fuzzy boundaries today, and many diverse figures in psychology and psychiatry assemble under its standard, there are sufficient features held in common to make Maslow's third force a recognisable entity. A helpful initial step in considering the third force is to examine its philosophical roots in existentialism.

Existentialism[18] is more a style or way of approaching the study of Man than a distinct school or systematic theory of knowledge. Indeed, under its rubric sit a whole range of ideas and attitudes, some of them quite contradictory – from the atheism and Marxism of Jean-Paul

Sartre to the intensely religious traditions of Martin Buber, Gabriel Marcel and Paul Tillich. But as a philosophical style, existentialism is reasonably consistent and encompasses themes common to most of its contributors: the inevitability of death, the freedom to choose and act, taking responsibility for one's life, and the centrality of meaningfulness and purpose.

A basic tenet is that the lived experience of a person is the touchstone of all knowledge and, moreover, constitutes the only valid criterion of truth. There is no truth except in relation to the experiencing man. The origin of this principle, in the last century, was a reaction against the overwhelming dominance of Rationalism. Martin Heidegger, for example, attacked the idea that anything could be explained by reasoning. Rationalism was altogether too materialistic and reductive a view of Man. Edmund Husserl, through his discovery of the phenomenological method, paved the way for the existentialist approach. Husserl rejected the subject-object division and argued that we know the world only through the active experiencing of it by our consciousness. We are what we are through our acts, through the fact that we constitute our world. All knowledge is in relation to the man who finds it and only he can give a sense of the world to himself.

I mentioned the common themes shared by diverse figures in the existentialist tradition. What are these themes?

1. Before any other consideration about the nature of Man, he exists. The famous Cartesian formula: 'I think, therefore I am' is reversed so that, as Sartre puts it: 'Existence precedes essence' or 'I am, therefore I think'. Man first exists, then encounters himself, and only on this encounter begins to define himself. The term 'exist' is derived from *ex-sistere* – to stand out – that is, to stand out from nothing or to stand out somewhere, in time and place. Heidegger's succinct phrase – *dasein* or 'being there' captures the essence of this concept.

2. Existence implies non-existence or non-being and non-being brings with it the phenomenon of *Angst* or existential anxiety. We suffer dread and anguish because we are threatened every second with non-being. We are cast or thrown into the world without our consent, Heidegger points out, and we must leave it in the same way. (There is the obvious exception in the act of suicide.) Moreover, our state of being may be removed at any moment. Faced with this unpredictable and finite span of life, we can choose between confronting this 'human condition' and thus live authentically, or avoid the reality of the threat

of non-being and live inauthentically. Two important concepts are incorporated here: the freedom and responsibility we have to choose; and how authentically we live our lives.

3.   Man is free to choose to live authentically or not and has a certain responsibility in his decision. Soren Kierkegaard, a Danish theologian and one of the forerunners of twentieth-century existentialism, addressed himself to this question when he stated: 'Man is not the simple working out of a plan, but is free to make his own choices'. He must face the nature of his existence by 'immersing [himself] deeper in existence' and in doing so he alone is responsible. For Kierkegaard the authentic man accepts responsibility for his life, his future and for his entire world since he is the author of this world and only he constitutes it. He accepts the finiteness of awareness: that we do not and cannot know everything, and that there is always uncertainty. The authentic person faces his *Angst*, and by taking it into himself, lives resolutely, in a positive way. The possibility of living life inauthentically brings us to a brief consideration of the clinical implications of existentialist philosophy.

The existentialist view of neurosis

There are a number of apt expressions to convey the existentialist view of inauthentic being. Sartre refers to the inauthentic person living in 'mauvaise foi' or bad faith; Nietzsche refers to such a person following the herd; for Erich Fromm, it is a question of the fear of freedom; Heidegger refers to the inauthentic person losing himself in 'das Mann' – that is, in chatter and the diversions and distractions of life.

Avoidance of facing and grappling with *Angst* or existential anxiety, is managed by a retreat into neurotic forms of anxiety whilst the dread of losing one's being is diverted into a fear of losing one's neurotic defences. Although therapists in the existential school have little room for clinical diagnosis or classification they do use certain diagnostic terms in their writings. Thus, a specific neurotic manifestation can be identified and understood in existentialist terms.

Let us consider four typical neurotic features: obsessiveness, depression, guilt and the phenomenon of being driven. The obsessive is typically rigid, constricted, orderly and intolerant of uncertainty and ambiguity – all qualities which aid him in containing and keeping *Angst* at bay. The neurotic depressive (we are not considering serious cases of depression which are often associated with biological abnormalities), because of his fear of commitment to authentic living, abandons any semblance of independent development and retreats into a state of helplessness and dependency. The greater this retreat, the greater his sense of ineptitude and worthlessness and the lower his self-esteem. In his effort to avoid life and the threat of non-being, the depressive ends up *as if* he were dead. The guilt-ridden person senses his inauthentic mode of living. He has opted out of choosing and acting responsibly. The driven individual cannot pause for even a moment. He is busily initiating and planning for the future and in the course of his intense activity there is no time to stop and ponder over his real fate.

These are individual neurotic features. Existentialist therapists also recognise an existential-type syndrome. Perhaps one of the reasons why humanist-existential psychotherapy has attracted a following in the United States is the common experience among middle-class, reasonably successful people, of a general discontent or malaise accompanied by perplexity over what meaning their lives have. With basic physical and materialistic needs more than satisfied and traditional religious practices lacking in inspiration, the ultimate concerns of existence come into view and stubbornly refuse to budge. The existential syndrome, or 'existential vacuum' to use Viktor Frankl's term, seems to be a recognisable entity and embraces the following features: a general sense of discontent, a feeling of emptiness and uncertainty, a lack of meaning and purpose in life and an absence of direction, a lack of spontaneity, a sense of alienation and detachment, and a concern over whether life is worthwhile.

Irvin Yalom has lucidly described these features in his book *Existential Psychotherapy*.[19] He refers to the four ultimate concerns about existing in the world which can overwhelm a person. The basic conflict stems from the individual's 'confrontation with the givens of existence' and with the anxieties that these givens or facts generate. The conscious and unconscious defences deployed to cope with the anxieties are but palliative and the price in terms of a constriction in experience and personal growth is costly. We have already discussed these ultimate concerns in a philosophical context and now it would be useful to mention them in a clinical framework:

1. The inevitability of death is too much to bear and efforts to evade it by all manner of tactic are made, without success.
2. There is a meaninglessness about life. Efforts to locate meaning brush up against the bald facts that life has no predetermined purpose and that no one can offer meaning and purpose to another

individual.

3. A basic sense of isolation faces every man. The wish to be protec-
ted and to be a part of a larger whole is opposed by the fact that each
one of us enters the world alone and dies alone.

4. There is a fear of freedom to assume responsibility for one's life.
The person must grapple with the absence of a secure, compre-
hensible framework or design and face the prospect of creating
his own life through personal choice and backed up by personal
action.

Yalom contends that existential 'psychopathology' is not separable
from normality in that no one can escape from the reality of having to
face life's ultimate concerns and deal with the human condition. It may
well be a matter of circumstance, even chance, whether a person enters
psychotherapy in order to examine his existential 'frustrations', seeks
a solution elsewhere, or strenuously ignores the frustrations.

Existential psychotherapy in practice

How does the humanist-existential psychotherapist set about treatment? Like the term existentialism, the psychotherapy derived from
this philosophy refers more to an approach to the therapy of Man's
human condition than to a formal school of psychotherapy with a body
of systematic theory and method. The literature of existential
psychotherapy contains only sparse comment on the subject of
technique for example and, if anything, tends to question its value.
The result is a group of related therapies which share certain theoretical propositions but differ widely in how they are practised. They
include the client-centred therapy associated with Carl Rogers, Gestalt
therapy founded by Fritz Perls, the logotherapy of Viktor Frankl, and
various forms of encounter group. Space does not permit discussion of
all these constituent sub-schools[20] although I do cover encounter
groups briefly in Chapter 5. Let me rather identify those elements of
treatment that they have in common.

Firstly, how are the goals of therapy construed? These are inextricably linked to the basic elements of existentialist thinking. The therapist seeks to promote in his patient an expanded, albeit realistic
appreciation of his situation in the world in order that he may become
– and the emphasis is on 'become' and not on 'be' – more spontaneous,
responsible for his life and actions, aware of some personal meaning
and purpose, whole, aware of his creative potential and able to exploit
it, open to new experience and free to grow. (It is no accident that a

seminal work by Carl Rogers is entitled *On becoming a person*.)

There is a discernible overlap between many of these objectives. Indeed, we could subsume them all under the umbrella of the authentic person. The notion *of becoming* and the importance of the authentic life is particularly well captured in the title of a book by James Bugental (a leading figure in the humanist-existential movement in Northern California) – *The search for authenticity*.[21] The attainment of this objective also presupposes that the patient will discard his neurotic defences as he permits himself to face up to his fundamental existential anxiety.

How are these goals striven for? Indubitably, the relationship between patient and therapist is the cardinal feature of existential psychotherapy. This relationship has particular qualities, best summed up in the term 'encounter'. Therapy is a collaborative and shared venture in which both patient and therapist are completely open to the experience, honest with each other, and act as authentically as possible. It is what the therapist *is* rather than what he does, and the way in which he accepts his patient that matters. This therapeutic stance is especially well illustrated by the Rogerian idea that the therapist's positive regard for his patient, his capacity to empathise with him, and his genuineness are the necessary and the sufficient ingredients of psychotherapy. I dealt with this fundamental position in the previous chapter and will not pursue it further here.

The therapist's task is to attempt to understand the private meaning of the patient's existence, his way of 'being in the world'. He follows the patient by communicating his authentically-perceived reflections on the significance of the actual events that take place during the therapy session. This amounts to a clarifying process rather than an analysis: interpretations are limited and based on what the patient is experiencing in the present. A particular aspect of the patient's behaviour in the session which is monitored carefully by the therapist is the resistance displayed by the patient in his effort to avoid existential anxiety. The therapist works to uncover layer after layer of symptoms to reach this elusive *Angst*.

Unlike psychoanalysis which delves into the past and is tantamount to a sort of archaeological dig to discover how particular patterns of personality and behaviour originated, existential psychotherapy is concerned with the patient's present and future. The historical process is merely incidental. This is especially obvious in Gestalt therapy where the focus is only on the present and the therapist directs his patient into immediate awareness of what he is experiencing. The future is as important as the present in that the patient comes to recognise that non-being can come at any moment and that only he has the power to choose what to do about the way he lives his life.

A flavour of what is required of the patient is seen in the following passage where James Bugental indicates what the patient should be doing during the session of therapy:

Tell me what is of concern to you, what matters to you in your life today right now as you lie here. What is it that you want to think through? What is it in your living that you want to make different? As you talk to me about your concern let yourself be open to mention any other awarenesses that come in whether or not they seem pertinent to what we are talking about. Sometimes these other awarenesses will be memories, sometimes physical sensations, sometimes emotions. Whatever they may be let yourself mention them and then continue with what you were telling me about, or follow whatever you find is of concern to you at that point. Talk to me about what concerns you in your life.[21]

The patient, following basic existentialist principles, is responsible for himself in seeking to change and in accepting the existential task. The therapist cannot, and will not, infuse him with change; change will not occur to him. The patient must remain the author of his world and be responsible for his life and his future. As Frankl puts it: 'man is ultimately self-determining. Man does not simply exist, but always decides what his existence will be, what he will become in the next moment ... every human being has the freedom to change at any instant.'[22]

If you have found my account of the existential approach somewhat imprecise, I would not be surprised. A criticism frequently levelled at the existential psychotherapist is the diffuseness of his theoretical position and the poor definition of the techniques applied. It would be a contradiction in terms if members of this psychotherapy school were to lay down unduly specific guidelines since the intrinsic quality of treatment would be undermined. This may be an injustice to existential psychotherapists who know what they are setting out to do but it would be fair to say that they often write about the nature of their activities in a vague way, and use much jargon.

Another judgement made on the school is concerned with its remoteness from common clinical problems. Are all patients who have neurotic symptoms or problems actually suffering from existential anxiety? It would seem highly unlikely. This is not to negate the possibility that existential-type issues and themes should be raised in psychotherapy. The question is whether such issues should constitute the core of treatment whatever the patient's difficulties. On the other hand, there is no doubt that, at least in contemporary Western society, there is a growing group of people who seek psychotherapy and whose problems are existential in type. The existential approach is probably most appropriate for these sorts of patients, who are preoccupied with such issues as lack of meaning, purposelessness, general discontent and a feeling of emptiness.

THE BEHAVIOURAL SCHOOL

Behaviour therapy is a conception of psychotherapy diametrically opposite to the psychoanalytic and existential schools. This third main school of psychological treatment, variously known as behaviour therapy, behavioural psychotherapy or behaviour modification, has undergone an enormous expansion during the last two decades. Its speedy development is seen in the several journals that have been founded on the subject, the growing library of books dealing with various aspects of the behavioural approach and the widespread application of the treatment in psychiatric hospitals, clinics, schools and prisons. It has been estimated that in the mental-health setting, probably twenty-five per cent of patients with neurotic complaints receive some form of behaviour therapy, particularly patients suffering from phobias, obsessions, compulsions and sexual problems.

Two key figures have spearheaded this rise in interest in behaviour therapy. Hans Eysenck, professor of psychology at the Institute of Psychiatry of the University of London has served as perhaps the most ardent proponent of behaviour therapy in Britain. In the 1950s he embarked on a campaign in which he argued that psychotherapy based on psychoanalytic theory was only minimally useful in the treatment of neurosis. Behaviour therapy by contrast was distinctly superior. We shall have more to say about Eysenck's attack on psychoanalysis in Chapter 6. Here we are concerned with Eysenck's espousal of behaviour therapy on the grounds that it is, in his view, based strictly on demonstrable experimental work from the psychology laboratory and that it does not become bogged down in irrefutable concepts such as the 'unconscious' or 'underlying psychic conflict'.

Joseph Wolpe, the other chief figure in the rise of behaviour therapy, first worked as a psychologist in South Africa and later continued his experimental and therapeutic research at Temple University in Philadelphia. 1958 saw the publication of his pioneering work, *Psychotherapy by Reciprocal Inhibition*,[23] which has since become something of a classic in the literature of behaviour therapy. Wolpe presented his clinical experience of treating various neuroses, principally phobic conditions, along what he considered were well-defined principles, and with precise and systematic methods.

With the explosive growth of behaviour therapy has come the problem of definition – what exactly is behaviour therapy? Some members of the behavioural school would argue that its methods are characterised by their exclusive focus on overt behaviour. Since the patient's symptom or problem is the focus for therapy there is no need to concentrate on such issues as conflicts and motives which may underlie the symptom. Others would prefer to define behaviour therapy in terms of its relationship to learning theory, that is to say, it is a method of treatment closely aligned to the theories of Pavlov, the discoverer of classical conditioning, or B. F. Skinner, responsible for the theory of operant conditioning, namely, that we learn by acting on our environment and repeating behaviour which evokes a positive response. We will return to both these theories of learning shortly. Still other behaviour therapists are more concerned to define their school of treatment in terms of the techniques they use.[24] This technique-oriented way of defining behaviour therapy is not altogether surprising.

In recent years behaviour therapists have broken through the school's original boundaries, and the methods catalogued under its rubric do not necessarily share the same theoretical basis. Particularly noteworthy here is the absorption under behaviour therapy's wing of the cognitive therapies in which the distorted ways in which the patient thinks about himself and his world are considered to be the basis of his neurotic state. These cognitive therapies, the best examples of which are the Cognitive-Behaviour therapy model of Aaron Beck[25] and the Rational-Emotive therapy approach of Albert Ellis,[26] go well beyond classical learning theory and focus on the patient's thoughts as much as, if not more than, his behaviour.

The problem of definition also involves the question of whether behaviour therapy is to be classified with the psychotherapies generally or as something quite distinctive. It does seem clear however that behaviour therapy and the sorts of psychotherapy we discussed earlier in this chapter share a considerable number of features in common. Interestingly, there has been a growing wish to create bridges between the behavioural school and other psychotherapies. Moreover, it is likely that in actual clinical practice, there are many therapists who incorporate principles and strategies from both the schools of behaviour therapy and psychoanalytically-oriented psychotherapy. Some critics assert that behaviour therapy cannot be properly defined because its boundaries are so obscure and blurred.

Theory

Although we can see from our brief discussion of problems in definition that behaviour therapy is not as straightforward a concept as some of its protagonists would believe, the following features are probably cardinal. All human behaviour is learned. There are differences of opinion as to whether this learning occurs through classical conditioning, operant conditioning or modelling. Neurotic symptoms are in essence examples of maladaptive behaviour and result when faulty learning has taken place. Neurotic symptoms in other words are learned bad habits. The goal of treatment in behaviour therapy is to unlearn specific patterns of behaviour and to replace them, through new learning, with more adaptive patterns.

We have already noted that learning theories are far from straightforward and that different views compete to explain how faulty learning takes place. There are at least four models.

1. *Classical conditioning*

The first model is most commonly associated with the name of Eysenck. In his theoretical approach classical Pavlovian conditioning is considered to be at the basis of both normal and abnormal behaviour. Neurotic responses occur when a neutral stimulus is paired with a stimulus that produces anxiety. Ultimately this neutral stimulus produces a similar response to the original anxiety-provoking one. Thus, in Pavlov's classical experiments, dogs were conditioned to become anxious on hearing a certain noise in the absence of the fearful stimulus with which noise had been initially paired. Similar experiments in man have been surprisingly rare. Eleven-month old Albert is probably one of the most cited research subjects in the entire literature of psychology. Watson,[27] the father of behaviourism, reported on Albert in the 1920s. His play with a white rat was quite amiable until a loud noise was introduced. After a few trials in which noise and rat were paired, the rat alone was able to induce fear into Albert, a fear which was also felt in the presence of other furry objects and animals and which persisted over several months. Watson suggested counter-conditioning as a way of treating such fear, namely, presenting the rat in association with a pleasant stimulus in order that re-learning could occur. Watson himself did not engage in the development of such therapy and it was not until the 1950s that the idea of counter-conditioning was re-introduced.

Indeed, counter-conditioning is the basis of Wolpe's behaviour therapy by reciprocal inhibition. Wolpe argues that the pairing of a fearful stimulus with a feeling in opposition to the anxiety which that stimulus would normally provoke is the basis for eliminating the fear. In practice, the most appropriate opposite feeling is a state of relaxation. The rationale for reciprocal inhibition becomes impressively clear. Consider a patient who has an excessive fear of thunder. He feels acutely anxious in the midst of a storm and even the thought of thunder makes him quake. Instruct the patient in some method of relaxation. Such a state is obviously the direct opposite of anxiety and will inhibit its occurrence in the face of the fearful stimulus. Wolpe went further and elaborated a methodical approach to the treatment of neurotic symptoms, particularly phobias. The procedure, named systematic desensitisation, involves relaxation training and the presentation of the fearful stimulus in a gradual fashion. Therapist and patient work out a graded hierarchy of anxiety-provoking stimuli. In the example of our thunder phobic, the least frightening stimulus might be the thought of a mild storm in a far-away place and the most anxiety-provoking stimulus the image of a particularly severe storm with gigantic claps of thunder. Between these two items would be placed a series of progressively increasing anxiety-provoking images. The patient is gradually desensitised to the thunder by facing the items on the hierarchy in a state of relaxation until each item is successfully coped with.

Behaviour therapists are assiduous in their research efforts. This is particularly evident when studying the literature on the evaluation of Wolpe's procedure and its many subsequent modifications. Important knowledge has accrued as a result. For instance, it has been shown that none of the acutal components in systematic desensitisation is essential – relaxation is not always necessary and the hierarchy items do not have to be presented in a graded way. It has also been shown that better results are obtained when the patient is desensitised to the actual anxiety-evoking stimulus rather than to the stimulus imagined. Thus it is now customary to place the patient directly in the situation he fears rather than have him imagine that situation – this is referred to as treatment *in vivo*.

Some modifications of the original treatment by Wolpe are almost tantamount to its opposite both theoretically and practically. The most noteworthy of these is flooding or implosion. This treatment entails the total immersion of the patient in the fearful situation with no attempt to prevent his experiencing anxiety or even panic. The person fearful of entering a shop, for example is placed in the middle of a busy supermarket and prevented from withdrawing. Alternatively the patient is encouraged to imagine in great detail the situation in which he experiences maximum anxiety. The resultant diminution in anxiety is thought to be due to extinction – the person comes to recognise that he will not be overwhelmed by the situation and that there is no need to avoid or escape from the originally anxiety-evoking stimulus. The research findings comparing flooding and systematic desensitisation are rather puzzling: some studies show a superiority of one treatment over the other whereas others show no difference between them. Also baffling is the adoption of polar opposite principles as a basis for treatment, both emanating from the same basic model of learning theory.

The formerly confident postulate that behaviour therapy is based on learning theory must be seriously reconsidered. A tradition of rigorous empirical research and clinical pragmatism is one answer in the face of the lack of a unified theory. The work of Isaac Marks, a British behaviour therapist, illustrates this trend. Based on his own impressively prolific and rigorous research, he honestly admits his uncertainty about the origin of neurotic symptoms and questions whether the Eysenckian view, as we earlier described it, is tenable. For Marks the evidence is insubstantial.[28] Instead of a reliance on classical conditioning to explain behaviour, both adaptive and maladaptive, Marks has preferred to make no assumptions about the causes and antecedents of neurotic symptoms. As far as he is concerned, their origin could be genetic, biochemical, developmental or learned: exact pinpointing of cause is not of primary importance and unnecessary to determine appropriate treatment. Thus the original Pavlovian sequence of learning is replaced by a much more obvious formula: an evoking stimulus such as entering a busy supermarket, triggers off a particular response, in this case a phobia or irrational fear to shop. This so-called evoked response can itself become a further evoking stimulus, so setting up a vicious cycle, with the person experiencing anticipatory fear of fear.

The many clinical trials conducted by Marks and his colleagues lead them to conclude that the chief therapeutic factor at work in behaviour therapy is graded exposure. The patient with obsessions or phobias is encouraged to face the evoking stimulus albeit in a step-by-step fashion. Training in relaxation is not required and the construction of a graded hierarchy of stimuli is unnecessary.

In addition to Marks, a growing number of behaviour therapists have questioned the simple conditioning model, pointing out that the neurotic's attitudes to himself and his environment are crucial. There is thus recognition that a cognitive element enters into the maintenance of neurotic behaviour such as poor motivation to change, the welcome sympathy and attention gained by the patient by virtue of his suffering, and the use of symptoms as an integral part of complex and disturbed family relationships. If it were not for these cognitive aspects, it could be argued that all patients with neurotic symptoms should respond to methods like graded exposure and that they should then maintain the adaptive habits they learn. The entry of behaviour therapy into this arena brings it close to psychoanalysis for in psychoanalytic theory and practice, the cognitive world of the patient, particularly his resistance to change, has long been recognised as salient. Discussion shortly of cognitive approaches in behaviour therapy will remind us of this convergence.

2. *Operant conditioning*

B. F. Skinner[29] has provided a theory of learning which differs from the classical Pavlovian model. He postulates that we learn by acting on our environment and repeating any behaviour which evokes a positive response. By contrast, we avoid behaviour which generates a negative response. In the first case positive reinforcement of behaviour occurs and in the latter negative reinforcement. Skinner supports his operant conditioning theory with simple animal experiments. His famous pigeons soon learned how to peck at a lever in order to obtain pellets of food. So long as the pellets were provided, the pecking continued – a particular piece of behaviour was reinforced by the provision of food. When positive reinforcers such as the food were withdrawn or reduced, the behaviour originally evoked correspondingly diminished and became extinguished. Similarly, when a negative reinforcer such as pain was withdrawn, the behaviour evoked by the pain eventually ceased. In Skinner's model, there is no mediating process; it is all a question of overt behaviour shaped by a programme of reinforcement.

Even the most complex human behaviour including the acquisition of language is, in Skinnerian theory, associated with a person's 'operations' on his environment and a consequent behaviour according to the responses of those operations.

There is little doubt that reinforcement is a powerful factor in human behaviour and it is probably a feature, albeit implicit, of all psychotherapy. A patient is likely, for example, to repeat behaviour of which the therapist approves. But the chief explicit application of operant conditioning is in the modification of behaviour of such disabled people as the mentally retarded, and chronic, long-stay patients in psychiatric hospitals. The most notable example is the token economy,[30] which was introduced into psychiatric practice at the Anna State Hospital in Illinois. First, the therapist establishes the desired behavioural components. In an institutional setting, these usually mean self-care, personal hygiene and participation in occupational therapy and other hospital programmes. A reward, namely some positive reinforcer, is given when the desired behaviour is performed. Reinforcement is contingent on this behaviour. In the classical token economy, the reward is tangible, consisting of tokens which can then be exchanged for money, material objects or special privileges like weekend leave, access to the hospital grounds or the use of television.

When the token economy was first introduced, it attracted much attention as it seemed particularly helpful in hospitals where patients had customarily become withdrawn and apathetic. More latterly, there has been some question as to what is the effective ingredient of a token economy. Some would contend that it is not the rewards that were helpful in early programmes but the enthusiasm among the staff that accompanied the innovation. The result has been a trend to dispense with the use of actual tokens and to promote an active rehabilitative atmosphere. Perhaps patients who are rewarded more naturally with compliments, attention and praise are as likely to demonstrate the behaviour desired by the staff as much as if they were offered concrete rewards.

More recently a procedure referred to as contingency contracting has been devised which is another application of operant conditioning theory. The method is especially relevant when the problem is centred on an interaction between specific persons, most commonly a married couple. There is a premiss that in a successful marital relationship each partner exchanges positive reinforcements with the other. The therapist's role in a disturbed marriage is to assist the couple to avoid the exchange of negative reinforcement or punishment and to help them to trade positive reinforcements. Each spouse ascertains what the other desires and expects and then tries to fulfil those wishes and expectations. Often, such punitive behaviour as constant criticism or withdrawal into silence can be avoided and replaced by more reasonable patterns. This approach seems rather facile and possibly unsuited to what may be a complex relationship. But its advocates argue that by modifying behaviour even at this simple level, other dimensions of the relationship benefit. Indeed, there is a prevalent view among many behaviour therapists that by tackling problems at the behavioural level, other changes in attitudes and feelings inevitably follow.

3. *Social learning theory*

A third type of learning is based on the assumption that learning is a social activity and comes about as a result of an individual's relationship to his environment. Albert Bandura[31] of Stanford University is the chief innovator of this approach. He has attempted to demonstrate in various research studies that learning consists of observation and subsequent imitation. Moreover, such socially-based learning is especially effective if the learner is an active participant rather than a mere observer. The apprenticeship model of learning is a good illustration of Bandura's theory. Traditionally, the apprentice observes his master at work and then actively imitates him. A typical clinical application of social learning theory involves the patient with a specific phobia. For example, Bandura has shown the effectiveness of imitation by participation in patients who are fearful of snakes. The therapist acts as the model and demonstrates to the patient, using a graded approach, how to approach the snake and handle it. Step by step, he encourages the patient to imitate his own behaviour and offers positive reinforcement of the patient's efforts. With increasing success on the part of the patient, there is a corresponding diminution in the therapist's guidance. The handling of an actual snake is an example of *in vivo* imitation and this is probably the most effective method. Alternatives are the use of filmed material or imagining the fearful object or situation.

Social learning theory appears to be limited to simple phobias, when used in a pure form. But there is little doubt that modelling is an omnipresent feature of psychotherapy generally. Patients covertly imitate the values, attitudes and behaviour of their therapists who are identified as models. A similar pattern of modelling occurs in group therapy which provides the opportunity for a patient to note how fellow patients tackle problems shared in common or react to particular circumstances within the group itself. Thus, the rather meek, unassertive patient may take note of a peer who is particularly talented in the area of assertiveness and attempt to imitate him.

4. *Cognitive theory*

This approach to learning theory is something of a departure from the traditional views of learning theorists. Unlike the theories of learning already discussed, cognitive theory postulates that a person's thoughts (cognitions is usually the term used) primarily determine behaviour. In neurosis, and especially in depression where low self-esteem is such a common feature, the notion is advanced that the patient's thoughts about himself are incorrect because of faulty learning. Erroneous premises and misconceptions are the root source of the neurotic's thoughts about himself: for example, that he has little to offer or has achieved nothing or deserves criticism. Aaron Beck,[25] for instance, believes that a depressed person has misinterpreted aspects of reality through processes of distortion and exaggeration and that the resultant thoughts have become automatic, something of an entrenched habit. In Beck's approach to the therapy of such a patient, the main priority is to 'correct faulty conceptions and self-signals' thereby abolishing the negative automatic thoughts and promoting realistic thinking. The important development in cognitive theory is that the therapist attends to emotions, such as depression and anxiety, through thoughts.

The therapist is almost tantamount to a teacher. He adopts an active role by directing the patient to his faulty thinking. The task is to make the patient aware of his automatic thoughts and to get him to realise that they have no validity. The patient who, for example, is convinced that he has little to offer to others is made to recognise that this is a distortion of reality. He is encouraged to examine himself and his qualities accurately in order to detect those attributes he does have. Needless to say, the assumption is made that no one is utterly devoid of some positive qualities, even if they are in short supply.

It is not entirely clear why cognitive theory is advanced as an example of behaviour therapy because the target of modification is thought and attitude rather than behaviour. In the sense that faulty cognitions have arisen through faulty learning, and this learning must be unlearned, the cognitive approach does bear some resemblance to conventional behaviour therapy. Also, the cognitions involved are within the realm of the conscious level of mind and the unconscious is not of any consequence. Finally, there is an assumption that the correction of faulty thoughts invariably leads to behavioural change.

Cognitive theory is a notable development in the evolution of the behavioural school of psychotherapy in that it is tending to influence more traditional practitioners in their approach to patients. The notion of stimulus-response without any mediating variables such as a person's attitudes or feelings is being examined more critically. The practical implications are profound – behaviour therapists are increasingly taking attitudes like motivation into account in their treatment programmes. There is a paradox here. Originally Eysenck mounted a stinging attack on the value of psychoanalysis. Now, with the advent of cognitive theory and its implications for the behaviour therapist, there is a growing recognition that an exclusive preoccupation with behaviour and its modification constitutes only a partial view of a person: his thoughts and feelings also have to be taken into account.

Before concluding our consideration of the behavioural approach, we should point out the advances it has spawned for psychotherapy in general. The concept of a behavioural analysis is especially noteworthy. Behaviour therapists diligently make a detailed and comprehensive assessment and analysis of the behavioural problems in their patients. They ask questions like where and when the problem arises and, very importantly, what maintains it? The rather obsessive preoccupation of the psychodynamic school with *why* a problem exists and how it has come into being is obviated. It may well make more sense to establish what factors contribute to the maintenance of a problem rather than to speculate on how it arose in the first place. The latter is always likely to remain an inferential exercise.

Another useful contribution to the psychotherapies is the notion of a contract. Following his behavioural analysis, the behaviour therapist determines an explicit agreement with his patient which helps to demystify treatment and enables the patient to appreciate what lies in store for him. Thus, agreement is reached on what objectives to set and on how to go about achieving them, and a clear explanation is provided of the specific procedures involved. Furthermore, the roles of therapist and patient are identified as clearly as possible. The explicitness of the contract is complemented by specific features that typify the treatment once it is in progress. The most important ingredient is 'homework'. It is as if the therapist assumes the role of teacher in the therapeutic session with lessons carried out between treatments. The emphasis is on self-efficacy. Ultimately it is the patient who must carry out the newly learned behaviour and accept chief responsibility; the therapist serves merely as teacher and guide. Also, during the course of treatment, the importance of regular reviews is highlighted. This entails careful monitoring of the patient's progress. If treatment is proceeding well, the patient's progress can be positively reinforced. If on the other hand, progress is patchy or erratic, the question can be asked – what is going wrong? The monitoring procedure is relatively straightforward in that behavioural change is the sole criterion of improvement. (This becomes more complex when cognitive-behaviour therapy is practised.)

All these features of the behavioural approach point to a therapy which is tailored to the individual patient. The behavioural analysis for instance is uniquely conducted in each case. Similarly, the setting of goals and the selection of specific treatment procedures are determined by the particular needs of a patient. It is arguable whether other psychotherapy schools are so attentive to the close matching of the procedure of treatment with the particular set of problems a patient has. The psychoanalytic school is more apt to determine what sort of patients are suitable for therapy and then to adopt a fairly standard therapeutic procedure. This is the case at least theoretically. In clinical practice however the degree of flexibility in therapeutic approach among analytically-oriented therapists is probably high.

Summary

We have looked at the three main schools of psychotherapy in order to discern what is different about them. It would be wise to remind ourselves that their distinctive features are in all likelihood of less consequence than the factors which the three schools have in common. We dealt with these factors, the so-called non-specific factors, in Chapter 1. A greater acceptance of these non-specific factors by adherents of different schools would do much to reduce some of the intense ideological battles that have been waged over the last three decades. The warfare has done little for the discipline of psychotherapy overall. On the contrary, it has tended to undermine its image, an image which has become rather tarnished. It is very likely the case, as we discussed in Chapter 1, that a therapist sticks staunchly to his school in order to preserve his belief in the rationale of that school. But if practitioners of psychotherapy were more inclined to weigh up the evidence for the usefulness of particular theories and treatment methods the subject would gain immeasurably. This is a matter of no small importance and one to which I return in the final chapter.

In our consideration of the three dominant schools of psychotherapy, I referred to the therapist and his patient. By implication, I suggested that these approaches are applied to the individual seen on his own. This was partly a matter of convenience and partly a reflection of the inclination of the psychoanalytically-oriented therapist, the behavioural therapist and the existential therapist to practise individual psychotherapy. None the less, practitioners in all three schools have applied their methods to groups. The next chapter deals with the group psychotherapies by focusing on three common forms of them – small group psychotherapy, family therapy and conjoint marital therapy. I also briefly consider two important social movements in which the group approach is paramount – the encounter and self-help movements.

5 The group approach

We live, work and play in a wide range of social groups. Not unexpectedly therefore, many of the emotional problems encountered in psychiatric practice stem from disturbed relationships within these groups. With the increasing appreciation of how important interpersonal factors are in psychiatric theory and practice has come the swift development in recent years of psychotherapy treatments which deal with the problems that exist *between* people rather than within the individual alone. Thus, family, marital and sex therapy among others, are expanding year by year. Apart from these naturally occurring groups the group process has also been applied to a number of other settings such as the wards of psychiatric hospitals, the out-patient clinic and the private psychotherapist's office. Today the group therapies, probably a better term to describe the broad range of treatments in which the group format is used, are among the most commonly used psychological treatments.

The systematic use of groups in psychotherapy is relatively recent. But the healing qualities of groups have been recognised for centuries, particularly in religious practice. The shrine at Lourdes, for example, is intrinsically an example of a group healing ritual. The founding of clinical group therapy[1] is usually attributed to a Boston physician, Joseph Pratt, who at the turn of the century brought together patients suffering from chronic tuberculosis to instruct them on medical aspects of their illness. Beyond this educational component he also promoted a group climate whereby members could provide mutual support to one another. Some years later a handful of American psychiatrists adapted Pratt's ideas in their treatment of the mentally ill. Lazell and Cody Marsh, for example, both incorporated Pratt's model when they formed highly structured groups of patients who were approached as 'students' and tutored on aspects of mental ill health. This educational approach was soon replaced by the early efforts of psychoanalysts to apply their theories to groups of patients. Freud himself was obviously appreciative of the importance of group phenomena as seen in his classic *Group Psychology and the Analysis of the Ego*,[2] published in 1921, but he did not actually practise group therapy. Jung was distinctly prejudiced against the use of the group approach. He regarded psychological illness as an individual experience which required individual analysis. Adler, by contrast, argued for the inclusion of social factors in treatment and applied the group format in child guidance centres and with alcoholics. The application of psychoanalysis to groups was mainly an American phenomenon and during the 1930s in particular, several notable analysts experimented with the treatment of patients in a group setting.

Undoubtedly the chief spur to the development of group therapy was the Second World War. Treating large numbers of soldiers was obviously more economical and efficient when conducted in groups. Some distinguished British psychoanalysts had an influential impact on clinical practice with their group work. The Northfield Military Hospital in particular was a centre of much innovation and there leading theorists and practitioners like Wilfred Bion, Michael Foulkes and Tom Main tried out new approaches to group therapy. Bion's work subsequently influenced clinicians at the Tavistock Clinic in London while Foulkes went on to found the Institute of Group Analysis, the chief training centre in group therapy in Britain. Another key innovator, active during the war, was Maxwell Jones, the founder of the concept of the therapeutic community. He showed how the staff and all the patients in an institution could collaborate together and use the resultant group forces for therapeutic purposes.

Another key contribution, this time in the United States, derived from a social psychology tradition. Kurt Lewin and his colleagues propounded a theory which was to serve as the basis for extensive research into the processes of groups. Lewin's Field Theory posits that an individual's personal dynamics are intimately bound up with the nature of the social forces around him. Immediately following the Second World War, Lewin was invited to translate his research ideas into practice by training community leaders in their efforts to grapple with inter-racial tensions. This was the prelude to the creation of the so-called Sensitivity Training Group or T-group. In 1950 the National Training Laboratory was founded as a centre for training in human relations and group dynamics. The basic notion was that group participants from various backgrounds – teachers, industrial managers, government officials – could have an opportunity through the medium of a special conference to experience and study the function of groups and interpersonal dynamics. The ultimate goal was that they might act more effectively in leading their home-based groups.

In the 1960s the emphasis in the National Training Laboratory shifted from group dynamics to personal dynamics, a reflection of the mounting interest in humanist psychology and the human potential movement. The goals of sensitivity training groups now became greater awareness in the self and personal growth. Soon the sensitivity training group gave birth to the encounter group movement and with it the development of the 'growth centre'. Esalen, one such growth centre in Northern California, opened in 1962 and became the prototype of dozens more centres throughout the United States and elsewhere. We return to the encounter group later in this chapter.

It would be a Herculean task to describe and comment on all group therapies that are practised currently. Instead, I will focus on three commonly applied uses of the group – small group therapy as conducted in the out-patient clinic or private psychotherapist's office, family therapy which has over the last decade attracted tremendous interest, and marital therapy. Brief consideration is also given to the encounter group movement and self-help groups.

Small group therapy

Small group psychotherapy is commonly practised in psychiatric out-patient clinics and privately, and most of the mental-health professions are represented among the ranks of those who conduct such groups. As with the psychotherapies generally, there is a plethora of theoretical schools which determine the practice of small group treatment. Despite the diversity of theories, many features of group therapy are held in common. An account of one particular approach which has attained a great measure of popularity – the dynamic interactional or interpersonalist[3] – provides a picture of how the small group process has been applied to the treatment of patients with neurotic and personality problems.

The interpersonalist view derives from the work of the neo-Freudians whom we discussed in Chapter 4. Harry Stack Sullivan is probably the most important influence in this context. He believed that personality is mostly the product of one's interaction with other significant people. A person's psychological growth entails the development of a concept of the self which is based to a large extent on how he perceives the appraisal of himself, by others. Sullivan argued that 'psychiatry is the study of processes that involve or go on between people'; mental illness is to be viewed in interpersonal terms and treated accordingly. Bringing a small number of people together in order that they may examine themselves in the ways they relate to one another follows logically from Sullivan's position.

A typical therapy group comprises six to eight members balanced for sex and with no extremes of age, intelligence or psychological sophistication. The group meets weekly with one or two therapists for an average of one and a half hours. The group may be open – accepting new members as it progresses and permitting their departure at different times, or closed – the group begins and ends its life with the same membership.

The members are encouraged to define their own personal goals and the problems which they would like to tackle in the group. Although these differ from patient to patient, there are usually certain basic themes common to all and they are not very different from problems tackled in any other form of insight-oriented therapy: poor self-esteem, difficulty in initiating or maintaining intimate relationships, a sense of purposelessness and lack of direction, demoralisation, some specific interpersonal conflict such as with a parent or spouse, difficulty in expressing or controlling feelings, and a lack of personal identity.

The group works on the assumption that a central difficulty for all its members is relating to others. Patients are told that the group is a special social microcosm where honest exploration of relationships between them is not only permitted, but necessary. If people have problems in the way they relate to others, then obviously a social forum which encourages honest encounters can provide them with an opportunity to learn valuable things about themselves. Patients are also told that working on one's personality and ways of relating is not easy and, indeed, may intermittently be stressful and unpleasant. Members must understand that some stress is a necessary condition for long-term improvement. Certain stumbling-blocks exist along the way: as there is no agenda or distinct structure to the meetings, the patient may initially feel puzzled and even discouraged, but it is necessary for him to weather this phase and to adapt to the unique process of the group.

Four features highlight the group process:

1. Members are encouraged to be honest and direct with their feelings, especially towards other members and towards the therapist. In

many ways this can be regarded as a central element of the therapy, and it becomes possible with developing trust in, and cohesiveness of the group.

2. Revealing intimate aspects about oneself is not mandatory and a forced confessional is not sought. But members do have to share their problems if the group is to be able to provide any help.

3. The group is a forum for risk-taking and experimenting with new behaviour. Members must recognise that the group is probably the safest place in which they can change their attitudes and behaviour. The group can tolerate this experimentation and provide profitable feedback about its effectiveness.

4. A basic aim of the group is that each member strives to accomplish his personal goals. Since the problems requiring change have usually been many years in the making, it is essential that the patient agrees to work for a prolonged period, usually one to two years, and then to review how effective the group has been and to what extent goals have been achieved. Reviews should also occur periodically during the course of the therapy.

The keystone of group therapy in the interpersonalist model is interpersonal learning: the members learn from one another, along a series of clearly identified steps: (a) here is what an aspect of a patient's behaviour is like; (b) his behaviour evokes these reactions in fellow members; (c) the members disclose their reactions to the patient involved and evaluate his behaviour; (d) the patient participates in this evaluation and attains insight into the nature of his behaviour; (e) he then weighs up the alternative of maintaining the behaviour or trying to change it; (f) if he commits himself to change, he then uses the group to take risks as he experiments with new substitute behaviours.

This process of learning is achieved by a focus on the present. Although material from the members' lives is important to consider, the events, mood and tone of the group at the time it meets are the most important elements to study. The premiss is that a patient's behaviour in the group in all likelihood reflects his behaviour elsewhere. It is this behaviour in the group that can be directly observed and reacted to, with the knowledge that similar behaviour occurs in the patient's general life. This makes group therapy a present and future-oriented activity with little emphasis on factors which led to the patient's problems in the first place. There are types of group therapy however – usually some application of the psychoanalytic method – in which the historical sphere is emphasised and the original causes of current behaviour are sought so that they can be clearly understood by the patient.

Claire's case is an apt illustration of how the interpersonalist model works. Claire, a forty-year-old clerk with three teenage children, enters a group complaining among other things of difficulties in maintaining relationships with others, especially men. There is a failed marriage in her past and the relationship with her second husband is far from satisfactory. It soon becomes evident that she is extremely distrustful of the male leader as well as of other group members. Consistently suspicious and defensive, Claire keeps a safe distance from the group. The members become restless and frustrated with her and before long express their feelings. They point out that her remoteness is responsible for their reaction. Could this not play a part in her failure in relationships outside the group? Claire considers the feedback and during the next few meetings comes to accept its validity. Over the ensuing months, she gradually makes efforts to be more open and less remote in the group. The group points out this improvement which positively reinforces it. Clare later reports that in relationships outside the group, including her marriage, she has also made progress.

This process normally takes many months and it is not necessarily smooth. It could well be that at various points, such as during a period of stress, Claire could again exhibit defensiveness. The group may then offer their support but also remind her of the original problem and how she successfully overcame it.

In order to optimise group conditions for change in the patient, the therapist has a number of tasks. These are to instil a climate of trust and cohesiveness (well recognised as an essential therapeutic factor), to encourage the group to focus on the present, and to promote interpersonal learning chiefly through the process of feedback – both the giving and receiving of it. He is primarily concerned with how patients act, especially in relation to other members. What is actually spoken is less relevant. For example, it is more important for the group to examine how a member dominates every meeting rather than to focus on what he says. The verbal content of course may be highly pertinent at times, particularly when problems are being shared, but tends to remain secondary.

The leader provides a temporal perspective of the patient's progress and can point out how, for instance, in the case of Claire, she no longer withdraws defensively in the group. He can compare a patient's current and past behaviour in the group.

The therapist is essentially a facilitator – he assembles the group, shapes its norms, and promotes interaction between its members. He must however remain constantly aware that the members themselves are the main agents of help and change.

The following summary of a typical group meeting conveys some idea of how groups function. Of the group of three men and three women, James is away writing examinations. Peter, the group member in the 'spot-light', has tended to keep to the periphery in the nine weeks of the life of the group.

Group meeting number 10

James was away writing examinations and we look forward to his return next week. Rather predictably Debbie invited Peter to use some group time for himself. He showed some tentativeness about this, whereupon the three women proceeded to suggest ways in which the group could be a more relaxed place. Suggestions were made about seating arrangements and soon legs were placed over chairs and shoes were removed. This was obviously a genuine effort to try to help Peter. Although he got lost in the new arrangements, he gradually began to participate. Initially he shared his concern about leaving the hostel and living on his own. This would be the first occasion that he would be on his own in digs. Various members either questioned him about his fears or made suggestions about how this could be a positive move.

The rest of the meeting was much along these lines with the women members playing an active role in bringing Peter into the group. Roger was noticeably quiet through most of the meeting; we wonder whether this reflected his concern not to use up more group time for himself considering that he had been the focus of the entire meeting the previous week. Indeed he was most active in responding to Peter's later feeling of guilt in having hogged this session. Roger felt that this guilt was unwarranted since the group had asked questions of Peter. There was recognition that guilt is a common response in members to using group time – the question arises as to who the group is for and comments were made that Peter was perfectly justified in having a session devoted to himself since he was an 'equal' member of the group.

We learnt a tremendous amount about Peter in this week, indeed more so than in the previous nine meetings combined. It was encouraging to see how he required less time before replying and by the end of the session, he was more spontaneous than he had ever been before. Among the important things he shared with us was something about his background. He came from a working-class background, his father was a labourer and the domestic circumstances limited, for instance he had a shared room with two brothers until aged seventeen. He used the word 'deprived' when reflecting on his experience and there seemed an element of resentment that this had been his lot. All this was related to his feeling of inferiority in the group – he had lumped the rest of us into a class different from his own. This differentiation was based on behaviour he saw in the group like good manners and politeness. He felt himself to be a much more earthy and basic individual who did not care for the contrived and ritualised behaviour of 'the middle class'. In talking about this, he swore a couple of times in a very natural way. This was in fact the first time that such language had been used in the group and it made the rest of us wonder if we had not been too formal. Ann certainly indicated that she swore all the time and was relieved that she might be able to do so in the group as well. The discussion also revolved around the use of accents and style of speech. There seemed to be a good measure of agreement with Peter about his dissatisfaction with the 'mannered class' and in fact Ann and Pam entered into what was becoming a dialogue on sociology. Ann shared something about her own home background – she recognised what Peter was saying having come from a middle-class home and having seen other modes of living since leaving home. Another important issue regarding Peter's parents was the fact that they had not expressed their feelings about what he thought of as his difficult situation. It was his belief that they did care but they had no way of showing their feelings. There was a lot of support expressed for Peter, particularly from Ann who spoke in rather general terms about the generation gap and how perhaps parents did not really understand the needs and wishes of their children. Here she might have been talking more about herself than about Peter and she may want to pursue this later.

Peter also spoke about his relationships in general. He had not entered the activities of the group because of his basic lack of trust. He was scared that he would be disliked or that people would use whatever he said against him. He seemed to deal with this problem of distrust in one of two ways: he either qualified all his comments so that he could be sure they would not offend (he seems to have done this in the group, for example, long pauses before his contributions) or by acting aggressively. Nancy (one of the two therapists) reminded him of an example of this attitude in that in an earlier meeting his comment that he felt bored was really a way of expressing his anger with the group.

In a way similar to the previous meeting in which Roger had invited maternal responses, Peter seemed to provoke the women much more than the men. The therapists were also responsive to Peter. Of the women, Ann expressed a sense of identification with Peter and felt with him much of the time – she was sensitive to what he was saying; Debbie was very helpful in bringing Peter into the group and she did this somewhat like an interviewer without giving much of herself away; Pam acted in a particularly supportive way, for example commenting that she had had some of the problems raised by Peter but had since overcome them, implying that he could do so as well. Nancy expressed how impressed she had been with Peter's honesty and saw this as a strength.

Sam (the other therapist) agreed and added that he felt closer to Peter than he had in any of the past nine sessions. Peter himself, as mentioned above, indicated that he would leave the meeting feeling guilty and this was where Roger tried to assuage this guilt. Were there any other feelings he would take away? It was back to the guilt although on more questioning, he indicated that he would feel slightly closer to the group. This was an honest response – he could have exaggerated this response because of group pressure but did not. Yet it is significant that Peter used almost a whole meeting for himself, became much more spontaneous, shared a tremendous amount of important material with us, and seemed to be able to trust us more at the end. It was our impression that the whole group felt closer to Peter and had got to know him much better.

Other theoretical models

The interpersonalist model clearly places the main source of change in the interaction between group members – the patients learn from one another. Another model, difficult to label, and whose main representative is Wilfred Bion,[4] emphasises the relationship between the 'group as a whole' and the leader. The group in a sense is anthropomorphised and its relationship with its therapist leader becomes the subject of examination and analysis. The therapist behaves in such a way as to stimulate group responses. Bion distinguishes between two types of groups: the work group which sets about its task effectively and rationally and the basic assumption group which acts more primitively and in which members are unaware of certain forces opposing its becoming a work group. The basic assumption group behaves as if there were some unstated assumption on which it is operating. These assumptions are dependency, usually on the leader or a particular member for decisions and getting the work done; pairing in which the group relies on two or more members to sub-group together and produce solutions for the group as a whole; and fight or flight in which the group either resists the task it should wrestle with or finds some extraneous 'enemy' to divert it. The therapist's task is to help patients become effective members of a work group. The limitation with this approach is that although Bion's observations are generally accepted, they are only part of the experience of the group. Inevitably, the newly established group progresses through a period of development in which phenomena like the basic assumptions occur. However, a group generally reaches a point of maturation and then works in a more or less rational way. Even then, it may indulge in resistance and avoidance of the task at hand but this is noted and dealt with. Thus the type of group therapy which places so much emphasis on the relationship between the group as a whole and the therapist seems to be more interested in the issue of group dynamics rather than in group therapy *per se*. This type is ideally suited to staff groups or professional training groups where the objective is to experience and study group processes.

In the applied psychoanalytic type, the emphasis shifts to the relationship that is established between each group member and the therapist. In its true form, group analysis amounts to the analysis of each individual group member, particularly the transference feelings he develops towards the therapist, and to a lesser degree the feelings he develops towards fellow patients. The therapist, as in individual psychoanalysis (see Chapter 4) encourages free association and makes interpretations of such phenomena as the transference and resistance. The ultimate aim is the attainment of insight on the part of the patient into the nature and origins of his difficulties. Group analysis differs from individual analysis in that patients help one another, the transference between patient and therapist tends to be somewhat diluted because the therapist is shared by many patients, and the group format is less intensive with changes in personality perhaps less substantial.

There are a variety of other theoretical approaches which rely on the group method. They include Gestalt therapy, transactional analysis, the therapeutic community, and psychodrama. The reader is referred to the bibliography for recommended reading on these various approaches.[5]

Family therapy

Unlike small group therapy in which strangers are brought together in order that they may form close relationships and learn from the ensuing interactions, family therapy involves a naturally-occurring group, one that has a past history and will continue long after therapy has ended. It is perhaps remarkable that group therapy with strangers evolved half a century before family therapy. Doubtless, psychoanalysis had something to do with the lengthy delay. Psychoanalysis was devised after all as a therapy for the individual, and although the assumption was made that neurosis commonly had its roots in early childhood and in a particular family matrix, the process of therapy entailed a patient's independent journey into his past. The destination of the journey was invariably the original family home.

There the patient would re-experience important episodes from his early life and in so doing come to understand the complex origins of his current symptoms and problems.

With the advent of the child guidance clinic in the 1920s, it followed logically that analytically-based therapy of the child would be conducted with child alone. However, a child guidance tradition was soon established of working with the child's mother as well but the two family members were treated quite separately and by different therapists. Only occasionally was the child's father seen. This remained standard clinical practice for many years until, in the 1950s, new influences came to bear in child and adolescent psychiatry. Most influential were the theoretical advances and the clinical observations of a number of American workers investigating the possible social causes of schizophrenia. Bateson and his colleagues[6] in Palo Alto devised the now famous double-bind theory to account for schizophrenia. They postulated that the communication between parent and child was of a particular quality – ambiguous and contradictory. The child at the receiving end of such communication became confused because of the inconsistency of his parents' messages. The covert communication differed markedly from the overt message. Although the double-bind theory is probably not a causal factor in schizophrenia, it is certainly observable in families with a schizophrenic member. The other development of note occurring at the same time, was the work of psychiatrists at Yale University[7] who were painstakingly examining the dynamics of families containing a schizophrenic child. Again, the search was for a possible cause of schizophrenia in the family. It seems more likely in the light of subsequent knowledge that the various phenomena described by the Yale group are secondary to the presence of the schizophrenic family member.

This work seems to have inspired a handful of therapists to develop a notion that for certain clinical problems, the family group was the most suitable target for therapy. One of these clinicians was Nathan Ackerman who in 1958 published a seminal work _The Psychodynamics of Family Life_.[8] Ackerman ingeniously applied his psychoanalytic experience to the treatment of the family. His publication seemed to pave the way for a number of other theoreticians and psychotherapists to develop alternative models and practical approaches in the treatment of families. Over the next two decades, a growing number of schools of family therapy resulted founded by figures such as Salvador Minuchin, Jay Haley, Virginia Satir, Robin Skynner and Murray

Bowen. The various theories and techniques advocated by these schools may differ widely. None the less, they all share one basic feature: the goal of any form of family therapy is to change the dynamics of the whole family or of what is commonly known as the family system, and not to concentrate on change in any individual member exclusively. Since there is no comprehensive all-embracing theory of family therapy as yet, it seems likely that multiple schools will continue alongside one another. We will look at the main schools of family therapy later.

Who benefits from family therapy? The family approach has become so popular since the mid-1970s that many therapists have come to regard it as something of a panacea for ills of all kinds. As is typical of new treatments in psychiatry, after the initial fanfare enthusiasm has been tempered with a touch of reality. The intrinsic nature of family therapy – assembling a natural group in order to explore and change its qualities – makes it ideally suited to a wide range of mental-health problems but certainly not to all.

Family therapy is not appropriate when the patient has a severe disturbance which as far as can be ascertained is unrelated to the family but linked to factors in the individual himself. Obviously, the family may be affected secondarily. If for example a child is the patient and a diagnosis is made of infantile autism (a severe psychiatric condition characterised by social withdrawal, abnormalities of language and ritualistic behaviour), this certainly means that the child warrants treatment in his own right. Similarly, if a parent has a well-defined psychiatric disturbance, particularly if this precludes an undistorted perception of himself and his relationships within the family, individual psychotherapy would seem more apt. Families are not necessarily bound together for life; therapists must recognise that sometimes they encounter a family on the verge of breakdown: the parents are intent on divorce or one or more children have decidedly left home. Forcing such a family together may not only complicate matters but is ethically indefensible. More pragmatically, should one or more family members express hesitancy or reluctance to participate in family therapy, it will serve little purpose to push such waverers or resisters into the treatment room. The result of such pressure is inevitably sabotage of treatment and consequent failure.

These questions must be considered in assessing suitability but a complementary and more positive approach is to try to establish what sort of families with what sort of problems are likely beneficiaries of treatment. The picture here is not as straightforward as one would like. As Tolstoy declares in the opening paragraph of *Anna Karenina*: 'All happy families are alike but an unhappy family is unhappy after its own fashion.' Very true. Family problems come in myriad forms, determined by the size of the family, personalities of the members, social class, ethnic and cultural features, and so on. None the less it is possible to identify commonly occurring problems which lead to disharmony or disability and which lend themselves well to a family therapeutic approach.

In child psychiatric practice, a whole host of symptoms and problems in children and adolescents are inextricably bound up with psychological disturbance in the family as a whole. A child with a disorder in behaviour or a psychosomatic illness like asthma in which psychological factors contribute to the cause or maintenance of the physical symptoms, or an educational problem such as a refusal to go to school, commonly serves as the standard-bearer of a disturbed family. Intervention at the level of the family leads to an improvement in the child's problems as well as to positive changes in the family group. Particular relationships within a family may be marked by conflicts and tension, with ripple effects on the other members of the family. The most obvious example is marital strife, which inevitably has deleterious effects on the couple's children. As we shall see later in the chapter, problems in marriage can be tackled through marital therapy without the participation of the rest of the family. Strife may occur between any members of the family, again serving to destabilise the family as a whole. Particularly common is tension between the generations – the adolescent child developing his own sense of values and attitudes which clash with those of his parents. Finally, the family as a group may become unbalanced in the face of some major stress such as the serious illness or death of one of its members, unemployment in one or more members, or moving to a new home.

It is obvious that these four indications are couched in general terms. Precise definitions remain elusive because of limited knowledge about the classification of disturbance in the family. The family therapist cannot simply apply the conventional classification of psychiatric disorders to the family problems he deals with. Conventional classifications focus on the individual; only recently have there been efforts to widen the range of categories so as to include problems in relationships. A systematic categorisation of family disorders is one of the important tasks facing the family therapist. The World Health

Organisation began to grapple with the whole question of diagnosis in child psychiatry in the late 1960s and some useful advances have already been made. For instance, a multi-dimensional approach to classification has been proposed which considers more than the mere psychiatric disorder diagnosed. The child's intellectual level and the identification of biological and social factors in relation to the disorder are additional features of the classification.

In the endeavour to tease out various patterns of dysfunction in a family, we need first to distinguish between what constitutes normal and abnormal functioning. To some extent, this difficulty is lessened by the assumption that families who ask for help not uncommonly need that help. But this is a crude and sometimes misleading criterion.

Before we look at family therapy in practice, it would be as well to tackle the question of whether there is such an 'animal' as the normal family. Here is not the place to enter into all the complexities of such an issue. It is possible however to consider the Tolstoyan notion that 'all happy families are alike' by amalgamating contributions from a variety of sources on what features in a family are regarded as desirable. I have found the writings of Nathan Ackerman, Virginia Satir and Salvador Minuchin – all notable figures in the field of family therapy – especially useful for this purpose.

The family is a social system in continuous transformation. An important requirement therefore is that it has the capacity to face new experience adaptively and creatively, and to act flexibly in the face of ever-changing circumstances. The arrival of a new baby, the advent of puberty in the children, illness, and loss of a grandparent are but a few of the incessant series of transitions and demands that every family must cope with. The concept of stability is highly relevant here: the family must not only tolerate various changes that constantly occur but must also accommodate itself to the change and regain its former stability. Families, by contrast, which are static, rigid and cling to old patterns or the status quo are likely to be overwhelmed by new experiences.

In the healthy functioning family, the self-esteem of each member is both promoted and maintained. Thus, each person has a sense of self-worth which is recognised and reinforced by the remaining members of the family. The family can praise and compliment the achieving member as well as support the development and creativity of all its members. In a troubled family, self-esteem is often at a low ebb or indeed non-existent.

In the concepts of many notable theorists, communication of a particular kind is the nub of the healthy family. Communication, both verbal and non-verbal, is typically direct, clear and honest. Furthermore, responses are readily forthcoming, contrary views can be expressed without fear, family members can express their needs, and messages, when appropriate, are supportive. As we shall see in a moment, some important schools of family therapy set out to identify faulty patterns of communication, make the family aware of these, and replace them with these positive styles of communication.

The healthy family caters for the needs of every one of its members. These needs may exist at any level, from the most fundamental – for food and physical comforts – to reassurance, encouragement and support. Obviously, the fulfilment of these needs is not perfectly symmetrical. Parents have certain responsibilities which are not reciprocated by their children and the young child is not necessarily in a position to fulfil the needs of his siblings. There is an implication however that the environment of the family facilitates the development of qualities such as empathy, receptiveness and sensitivity in all members. Requiring special mention is the need for each person in the family to establish his own identity. A common term used in this context is boundaries. Boundaries clearly exist between members so permitting their separateness although these boundaries are permeable. Disordered families are commonly typified by boundaries which are impermeable – each member is totally independent of the others and intimate relationships fail to evolve – or by the complete absence of boundaries in which case the family is enmeshed.

Finally, the healthy family has the ability to tolerate conflict within its ranks. In a group where there are inherent differences in attitudes, values and life-styles, the differences are tolerated. However, when conflict between two or more members does arise, such conflict is squarely faced. Some solution is sought, and if necessary compromises are arranged.

Family therapy in practice

The initial interview of the family is often tricky in as much as the experience is so utterly novel. And yet the interview is critical in enabling the therapist or co-therapists to ascertain the nature of the problem and to map out an approach to treatment. The therapists must also equip the family with some rationale and do so, not uncommonly, in the face of resistance: 'Isn't it Peter who needs the treatment? After all, he is the one that refuses to go to school.' Or: 'I am sure my wife could deal with this. My work would make it awfully difficult for me to attend the therapy sessions.' In some cases, assessment is a stepped procedure. Mother and her child, the patient, attend in the first instance. Thereafter, the father is encouraged to meet with the therapists, and subsequently, the other children. There are various strategies to involve the entire family with the ultimate goal of obtaining a commitment from each member to engage in treatment.

Most family therapists favour the participation of the whole nuclear family but there are variations in practice. For example, it is not entirely clear that very young children should attend and the question does arise of whether any risks may be attached to their participation. Most family therapists assume that the risk factor is negligible and argue that only with the whole family can the full picture of faulty interactions be recognised and tackled. Following this line of thought, certain schools favour the presence of the extended family, and grandparents in particular may therefore be invited to participate. One pair of therapists, Speck and Attneave,[9] have gone so far as to bring into therapy not only the family and the extended family but also relevant neighbours and friends. In this approach, network therapy, up to three or four dozen people may congregate together! Large numbers may also result from an approach known as multiple family therapy. Here a few families, three or four, are brought together on the premiss that the resultant group offers a forum whereby each family can observe how other families experience their problems and try to find solutions to them. Not only is there this vicarious learning but also the recognition that other families have problems too and these are commonly of similar type.

In the more usual practice of working with the nuclear family, various groupings and re-groupings can be arranged during the course of treatment. This flexibility is especially favoured by Minuchin, whose approach is discussed a little later. Minuchin arranges for all children to be present at the initial session, and grandparents as well if the family is an extended one. This is on the grounds that observation of the total family enables him to identify the various ways in which different members contribute to the disturbed patterns of relationships. Also demonstrable is the power of different members to obstruct or facilitate change in the family.

The average frequency of family therapy sessions is once every three weeks. This interval, which is in contrast to the customary weekly meetings of individual and group therapy, is intentional as it allows the family to continue to work on the issues raised in the sessions. Therapist and family also have the chance to assess progress by looking at the experiences of the family during the periods between treatment. As for the length of therapy, this varies according to the goals that are set. Many family therapists claim that a programme of ten or less sessions is sufficient. This is probably the case for problems which are not too severe; or when the aims of treatment are reasonably modest – improvement in particular symptoms or problems for example. More ambitious therapists who seek to achieve structural change in the family with parallel changes in each member tend to work with the family for a much longer period than their problem-oriented counterparts.

Therapeutic approaches

As already mentioned, no universal theory of therapy has yet evolved. Therapeutic approaches and the corresponding styles adopted by therapists vary considerably as a result. There is one quality in a therapist, however, which probably permeates all approaches, namely, a greater level of activity compared to more traditional psychotherapy. None the less, it is also on this dimension that family therapists can be distinguished. Beels and Ferber[10] have attempted to differentiate between two styles of therapist – conductors and reactors. Conductors are more active and dominant and lead the family group. They are also inclined to serve as guides, pointing out processes to the family such as their faulty patterns of communication. Reactors are non-directive and more passive. They are apt to react to what they note rather than to lead the family. Thus they weave in and out of the family, at times registering the feelings that are induced in them by the family: they may express their sense of bewilderment, impotence, anger, and so on. In an extreme version of the reactor style, one cotherapist of a pair allows himself to be sucked into the family's disturbance so that he may experience what it is like to be a member of the family under treatment. With this thorough immersion, he is in a position to offer feedback regarding what he has experienced. Meanwhile his co-therapist, remaining detached and in the role of observer, can appraise the events objectively. The observer-therapist can also bail out his reactor colleague should this prove necessary.

The family therapist who adopts a psychoanalytic approach in the therapy of families is best classified as a 'reactor'. The classical features of individual psychoanalytic psychotherapy are applied without much alteration to the members of the family. Sessions are held weekly and last one hour. The therapist's chief task is to interpret the transference projections (see Chapter 4) of each member of the family onto himself and transference projections that occur among the members of the family themselves. The assumption is made that the problems have their roots in early childhood experience and the perspective is consequently past-oriented. Therapeutic goals are insight and understanding of the underlying difficulties. This enables each member of the family to get beyond the original problems and to achieve personal growth. Typically, the psychoanalytically-based therapist issues no directives, does not assign the family any homework tasks, and offers no leadership.

In marked contrast to the analytic model are those in which the therapist is highly active, the 'conductors' of Beels and Ferber. Prominent among them are Virginia Satir, Salvador Minuchin and Jay Haley. Although there is some overlap between their three approaches they are all well known in the family therapy arena and each deserves a separate mention. Satir approaches the family in the first instance with an appreciation of how difficult it is to rear a family. As she puts it: 'I regard this as the hardest, most complicated, anxiety-ridden, sweat and blood-producing job in the world.'[11] In view of this attitude, it is not surprising that she offers a troubled family explicit leadership and guidance. In essence, she depicts herself as a teacher who has expertise in the field of communication. Her role is crystal clear – the family has failed in its ability to communicate satisfactorily and needs to be taught afresh. A new language must be acquired to resolve those problems in communication which Satir regards as the root of the family's woes. As the expert, she offers herself as a model, helps the family to set appropriate goals and points them out in the course of therapy. Moreover, Satir instils in the family a sense of hope and confidence that problems can be overcome and harmony restored. The approach involves much encouragement and reassurance. It is difficult to know how much of the therapeutic effect lies in these more non-specific factors and in Virginia Satir's obvious charismatic personality and how much is associated with the lessons she teaches about communication. The instruction is explicit: the family must learn to communicate with one another clearly, directly, congruently and honestly.

A climate must be created whereby the whole range of emotions can be expressed, including hurt, criticism and anger. Inevitably, the family must learn to take risks with one another. The expectation is that with improved communication, each member of the family will feel a sense of worth and individuality.

Salvador Minuchin likens his role as family therapist to that of the director of a family play. But he also sees himself as one of the actors. As director 'he creates scenarios, choreographs, highlights themes, and leads family members to improvise within the constraints of the family drama'.[12] In his book, *Families and Family Therapy*, he provides a clear account of what he regards as the nature of the problem in the troubled family and of the methods to achieve improvement. Minuchin views the family as a social system within which is contained a variety of sub-systems. These sub-systems can form on the basis of diverse dimensions such as age, sex, interests and values. An obvious sub-system is the parental one, another is that comprising the children. There may be many others besides – two adolescent siblings or mother and babe for example.

Difficulties arise for a family when its structure, that is, the arrangement of the various sub-systems, is faulty. One common pattern is enmeshment – there is poor differentiation between sub-systems so that family members are lumped together with no boundaries between them. There is thus no space in which a parent or child can make his own individual stamp. Conversely, the boundaries between members of a family may be completely rigid; the result is that each person is totally separate and constitutes his own sub-system: there is minimal or no inter-play between any of the family members. The system is governed by completely inflexible boundaries. A sub-system may exploit other members of the family to serve its own ends. For example, parents may deal with stresses in their relationship through one of their children. The result is that the parental sub-system is ostensibly intact but at the expense of the child. Any deviant behaviour in him is reinforced by the parents since such a strategy allows them to 'detour' their own problems. The child may be criticised and labelled as the culprit for the family's problems. An alternative device is for the parents to label the child as ill and in need of their protection; again, this allows the parental sub-system to avoid facing up to its tensions.

The emphasis on sub-systems and family structure provides a name for Minuchin's approach – structural family therapy. The target in treatment is the family system and the goal is a change in the organisation of the family. An assumption is made that with restructuring, each member of the family can be helped to benefit. 'Structural family therapy is a therapy of action', proclaims Minuchin. And indeed Minuchin's verbatim accounts of his work with families and the widely-known films of his approach testifies to the therapist's complete and active participation. As he strives to break previous patterns in family behaviour, he is an explicit agent and unashamedly directive. He becomes part of the family context and, in so doing, therapist and family join to form a new therapeutic system which intrinsically affects the behaviour of each participant. The perspective is the immediate present: exploration and interpretation of past history is regarded as unnecessary. The family's past has shaped it and therefore shows itself in the present. Moreover, the influence of the past can be replaced by a treatment that reorganises the present. Therapy is also future-oriented – structural transformation paves the way for the possibility of future change. Minuchin highlights the 'self-perpetuating properties' of families. Thus, the effects of the therapist's strategies will be maintained within the family in his absence. The family preserves the changes that ensue and these changes in turn provide a system which allows new possibilities for the family.

Minuchin has coined a number of terms which affect the therapist's activities. 'Joining' and 'accommodation' are two important examples. As an actor in a family play, the therapist actively joins various sub-systems and fits in with their behaviour. In joining a sub-system of children, he will talk with them using their style of talk; he may go further and sit on the floor with them and join in building towers. With a baby, he may again sit on the floor and tickle the infant. To point out the nature of a problem, the therapist may work with different sub-systems in different ways. The permutations are infinite. For instance the parental sub-system may be separated out and worked with alone because it is felt that the spouses require some privacy.

Joining and accommodation permit the therapist to gain knowledge of family patterns which are inevitably displayed before him. In order to appreciate the pattern, he must at times plunge into the family structure and at other times disengage himself and make sense of his observations.

The therapist, in setting out to restructure the family, can make use of a wide repertoire of techniques. For example, instead of talking about the difficulties facing the family, those difficulties are enacted: the accent is not so much on the content of the family's communication as on the way it is made. The therapist engineers who talks to whom, about what and how. Other forms of communication apart from words can be used. The most obvious illustration is the manipulation of space – the therapist can separate particular members of the family in the therapy room or bring particular ones together. He can, for example, place the parents in the centre of the room and arrange for the children to observe them from outside. An adolescent child who has dominated family life may be transferred to an observation room from which he notes how the family behaves in his absence. Tasks of all kinds may be assigned including homework. A husband may be instructed to choose his own clothes for the first time or a mother and adolescent daughter told to spend a specific period of the day in intimate chat.

There is a welcome flexibility in the methods of treatment used. Although Minuchin works within a theoretical framework, he is not constrained by it and roams widely to devise those techniques by which his therapeutic goals can be reached. All in all, this is a salutary lesson for psychotherapists (whether they work with families or not) who tend to be unduly inhibited by the theoretical postulates of their school. A risk is always entailed in the application of techniques in so far as the therapist may be so seduced by new techniques he stumbles over that he uses them indiscriminately and ineffectively. Techniques then predominate and foundations of therapy fragment. Such is not the case with Minuchin.

Jay Haley and his colleagues[13] follow a similar path in this regard in that their approach comprises a sensible blend of theory and method. There is much overlap between their theoretical position and that of Virginia Satir, discussed earlier. Communication theory is the nub of Haley's approach with its central concept that all behaviour is communicative, even silence. The notion is held that the exchange of messages between people, and obviously therefore between members of a family, defines the relationships between them. In addition, the relationships tend to be influenced by patterns of communication that occur in such a way as to maintain a balanced state.

Haley refers to his treatment as strategic therapy, and in this context it resembles the methodical, step-by-step approach of the behavioural psychotherapist. Haley sets clear goals and outlines the steps whereby these goals will be attained. As with the other 'conductors', Haley assumes a position of leadership as he attempts to alter the family system by getting members to communicate differently. The procedure is explained and a sequence of steps followed. First, from what is actually observed in the verbal and non-verbal communication of the family, the person or persons involved in a particular problem are identified and their roles therein clarified. Then a strategy is devised to change the faulty communication patterns, a strategy which differs with each type of problem. The therapist applies his methods directly and actively by setting tasks both during and between sessions. He may for instance instruct the parents to collaborate on a specific assignment. Haley includes a number of ingenious strategies which are beginning to attain wider popularity. One is the paradoxical directive in which the therapist instructs the family to exaggerate a particular facet of behaviour: a couple for example who constantly fight may be told to indulge in their skirmishing as much as they possibly can. The heat is soon taken out of the conflict as the couple realise what they are doing and how absurd their behaviour has been. Another seemingly potent technique is for the therapist to engage in alternate siding with two or more family members in order to force a conflict which has become stalemated into some form of resolution.

Whatever strategies are adopted, the therapist remains exclusively in the present. Haley is not concerned with the family's past nor sees future growth as a goal. Interpretations by the therapist are not called for as the family is not required to achieve any deep understanding of their problem. Haley is clearly determined to limit the therapy to a focus on communication and to achieve improved forms of it.

Let me conclude our discussion of family therapy with a brief mention of two other interesting approaches. That of Paul[14] chooses as its focus the 'three-generational system'. Paul postulates that the source of many a troubled family lies in feelings towards one of its number – usually a grandparent and hence the emphasis on three generations – which the family is unaware of and has not sorted out. Paul refers to the ghost which dominates family life and whose continued influence affects relationships within the nuclear family. The therapist identifies as much as he can with the particular family member, say the father, who may be re-experiencing sadness over the loss of an important family figure. A related feature of Paul's approach is to ensure that the rest of the nuclear family also empathise with the affected member in order to discover their rapport with him.

Finally, a word on multiple impact family therapy as originally devised by a group of workers[15] in Galveston, Texas. As the name suggests, the family is tackled on numerous fronts. It meets for two full days with a panel of therapists. During this time various sub-groups are formed according to a strategy worked out in the initial assessment phase. In what is an intensive, future-oriented treatment, various combinations of groups form and re-form so that complete examination of the family's problems is achieved. In ways similar to Minuchin's work, the object is to re-structure the family in order that the system is flexible enough to permit future change and development.

I believe we can conclude from our account of some of the major figures in family therapy that, while there are elements common to all of them – compare the non-specific factors we discussed in Chapter 1 – diversity is very apparent. This diversity is probably necessary for a new and blossoming field. It would be counter-productive to disregard either theoretical or practical alternatives when so little is known about normal families and their development, what characterises troubled families and how to categorise these troubles. I hope however that family therapists will not congregate into water-tight compartments but rather be open to new developments. A systematic study of different theories, methods and styles germinated during the 1970s. These seeds have developed into sturdy little saplings but nurturing over a long period will be required. In the interim, there is no doubt that the psychological management of selected problems through the agency of the family – while certainly not a panacea – is a significant addition to the psychotherapies.

Marital therapy

An obvious overlap exists between family therapy and marital therapy but the latter is indicated when the relationship between two spouses is disturbed and this disturbance is more or less independent of the rest of the family. Of course, the couple may have no children or marital therapy may be appropriate in conjunction with family therapy.

Until recently the professional interest in marital therapy was minimal. It seems as if there has been a long-standing ambivalence on the part of psychiatrists and other mental-health professionals towards working with couples. Marital therapy does involve a conceptual leap – from the notion that it is the individual patient with his internal conflicts who is the target of treatment to the notion that the problem resides in the sphere of the interpersonal. Here psychoanalytic influence has been marked, with its emphasis on the individual patient. Traditionally, the analyst has avoided any contact with the patient's spouse or family even though the effects on that spouse are potentially profound. Two other inter-related factors probably account for the professional's late entry into the field of marital therapy. For many years couples have sought the help of voluntary counsellors through such organisations as the Marriage Guidance Council. The priest too has often served as the comforter and adviser to a troubled pair. As a result of this 'voluntary' involvement, professional therapists may have regarded therapy with spouses as insufficiently prestigious. Now that marital therapy is established as a professional activity, the relationship between professional and lay therapist is unclear. It could be said that Marriage Guidance counsellors are more problem-oriented in their approach and that their work is more limited in scope but some professional therapists no doubt adopt very similar approaches. This raises the important question of who is best suited to provide psychotherapies of different kinds, a question I return to later in this chapter.

The growing interest in professional marital therapy, as seen in the expanding literature and research, has led to a proliferation of theories and techniques, as in the field of family therapy. As yet there is no unified conceptual scheme of what constitutes an abnormal marriage or of what the optimal therapeutic approach is.

We face a problem similar to the one I discussed in the section on family therapy. What is a healthy marriage, when does it become abnormal, and how do we classify marital disorders? Despite much interesting work on the sociology and psychology of marriage, the first question remains a knotty one. The concept of a marital life cycle is helpful in this regard. Marriage is obviously not a static phenomenon but an ever changing process. Fairly distinct phases can be identified: the initial step of a couple making a commitment, the first years before the arrival of children, the presence of young children, the presence of adolescent children, and the marriage following the departure of grown children. In each of these phases, the marital pair faces certain tasks and demands. Another helpful approach to the study of normal marriage is to tease out different aspects of the relationship. Jack Dominian,[16] a prominent British figure in the study of marriage and marital therapy, has suggested five important areas – emotional, sexual, social, intellectual and spiritual.

Some observers have described the qualities of the ideal marriage. Ackerman, the pioneering family therapist we mentioned earlier in the chapter, has suggested that in the ideal marriage: spouses share values to a reasonable degree and these values are realistic, stable and flexible; there is reasonable compatibility in the main areas of shared experience – emotional, social, sexual and parental; conflicts occur but they are not excessive or unrealistic; there is a tolerance of differences through mutual understanding and egalitarianism; and finally, there is a sharing of responsibility and authority. One wonders how many such marriages exist and also what to make of terms like 'reasonable', 'not excessive' and 'realistic'.

Turning to the disturbed marriage, there is little difficulty in recognising gross conflict and disharmony. The only drawback is that, at this level of severity, the marriage is inevitably on the verge of breakdown. Clearly there is a need to identify difficulties long before they become insurmountable and preferably soon after they appear. This is not to deny that some marriages are best terminated, even when children are involved. There is little point in a marriage continuing when one or both partners feel it as a constant torment or imprisonment. The partners may be completely incompatible with one another and any amount of therapeutic intervention is likely to prove futile.

The several attempts to classify different types of marriage are not that useful in pointing out which couples need help. The need for marital therapy is more usually determined by the partners themselves deciding, or being advised, to seek help. In addition, marital therapy may be recommended by a clinician when, in the course of his assessment of an individual patient's difficulties, he judges those difficulties to be associated with a marital conflict rather than being exclusive to the patient. Often, a young married woman complains to her family doctor of tiredness, headache, insomnia and tension but refrains from complaining about her marriage. It becomes obvious however on enquiry that her symptoms are entirely secondary to a troubled marriage. Another mode of presentation is the complaint by one or both partners about the sexual aspects of the relationship. Although sexual difficulties may be circumscribed and best dealt with by sex therapy,[17] in many cases the more appropriate target of treatment is the overall relationship. Perhaps the commonest pattern of marital disturbance lies in the area of communication – husband and wife simply fail to communicate clearly and unambiguously with each other. The inevitable result is friction and tension. In all these circumstances, marital therapy appears to be effective provided that both spouses are motivated to change and willing to commit themselves to the programme of therapy. If the situation has become intractable and one or both partners wish to separate, there may, paradoxically, still be a role for the therapist in helping them through this demanding process. Marital therapy is definitely not appropriate when one of the partners suffers from a severe form of psychiatric illness. In this case, individual treatment is called for although the partner may be involved secondarily.

Several schools of marital therapy exist and they are basically similar to the ones discussed in the section on family therapy. There, I paid more attention to those schools which emphasise the family as a social system, and in particular their pattern of communication. I commented less on the psychoanalytic, and not at all on the behavioural approaches. There is nothing arbitrary in my selection – it reflects by and large contemporary family therapy practice. The picture in marital therapy is somewhat different: the three schools are more or less equally represented amongst the ranks of marital therapists. There is a growing tendency however for an eclectic style which combines concepts and strategies from all three schools.

Marital therapists who rely on general systems theory are indistinguishable in their clinical approach from family therapists of the same school in that they are mainly concerned with the structure of the relationship. The focus is decidedly on the interaction between the spouses – the way they communicate, both verbal and non-verbal. Typically, the communication disorder involves misapprehension and misinterpretation because messages are indirect and confusing. Since the problem lies in the system and not in the people comprising it, treatment is geared towards changing that system. A whole range of strategies is applied, designed to make the couple aware of the faulty patterns of communication and to enable them to establish new adaptive modes of relating. I have discussed these practical aspects in some detail in the family therapy section.

The psychoanalytic school of marital therapy was pioneered by Henry Dicks. He and his colleagues began to apply psychoanalytical concepts to the treatment of couples in the late 1940s. His marital unit at the Tavistock Clinic in London was one of the first of its kind and from it stemmed important theoretical and clinical advances. Dr Dicks's *Marital Tensions*[18] published in 1967, describes the Tavistock work. For Dicks, 'modern marriage is perhaps the greatest challenge to [maturity]'. He sees marriage as a voluntary contract between two people to play certain social roles in order to satisfy their respective needs and the requirements of society. But Dicks regards another dimension of marriage as perhaps the most important – the fact that it is a transaction at a deeper level between the unconscious identities of the partners. From the very start, at the time when a man and woman select each other, the decisions to do so are largely unconscious. Social class, religion, education, age and other similar factors also contribute to the choice but not in the same measure as those factors which are unknown to the person choosing. In this regard, the Tavistock school is heavily dependent on the ideas of two prominent psychoanalysts, Melanie Klein and W. R. D. Fairbairn. This is not the place to enter into the content of their theories (see references 11 and 12 in Chapter 4); suffice it to say that both Klein and Fairbairn advanced the idea that Freud's instinct theory is inadequate to explain the complexities of human behaviour and that a person, from his earliest infancy, has an innate need and longing for relations with others.

When it comes to marriage, a person selects a mate based mainly on unconscious factors and these factors are in turn dependent on the individual's developmental history, in particular his early family experience. A person may therefore select someone whom he hopes will gratify his unfulfilled infantile expectations. There is an unconsciously-held hope to find those parts of the self which the individual misses or feels he has lost. For example, a passive, unassertive man may select a self-reliant, dominant woman in order to achieve these latter qualities. A man with a pronounced masculine image may select a dependent, soft and feminine 'little woman' with the unconscious hope of finding the tender and dependent part of himself which is lost to him. In some couples, the mating is what has been referred to as assortative – the partners appear to be matched in such a way that they complement one another. Thus, the passive husband not only selects a self-reliant and dominant woman; she in her own right has selected him to satisfy her unconsciously held expectations. The matching can prove satisfactory with an adjusted marriage the result. The unconscious factors in selection never surface and the needs of each partner are satisfied. Not uncommonly however, difficulties arise. A spouse requires of his partner that she behave in terms of the projected model he has of her; the spouse can only see the other as he expects her to be rather than what she actually is. If, in this case, the wife does not fulfil her husband's unexpressed hopes, disappointment and resentment is his response. The picture is even more complicated in that partners are chosen on the unconscious premiss that through the marriage an unresolved conflict will be magically resolved without their personal handicaps having to be exposed. This accounts for the common observation that a couple, despite incessant strife, will persist with each other. A neurotic balance is established which enables the two spouses to avoid their own personal hidden conflicts: better the tension of the relationship than facing up to their own inner problems.

The aim of analytically-oriented marital therapy is personal change in both spouses so that each recognises his or her own internal conflicts and the neurotic equilibrium characteristic of their relationship. The idea is that with personal insight, the partners will re-establish their marriage on a more mature and realistic footing. The psychoanalytic school of marital therapy thus seeks to ascertain and understand the underlying causes of the marital disorder and regards symptomatic improvement as superficial and temporary. Although the emphasis on personal change is obvious, the therapist does not lose sight of the need to consider the marriage as a whole in assessing outcome. Dicks, for example, requires evidence of substantial change in the interaction between the partners 'towards full communication at all levels'. This includes a satisfying sexual life, the capacity to quarrel in a mature way, a greater sense of identity in each partner with associated regard for the self and the other, the tolerance of differences and a more realistic perception of the partner.

The behavioural approach to marital therapy is in marked contrast to the psychoanalytic one. Much simpler and less ambitious, the couple is not required to understand their own psychodynamics or the dynamics of their relationship. Instead, the focus is exclusively on their problems and how to change them. Many therapists using a behavioural approach subscribe to three premises: (1) the existing pattern of interaction in the marriage is usually the one experienced as the most rewarding and requiring the least effort; (2) most couples expect to share the rewards and responsibilities involved in marriage; and (3) in troubled marriages this sharing process works poorly. The capacity of each spouse to reward the other is minimal and negative methods are used instead to get the partner to co-operate – silence, pestering and withdrawal from sex are common examples. Stuart[19] has devised an approach to treatment based on these assumptions in which principles of operant conditioning (see Chapter 4) are applied. The basis of treatment can be summarised in the phrase 'give – to – get'. After a thorough analysis of the problems facing the couple, the partners are asked to specify the changes they want in each other. For example, the wife may request a regular chat in the evening after dinner for some twenty minutes while the husband may want sex twice a week. It is important that the desired behaviours are highly specific precluding any confusion about what each wants of the other. The partners must agree to a clearly outlined system of rewarding each other. With practice, the power of the spouses to reward each other for positive behaviour is improved.

This approach may seem unduly mechanical and in many ways it is but the therapist works on the assumption that even with simple behavioural changes, greater harmony will follow and other facets of the relationship will improve. There is some research evidence to suggest that this is indeed the case.

The behavioural approach is likely to be more appropriate in couples whose problems are not unduly complex and therefore amenable to change with a comparatively superficial approach. Behavioural marital therapy is also suitable for couples in whom the level of psychological-mindedness in one or both partners is slender or where psychoanalytic-type interpretations are likely to cause anxiety with which the couple cannot cope.

Marital therapy in practice

Whichever theoretical model is used, there are variations in the practice of marital therapy. Each partner may be seen individually, by the same therapist or by two different therapists who collaborate over their plans for treatment. The idea is that each partner will change so permitting his or her re-entry into the marriage with a greater sense of maturity and realism. The focus none the less in the individual sessions is on the marital relationship. This individual approach is particularly useful if partners refuse to work together or their hostility to each other is so intense that it could prove hazardous. A much more common variation is therapy in which both partners are treated together. A single therapist or a pair of therapists, invariably one male and one female, may be involved. The focus here is on the present, that is observations are made by both patients and therapists of what transpires in the session of therapy. Because of this arrangement, personal exploration is more difficult to achieve.

A further variation is the so-called four-way session. Here each spouse has his or her own therapist but all four meet regularly as well. The model was developed by Masters and Johnson,[17] who pioneered the psychological treatment of sexual problems. Although there is some evidence to suggest that a single therapist is as effective as a pair in sex therapy, the four-way concept has intrinsic advantages: each spouse derives support from his or her own sex therapist who serves as something of an advocate, and the co-therapists can serve as models, particularly in the way they relate to each other in the sessions. Complications may arise, however, in respect to confidentiality. Obviously the co-therapists obtain information about both spouses and may therefore have knowledge which one or other spouse does not have. An explicit agreement needs to be reached about how information will be shared. Because of this handicap, most marital therapists favour the system in which no secrets can be kept and candid communication is prized. A fourth variation is group marital therapy. Three or four couples meet regularly together over a period of many months, usually with a mixed pair of therapists. Although concentration on a particular couple is hereby reduced, the group has certain intrinsic advantages. Couples soon recognise that their problems are not unique and feel less 'different' as a result. As the group becomes more cohesive, so the climate of trust and support grows; there is a sense of belonging and loyalty. Each couple can learn from the others by identifying with their problems and noting how they approach them or by imitating their assets and desirable behaviour. The couple also learns more about the nature of their problems by receiving feedback from the other couples and the therapist. The pair of co-therapists may serve as a model of how a couple should relate by implicitly demonstrating how they communicate. Co-therapists who are actually married to one another have conducted marital therapy, either with single couples or with groups, invariably doing so on the supposition that they can model positive patterns of behaviour.

With all these different possibilities, there is some confusion as to what is optimal. The growing body of evidence gained by research[20] suggests that individual therapy for marital problems is not very effective and may in fact cause more harm than alternative approaches. Couples seem to benefit most from the joint approach with group marital therapy a close rival. Although there would appear to be common-sense reasons for a couple to be treated by a mixed pair of co-therapists, research studies show little difference in the effects of treatment given by a single therapist or a pair of therapists; the sex of the therapist does not seem to be a crucial factor in outcome.

Encounter groups and self-help groups

In Chapter 1 we looked at various definitions of psychotherapy and noted that almost all of them referred to the *professional* relationship between a troubled person and a sanctioned healer. Szasz's definition by contrast compared the relationship in psychotherapy to a friendship and implied a more reciprocal process between the participants. The question of which definition is more accurate is impossible to resolve because it depends entirely on where the boundaries of the discipline are drawn.

The issue is important in view of the development and rapid growth since the 1960s of certain social movements which have a direct bearing on how people seek, and receive psychological help. I refer to the widespread popularity of encounter groups and self-help groups. Participants in these forms of group activity commonly do not regard themselves as patients but as either involved in the pursuit of personal growth or as wrestling with problems in living. Because of the impact of these new social forces, the conventional concepts of patient and healer are thrown into doubt. A brief account of the encounter group and the self-help group movements will enable the reader to appreciate the changing image of psychotherapy.

The *encounter group*, an American invention of the early 1960s, grew phenomenonly in that decade, peaked at the beginning of its second decade, but has subsequently lost some of its glitter. Notwithstanding, it continues to be an influential social phenomenon. In the heyday of the encounter group, as prominent a psychologist as Carl Rogers (see page 129) became so convinced of its potential that he could proclaim: 'The encounter group is perhaps the most significant social invention of the century – the demand for it is utterly beyond belief. It is one of the most rapidly growing social phenomena in the United States. It has permeated industry, is coming into education, and is reaching many professionals in the helping fields.'[21] Other commentators, similarly, have hailed the encounter group's virtues, with some likening it to a social oasis in a dehumanised society.

What exactly is an encounter group? Although a generic term for a heterogeneous collection of group experiences, certain properties are common to virtually all encounter groups. A number of people – anything from half a dozen to 200 – assemble for a period ranging from a weekend, the most usual duration, to several weeks. During this time they live and meet together in an intensive way. The purported goal is the achievement of personal growth. Terms commonly used in the encounter group literature which reflect its objectives include self-actualisation, self-awareness, exploration into the self, personal search for authenticity, meaningful communication and social sensitivity. Clearly the focus is on developing the self. Thus, one encounter group organisation in Britain comments in its advertising: 'Quaesitor sees its function as providing an open centre for creative group work, a framework for exploration of the self. The centre adopts no individual style except one of flexibility, and covers every reputable method of personal growth or else refers enquiries to the right place.'[22]

Who participates in encounter groups and why? It has been estimated that over five million Americans have experienced them in some form during the past two decades. Attenders appear to be chiefly upper- and middle-class whites, in their 30s, well educated and mainly from professional backgrounds. Although encounter groups are ostensibly designed for normal healthy persons interested in personal growth, there is little doubt that a substantial proportion of the participants attend for the same reasons which prompt others to consult a mental-health professional. Probably the most common problems shared by the two groups are of an existential nature: lack of meaning in life, basic loneliness, and sense of purposelessness, among others. Perhaps not unexpectedly, those who participate in encounter groups and clinical patients overlap to a considerable degree. In one illuminating survey[23] of over 400 prospective participants of encounter groups, it emerged that eighty-one per cent of them had previous or current experience of conventional psychotherapy. In other words the encounter group was a supplement rather than an alternative to traditional psychotherapy. Moreover, in comparison with a group of applicants to psychiatric clinics, the encounter group sample was found to have similar motives of seeking help and contained many people who were currently experiencing distress in their lives.

A commonly held notion that the patient attending a professional psychotherapist and the participants in an encounter group are different people is suspect. The question of what constitutes a patient as a result becomes much more problematical than hitherto. Pertinent in this context are the concepts of 'head-shrinking' and 'mind-expanding'.[24] Head-shrinking refers to the therapist's endeavour to reduce discomfort such as distress and dissatisfaction, and ineffectiveness such as ineptitude, inefficiency and unproductiveness; mind-expanding on the other hand involves an increase in pleasure – joy, love and verve, and creativity – energy, effectiveness and power.

Head-shrinking has typically been part of the conventional psychotherapist's approach, consisting of the professional healer and his methods of treatment on the one hand and the patient and his symptoms on the other. Mind-expanding is typical of the encounter movement in which it is assumed that participants are not ill in any sense, do not warrant designation as patients, but are there to expand their personal horizons. The conventional treatment model as a result of the encounter movement's potent influence has tended to creak along in recent years and may well become an anachronism before long.

The views of Carl Rogers, the doyen of the encounter group movement, on what constitutes a patient, are highly relevant in our discussion of the head-shrinking, mind-expanding dichotomy. His position is significant in so much as he straddles both conventional psychotherapy and the encounter group. Throughout most of his career, he has been active in developing a school of psychotherapy based on humanist and existential principles (see Chapter 4). The crux of his model is that the client is seen as an active collaborator in his own development. The name of the school – client-centred counselling – (formerly known as non-directive counselling), reflects a cardinal Rogerian tenet: respect for the patient's autonomy. Rogers eschews conventional treatment entirely. The person receiving help is not diagnosed in any sense, is not classified, and is referred to as the client, never the patient. The therapist, *as human being*, is regarded as the helpful agency and not his technical skills. The therapeutic relationship enables the client to realise his capacities. Rogers postulates a tendency to strive for self-development in all human beings, mainly, the 'inherent tendency of the organism to develop all its capacities in ways which serve to maintain or enhance the organism'. This tendency is regarded as the 'mainspring of life ... evident in all organic and human life'.[25]

This basic notion has an important bearing on the conduct of psychotherapy as practised by Rogers and on his style of leadership in encounter groups. In both cases, a highly optimistic view is taken of the client's predilection for positive change and growth. In essence, the therapist or leader creates a climate which facilitates the individual's inherent tendency to self-development. Little more is required since the actualisation motive is so potent. The chief characteristic that distinguishes client-centred psychotherapy from the encounter group is the number of participants. The encounter group obviously depends for its effects on the existence of a group with the leader filling the role of facilitator. Rogers appears, like many of his colleagues in the encounter movement, to have become exceedingly impressed with the power of the group force to promote the necessary conditions for participants to achieve personal growth. He comments: 'Individuals totally untrained in the helping relationship often exhibit a sensitive capacity to listen, an ability to understand the deepest significance of the attitudes expressed, and a warmth of caring that are genuinely helpful.'[26]

This 'sensitive capacity', 'ability to understand' and 'warmth of caring' on the part of untrained group members no doubt account in large measure for the attractiveness encounter groups have for their members. How do these characteristics evolve? Typically, the group assembles at a 'growth centre' (this is usually an autonomous institution set up especially for the purpose of organising encounter group experiences and quite separate from conventional psychiatric clinics). Initially, the members are all strangers to one another. A mixed sense of heightened expectation and anxiety flows through the group. The leader encourages members to share their immediate feelings and to overcome their defensiveness. The usual result is the fairly rapid evolution of a climate of trust which allows participants to be less inhibited and more open to new experiences. A stage is reached in which individuals can openly and honestly express their feelings towards one another. The result is that each member learns how he comes across and what impact he has on others. Soon, façades and defences are put aside and members allow their real selves to emerge. By now, there is a growing warmth in the group and members have developed a sense of intimacy with one another. Lest this sounds simply like a love feast, it should be noted that experiential learning is at the heart of the cohesive group: through active participation, members are learning about themselves, about their relationships with others, and about their potential for change.

This description seems impressive but are encounter groups actually effective? The testimony of participants and the convictions of leaders of encounter groups are certainly persuasive but it is to the only large-scale controlled study of encounter groups that we need to turn to ascertain more objectively the level of benefit that results. Over 200 students at Stanford University were randomly assigned to one of eighteen groups. These represented ten major schools. Each of the eighteen groups met for a total of thirty hours over a three-month period. The students were assessed before the beginning of the group, immediately after completing it, and again six months later. The battery of tests was extensive: questionnaires for the students covering such aspects as self-esteem, interpersonal attitudes, values, emotional expressiveness, and patterns of friendship; and assessments by the group leaders, by the group members of one another and by significant people in the student's life. Of the 170 students who completed the groups, the majority found them constructive and pleasant. At the six-month follow-up this enthusiasm had diminished somewhat but the evaluation remained positive. This finding is in accord with the commonly obtained testimony of participants in encounter groups. But what about actual change in the students? Outcome was categorised in terms of learning from the experience and here the study shows that one-third of the participants at follow-up achieved moderate or considerable positive change. Another one-third were unchanged while the final third comprised a group of drop-outs, those who changed for the worse, and casualties. By contrast, over two-thirds of a control group of students who were given a similar battery of tests but who did not participate in groups remained unchanged at follow-up.

The book in which this study is comprehensively described and analysed is entitled *Encounter Groups: First Facts*.[27] The title is most apt. At the time of its publication in 1973, these findings did indeed constitute the first objective knowledge on encounter groups. Nearly ten years later the study has not been repeated. We must therefore assume that the rather modest improvement that it was concluded encounter groups produce is probably correct. Glowing testimony is one thing, objective change is another. Perhaps the most notable finding of the investigation was the ten per cent casualty rate. Sixteen students were actually made worse as a result of their participation. We will turn to this important matter in the next chapter.

Now that encounter groups have been with us for over twenty years, what conclusions can we reach about them? Firstly, there is little doubt that encounter groups promise too much to their prospective participants. At the height of their popularity, the conviction grew that the encounter group was a spectacular new social phenomenon which could go far to reducing an individual's sense of alienation and malaise. Moreover, with members experiencing their real selves and through intimate encounters between them, a means was available to remedy many of the social problems facing contemporary society. Alas, the encounter group has achieved little in this regard. All we can say is that participants generally feel positively about the experience, particularly in the days that follow it but that any more substantial changes are uncommon or temporary. If any learning does occur, it does not appear to be of use in ordinary life. Secondly, what Rogers sees as the exquisite real encounter between people is something of a mirage. What appears to be more the case in practice is an exhibition of narcissism. Although the idea of encounter may be held in high esteem, what seems to over-ride it is the need for the individual to indulge primarily in self-gratification. The encounter group can be tantamount to an occasion of hedonism. The painful problems and challenges of real life are side-stepped and it is no wonder that participants attain so much pleasure from the group experience. In many ways, they are suspended from ordinary life and enveloped in a cosy social microcosm. I would not wish to infer that personal problems are not raised in encounter groups; far from it. The point is that ultimately a priority of the attender is the seeking of pleasure.

Another criticism levelled against the encounter movement revolves around the paradox that whilst members are encouraged to prize their autonomy, the nature of the experience is such that conformity is a prominent feature. An ethos pervades the group according to which all members, without exception, must 'let go', actively disclose personal information about themselves and develop intimacy towards one another. There is little or no room for individual privacy: everyone has to get involved. And yet the sharing and the valued intimacy call for no long-term commitment; these circumstances are desiderata for the duration of the group only.

We have already commented on the casualty rate. Encounter groups, unlike conventional therapy groups, entail no selection or screening procedure. Participation is entirely voluntary; leaders can have no idea about the members they will have in their groups. Perhaps even more critical is the commonly occurring situation of no screening of the leaders. Encounter group leaders are for the most part non-professionals and untrained. They generally hold strong personal convictions about the value of the encounter movement and steer clear of any critical arguments against it. There tends to be an anti-intellectual bias with leaders contending that their movement is beyond scientific appraisal, which can only bring with it dehumanising and limiting attitudes. The field is ripe for creative quackery.

Consider the case of one of the most prominent representatives of the encounter group – Werner Erhard. A former car salesman named Jack Rosenberg, Erhard devised in the early 1970s a therapeutic package entitled Erhard Seminar Training (usually abbreviated as EST). His programme consists of a pot pourri of techniques borrowed from just about every school of psychotherapy. The package is purveyed over two successive weekends to groups of 200 people who are willing to pay the fee of a few hundred dollars. Although Erhard refers to his activities as a form of training and not of psychotherapy, this is probably disingenuous of him because it is abundantly clear that the objectives of his programmes are intimately bound up with the mental health of the participants. There is little doubt that EST is a dressed-up therapeutic programme, marketed like a commercial product, whose purpose is to ensure that the consumers of the product enjoy a feeling of self-satisfaction. The argument could be offered that Erhard, or any other encounter group leader, has the right to peddle his wares and that it is the responsibility of the prospective customer to be circumspect prior to making his purchase. All well and good except that the unfortunate prospective participant may be quite ignorant of the encounter group's potential risks and inflated claims. I would not wish to allege that all encounter group leaders are charlatans, irresponsible or unintellectual. Far from it. I have already mentioned Carl Rogers on a number of occasions; his integrity is to be envied. No, the problem lies in the fact that anyone can offer his services and his sense of accountability may be slender.

Finally, the history of the encounter movement has witnessed a tendency to vulgarisation. We can see this in concrete form in the way in which gimmicks rather than a coherent model are pre-eminent. And so, as in the case of EST, a hotch-potch of techniques and 'games' consume the hours, ranging from the use of every conceivable Eastern religious practice to body massage and nude marathons. Interestingly, those encounter groups in the Stanford study which emphasised the use of various structured exercises had no influence on outcome. By contrast, the leader who understood group dynamics and the nature of his role proved most effective.

This sounds like a damning indictment but I should point out that the purpose of my critical evaluation is to place the encounter movement in a realistic perspective. This is not to negate its potential in helping a proportion of participants to achieve greater self-awareness and growth. I can testify myself to the value of an encounter group experience. In the early 1970s, I had the good fortune to participate in an encounter group on two occasions and found both experiences worthwhile. I learned a fair amount about myself and the way I came across to others and as a splendid bonus achieved considerable understanding of various group processes. I should also hasten to mention that these encounter groups were under the aegis of an excellent 'growth centre' – the San Diego-based Center for the Studies of the Person, founded by, among others, Carl Rogers.

Whatever the current status of the encounter group movement, its positive influences on conventional psychotherapy are discernible. Certainly, in the 1960s, with progressive disillusionment with psychoanalytically-oriented psychotherapy and the growing interest in humanist psychology and the human potential movement, encounter groups served as an important model for group therapy with patients and for conventional psychotherapy in general. The espousal by the encounter movement of a prominent humanising tradition left its imprint over almost the entire mental-health profession. Some fundamental assumptions of traditional psychotherapy were exposed, assumptions we mentioned briefly earlier in this chapter: the use of the classical approach in treatment, the emphasis on symptomatic relief, the use of psychiatric diagnosis, and so forth. Possibly another salutary effect of the encounter group has been the growing demystification of professional psychotherapy. The greater degree of openness among leaders of encounter groups has no doubt persuaded professional therapists to shed some of the mystique that surrounds them. Such leaders have also been confronted with new techniques and approaches which, at least during the 1960s, were inventive and sometimes ingenious. Some of this inventiveness has been absorbed into traditional therapy, in particular the selective practice of various action techniques or structured exercises. Therapists have come to realise that an exclusively verbal mode of communication in therapy, especially in the group psychotherapies, is highly limiting. The introduction of action techniques into small group therapy and family therapy would probably not have taken place as it has without the stimulus and model of the encounter group.

The influence of the encounter group approach on the conventional therapist has been further increased by the latter's participation in such groups. I mentioned my participation and its useful results in my own case. The encounter group using coherent principles and avoiding gimmicks and fads has served the excellent purpose of offering mental-health professionals the chance to study both personal and group dynamics.

Self-help groups

'Sensitive capacity', 'ability to understand', and 'warmth of caring', qualities that Rogers highlights in his account of encounter groups, also play a prominent role in self-help or mutual-help groups and probably contribute to the phenomenal success they currently enjoy. Groups of all types, small and large and including the family, the extended family, the clan, the tribe, the neighbourhood, among many have served as a vital healing agency throughout recorded history. Among them have been groups which rely on the help and support members offer to one another, without recourse to a designated leader.

The contemporary self-help group does not differ substantially from its predecessors. The main changes lie in its current widespread popularity – there are several dozen self-help organisations in most Western countries – and its socio-political significance. The last two decades have seen the tremendous growth of a consumer movement, one of whose features is a healthy scepticism of professionalism. No longer is it axiomatic that a consumer or client will take on trust what the professional has to offer; undoubtedly, a better informed public has become more cognisant of the professional's genuine skills rather than his ostensible skills, and of the inherent limitations of the professional's power.

A most interesting example in this regard is the case of the homosexual. Professional psychiatry first regarded homosexuality as a perversion, the very word reflecting a moral judgement. Later, the term sexual deviation was used to describe homosexuality, suggesting that it was an abnormal condition much like any other psychiatric disorder. In the early 1970s, a further change ensued, at least in American psychiatry when the abnormal connotation was modified and replaced by a new concept, namely, homosexuality as a sexual orientation disturbance. This meant that homosexuality was no longer regarded as a psychiatric illness; instead, homosexuals were regarded as potentially in need of psychiatric help if they were distressed by their sexual orientation or unable to adjust satisfactorily to it because of society's attitudes. This last change was almost certainly not an innovation conjured by psychiatrists themselves but followed in the wake of a self-help movement composed of homosexuals themselves.

The so-called Gay Movement which began to have influential social and political effects from the 1960s expressed in most articulate fashion its dissatisfaction with the traditional medical view of homosexuality and, in particular, psychiatry's approach to its treatment. Homosexuals began to turn towards one another for support and understanding – only fellow homosexuals could really appreciate what it was like to be homosexual and be in a position to offer help and guidance.

The evolution of a strong self-help movement among homosexuals is matched by other minority social groups who feel stigmatised, deprived, misunderstood or rejected by society. The Women's Movement for example developed during the 1960s in the context of the American Civil Rights Movement. Women began to recognise that their own civil rights had never been fully recognised as a result of the traditional, fixed role assigned to them and because of society's attitude towards women. Apart from the political consequences of this new movement, the chief development was the 'consciousness-raising' group. These groups, composed of about ten women, typically meet weekly to exchange views and feelings on topics such as relationships with men, sex, motherhood and femininity.

The Women's Movement and the Gay Movement are to a large extent ideological in type. Other self-help groups have sprung up for different reasons. Alcoholics Anonymous and Gamblers Anonymous – organisations which deal with a form of addiction – have probably evolved as a response to professional failure. Psychiatry has hitherto enjoyed little success in its efforts to help alcoholics and gamblers. What could be more logical than the disappointed patient of the professional attempting to grapple with his problem in an alternative way, particularly by turning to his fellow sufferers for support and help: 'The professional cannot help me, cannot even understand me; perhaps others with a similar problem can.'

The widespread break-up of the extended family and the decline in such traditional sources of support as the Church are other factors which contribute to the growing popularity of the self-help movement. Bereavement serves as the best example in this regard. Formally, a bereaved person could derive sympathy and support during his grief from a wide network including the immediate family, the extended family, the neighbourhood and the Church. Many of these traditional support systems have collapsed or undergone radical change. The result has been unfortunate – the bereaved person is often isolated and has no one to share his grief with. Perhaps not unexpectedly, the hiatus has been filled, at least partially, by new forms of social organisations, with the self-help group pre-eminent. One such organisation in Britain, Cruse, has established a national network of groups which offer widows and widowers an opportunity to meet with one another in order to share their grief and to overcome the effects of isolation and loneliness. Compassionate Friends is a similar organisation but founded specifically for parents who have lost a child. Founded in 1969 by a British chaplain, Compassionate Friends has grown into a large international organisation. It offers parents the chance to talk freely about their grief, to learn how to accept their loss, to recognise that other parents have undergone similar losses, and to be of service to other bereaved parents. Another example of self-help as replacement for declining traditional systems of support is the Post-natal Group. As the name suggests, new mothers band together in order to gain emotional support and practical guidance. In former times, grandmother or even great-grandmother would have played such a role. In their absence, the Post-natal Group is one contemporary substitute.

Accompanying the development of the self-help movement has been its systematic study by psychologists, sociologists and anthropologists, especially the attempt to define and classify self-help groups.[28] What have these studies shown? The review of the literature by Marie Killilea[29] is splendidly comprehensive and illuminating. Her account of the characteristics common to self-help groups is particularly noteworthy. The seven common properties are:

1. The common experience of the members – the participants in a self-help group, without exception, share the same problem. They are, for example, alcoholics, the parents of a chronically-ill child, overweight, homosexual, gamblers, child abusers, epileptics, bereaved, ex-psychiatric patients – the list is endless. This shared experience helps the sufferer feel he is not unique in having such a problem. Not uncommonly, a person with a problem such as these perceives himself as something of a freak, as if he alone was burdened or afflicted. The self-help group rapidly dispels this assumption. As important is the commonly stated experience that only fellow sufferers can really grasp and appreciate the nature of the problem. Professional psychotherapists have only occasionally experienced the problems of their clients and must rely on empathy to understand them. There is an important implication embedded here – is a psychotherapist likely to be more

effective when he and his patient are matched in terms of their experience, values, ideology, and so forth? It has been argued, quite persuasively, that matching of this kind on factors like social class and ethnicity allows for a closer therapist-patient relationship and more effective therapy as a corollary. It comes as no surprise to find that psychotherapists, by and large, work with patients from similar backgrounds in terms of class and race. Undoubtedly, therapists find it easier to treat 'their own kind', because of shared assumptions and values. In the self-help group, it is the common experience of a particular problem, affliction or stigma which binds the members.

2. Mutual help and support – at first sight it would appear unlikely that a person carrying a burden of some kind would be equipped to offer any form of help to another person. But this is decidedly not the case. We noted earlier in this chapter, in our discussion of the small therapy group, that most of the benefit stems from the process whereby group members give and receive support and feedback to one another. The same applies to the psychiatric hospital in which the principles of the therapeutic community are used – that the entire membership of the hospital community and above all the patients constitute the therapeutic agent. The self-help group also adopts this principle and assumes that its members are able, despite their own personal difficulties, to offer one another help and support through regular contact. Alcoholics Anonymous illustrates very well this pattern of mutual help. It effectively offers a small group forum in which members, having acquired an expertise based on their own experience of their drinking problem, can share that expertise with other members. Moreover, a new member is assigned to a veteran who helps to integrate him and to assist him in case of emergency. The longer-term goals in this process involve the novice himself becoming a sponsor after he has become an established member.

3. Altruism – mutual help and altruism are closely aligned as witnessed in the Alcoholics Anonymous illustration. It is common experience that when we attempt to help our fellows, we may derive as much from the experience as does the recipient. A self-help group member similarly gains considerably from his altruistic endeavour. The helper enjoys the sense of giving of himself: 'I can be useful to others and I am therefore of value.' Altruism also serves to reduce a person's undue self-absorption and to enhance his sensitivity to others.

4. Reinforcement of normality – a common experience of self-help group attenders is their sense that they are different or deviant. We

have already noted that the first common property of the self-help group is the creation of a feeling that 'everyone is in the same boat'. This sense is further extended when the group member notes that his peers with identical problems to himself can function normally in conventional spheres like work, marriage, family life and leisure. Persuasion that he is normal and can participate in normal social activities is not required – the evidence through the self-help group is highly conspicuous. Another advantage is in dealing with the stigma attached to mental illness. A sense of stigma and feeling different applies particularly to the psychiatrically ill towards whom a deep-seated social prejudice is commonplace. Recovery INC., a prominent self-help organisation composed of ex-psychiatric patients takes the fighting of the stigma further in declaring that one of its aims is to abolish the 'prejudice and superstition of the community against mental disease'. Similarly, homosexual activist groups like the Campaign for Homosexual Equality work hard to change social prejudices traditionally directed towards them. They fight for enlightened attitudes, including the understanding that a homosexual is as much deserving of membership of society as is the heterosexual or bisexual. All should be free to express their personality.

5. Collective will-power – it is not uncommon in the practice of psychotherapy to encounter a patient who has lost heart and the motivation to change. The self-help group by bringing people with a shared difficulty together enables them to look to each other for validation of their attitudes and beliefs. They can obtain testimony from their peers that their commonly shared problems can be faced, wrestled with, and overcome. Each member by his sheer participation, encourages others in their determination, especially the novice or waverer. In this way motivation for soldiering through difficult times or for solving problems is sustained.

6. Exchange of information – a prominent property of the self-help group is its use as a forum for the exchange of information. Members can obtain a greater understanding of the nature of the condition or problem they have through the provision of specific information about practicalities, about what to expect, and about different ways of coping. For example, a bereaved person can gather information from more experienced peers about funeral arrangements, business matters, and the nature of grief on anniversaries and how to cope with them. This sort of information is not always easily available from books or from experts. The educational aspect of the self-help group

also enables a member to look at his problem in new ways and to compare his attitude to, and management of, the problem with his fellows.

7. Constructive action toward shared goals – the emphasis in a self-help group is very much on doing and action of various kinds is commonly the main criterion of membership. Each member works in order to enhance both his personal welfare and that of the group. Passivity is discouraged and the assumption of responsibility for oneself promoted. Doing can take various forms, from the mere act of regularly participating in a social assembly to filling the role of a social advocate in the pursuit of political objectives.

I mentioned earlier that self-help groups have substantial implications for traditional psychotherapy. What are these implications? The issue of what constitutes 'a patient' is as relevant here as it was in our comments on encounter groups. The over-weight, the addicted, the homosexual, the gambler, the bereaved, the child-abuser, and a host of other traditional groups of patients, who attend self-help groups, do not usually regard themselves as psychiatrically ill. Instead, they see themselves as having to wrestle with, and surmount, problems of living.

A good illustration is the case of the bereaved. In recent years, the general practitioner, the psychiatrist and other mental-health professionals have worked with grief-stricken people. Even more recently, however, self-help groups have sprung-up composed of bereaved widows and widowers, or of bereaved parents. The manner in which the self-help group and the professional therapist operate in this context differs in major respects. For example, the therapist usually offers his help in the setting of a psychiatric hospital or clinic and this means formal registration as a patient, the opening up of a file, perhaps the payment of a professional fee – all hallmarks of the patient. By contrast, the participant in a self-help group is spared the label of psychiatric patient with all the implications that spring from it. Although, in practice, the therapeutic process in the self-help group and in the clinic may not differ much, the context and the trappings distinguish them. This is not to denigrate my own colleagues, who regard their help to the bereaved as appropriate. Rather, the question to be tackled is whether the bereaved and people with a whole variety of problems can obtain the same quality of help, perhaps even better, without designation as a patient.

The last issue is inextricably bound-up with a second vital implication of the self-help group for traditional psychotherapy, namely, who is best placed to act as the therapist? The seven common characteristics of the self-help group, mentioned above, do point to its immense advantages over conventional psychotherapy (although I should mention that in some important respects the self-help group and the traditional therapy group are similar). The advantages include the opportunity for a member to recognise that his problem is not unique, he can derive support from others who have undergone a similar experience, he can be of service to others who are in need, and he can observe the normal functioning of fellow members.

Despite these implications, there is little doubt in my mind that professional psychotherapy and the self-help movement are perfectly compatible and can co-exist successfully. A good illustration of such co-existence is Alcoholics Anonymous, which, over a period of nearly four decades, has co-operated with the mental-health professions. Such is not the case with all self-help organisations. Feminist groups and homosexual groups have, customarily, criticised psychiatry for its attitudes, and relationships here have been strained. And yet there has been a decided effect – an awareness among professionals that they have not always had the answers or the most reasonable attitudes.

There are other cogent reasons why self-help groups commend themselves to me, as a professional. Apart from a very few privileged areas, where therapists are available in reasonable number, the need for psychotherapy far outstrips resources. Even if this picture were to change, and it does appear to be doing so slowly, it is highly unlikely that services would ever catch up with needs. Thus, pragmatically, the self-help group can play an outstanding role in contributing to psychotherapy's resources. A related factor is the self-help group's preventative role. Instead of a bereaved couple experiencing their anguish alone and possibly suffering unduly, they could be encouraged to link up with an organisation like Compassionate Friends at the outset. Support at an early stage of their grief could well preempt the development of more serious problems and spare the couple unnecessary distress and dislocation. Similarly, a person sensing his growing and uncontrolled dependence on alcohol may seek out the help of Alcoholics Anonymous rather than wait until reaching 'rock bottom'.

I myself welcome the growth of the self-help movement particularly because it constitutes the revival of the 'natural' support system. Of course a self-help group is artificially created in the first place, but its mode of operation simulates such natural sources of support as the family, friends, neighbours and the Church. This 'naturalness' is a distinct advantage over professional therapy, although I could not possibly prove that greater effectiveness is a direct product. In any event, a movement which contributes to lessening the bureaucracy involved in providing mental-health care is eagerly welcomed. Psychotherapy, whether it is practised in institutions or privately, cannot escape at least a tinge of the bureaucratic despite the most well-intentioned efforts on the part of professional staff to avoid it.

For these reasons, among others, I predict that the self-help group has a spectacular future.

Summary

In this chapter we have looked at three forms of group therapy: small group therapy, family therapy and marital therapy. I selected them to illustrate the nature of the group approach in general because they are all so widely practised. I have also considered the encounter group and self-help group which, while not strictly speaking professional group therapies, have considerable implications for conventional psychotherapy: they raise basic questions such as what constitutes a 'patient', and whether a professional therapist is always necessary in mental-health care.

In this chapter, as in earlier ones, we have intermittently mentioned the relevance of research findings. We now turn specifically to the place of systematic, scientific research in psychotherapy and appraise the knowledge that has accrued thus far.

6 Research in psychotherapy

Systematic research in psychotherapy was long in gestation. Only in the late 1940s did investigation of the subject take off. During the first half of the century, there was no shortage of published reports written about different aspects of psychotherapy but these were mainly clinical in type: therapists themselves provided accounts of their clinical experience, some of them highlighting processes in treatment that they regarded as effective. A number of therapists also provided theoretical frameworks in an effort to explain the basis of their work.

Perhaps the most significant impetus to the potential researcher was the highly critical paper by H. J. Eysenck[1] published in 1952 in which he contended that psychotherapy of neurotic patients was not any more effective than no treatment at all: about two-thirds of both treated and untreated patients showed improvement with time. By extrapolating from twenty-four selected studies about psychotherapy that had been done before his review of the research literature, Eysenck concluded that seventy-two per cent of patients given general psychological care only and involving no specific psychotherapy improved whereas only forty-four per cent of patients in psychoanalysis improved. In subsequent surveys of the literature, Eysenck was even more critical of psychotherapy: its effects were minuscule. Although his attack led to considerable rancour and a prolonged dispute between psychoanalytically-oriented clinicians and behaviour therapists, among whom he featured prominently, a positive repercussion was the sense of challenge felt by the former group. For too long psychotherapy had basked in its own complacency – psychoanalysis and several of its derivatives were riding high, particularly in the United States – there was little question that Freud's concepts and guidelines for practice were in need of scientific testing. Rival schools, particularly the behavioural and the humanist-existential, were at an embryonic stage of development, quite unable to challenge psychoanalysis. Although Eysenck's interpretation of the research literature was seriously flawed, and is today widely discredited,[2] he had stirred a hornet's nest. No longer could psychotherapists automatically assume that their patients derived benefit from treatment, and even if they did, the precise source of the improvement could not be pin-pointed – was it the therapist's technique, his personality, chance, life experiences or one of many other factors?

Since 1952 the research literature[3] on psychotherapy has burgeoned and there is no doubt that the last three decades, in particular the 1970s, have witnessed a dramatic surge of interest among therapists in both the questions of whether psychotherapy works (outcome research) and how it works (process research). This development has not been entirely without incident. Some practitioners have challenged the appropriateness of psychotherapy as a subject for scientific study. They say that the encounter between therapist and patient is self-evidently unique. It involves two human beings in an intricate collaborative venture which is quite beyond, and should be beyond, the realm of experiments and the statistician. Psychotherapy in their view is an art and therefore not subject to scientific scrutiny. They point out, with some justification, that the neater and more rigorous the research design, the more trivial the study; adherence to scientific method can only be mechanistic and limiting. Moreover, any effort to study therapy objectively sabotages it by intruding into what must always remain a highly personal and private encounter. This point of view is reasonable enough as we shall see when we discuss the problems facing the researcher in psychotherapy, but in the case of some therapists their attack on research may be, at least in part, disingenuous. Eysenck questioned the basic efficacy of psychotherapy as a form of treatment and systematic research could conceivably be said to bolster the validity of his claim. What might this portend for the practising therapist? That his profession is not a profession, that what he purportedly achieves in the way of helping his patients is nothing but a sham, that the need for a demanding period of training is unfounded, and so forth. The attempt to establish facts about psychotherapy constitutes an enormous threat to many practitioners and it is not surprising that they may be ambivalent, even hostile, in their attitudes to research.

Can a subject like psychotherapy be systematically investigated? What problems face the researcher? Can these problems be circumvented? These questions can best be answered by considering first the research designs commonly applied in the study of psychotherapy (and indeed in the psychological sciences generally).

In the *experimental method* contrasting conditions are set up in such a way that a specified hypothesis can be tested. Ideally, two or more groups of patients, matched so that they are similar in as many respects as possible, such as age, sex, diagnosis, severity of illness and so forth, are given contrasting treatments (independent variable), for instance, a comparison between a specific type of psychotherapy and no treatment at all or a specific type of psychotherapy and another altogether different type of psychotherapy; and the effects of each treatment (or the absence of treatment) are then assessed on a number of specific measures of outcome (dependent variables). Thus we can answer the set question of whether treatment X is superior or not to treatment Y. Seemingly straightforward, the application of the experimental design in psychotherapy is fraught with difficulties. Before commenting on these, a brief word on alternative research design is required. In the *correlational* approach the investigator does not differentiate between independent and dependent variables; rather, he measures the phenomena that interest him and notes how they relate to one another through a statistical process of correlation which ranges from the relatively simple to the extremely complex. This method may, for example, enable him to discover that a patient's unrealistic expectation of improvement from treatment is associated with limited education or that the older a patient the less likely he is to benefit. No causal relationship can be assumed in these two examples. Age for instance is not necessarily the reason for poor outcome; it could well be that therapists are not as motivated to help the older patients whom they may regard as too rigid to allow substantial change.

A method of research with a long tradition is the *individual case-study*. Traditionally, clinicians have carefully observed their individual patients to note whether, and how, they change in treatment. The method was frowned upon with the advent of systematic research in the 1950s because of fundamental problems limiting its utility: the bias of the therapist-researcher and the findings not readily generalisable or repeatable. Recently, however, the approach has gained support particularly among behaviour therapists, albeit in a new guise – judges involved in treatment have observed and measured the variables under study with the use of audio or video recordings. The distinct advantage of the case-study is its respect for the uniqueness of each therapist–patient relationship. Moreover, the study of individual cases has the potential of generating new hypotheses for testing by other types of research.

Finally, another research design in psychotherapy is the *analogue* study. Because of the considerable difficulty in studying many facets of psychotherapy as it takes place, investigators have turned to research designs which attempt to simulate the psychotherapeutic situation. For example, students might be asked to volunteer for a project in which their expectations of improvement after a simulated first psychotherapy session are noted, or therapists might be shown tapes of typical patients in psychotherapy and be instructed to select a specific approach they would take if they were actually conducting the treatment. The predictable objections to the analogue design are based on the obvious fact that psychotherapy in practice is not studied directly and that the findings can, therefore, not be confidently extrapolated to it.

We have mentioned various limitations of each type of approach. Let us now consider the snares facing the psychotherapy researcher in general. Apart from the self-evident point that group research designs require an adequately sized sample of patients, a complex issue concerns the definition of the characteristics of these patients. As we saw in Chapter 2, patients come in myriad form and although they may share certain common features, their differences may be crucial in influencing their outcome. Thus age, sex, diagnosis, severity of illness, occupation, education, expectation of improvement, motivation, social adjustment, and previous response to psychotherapy are only a few of the factors which may be relevant in both the way the patient participates in his treatment and the response he shows to it. In conducting a study the researcher needs to identify as many of these characteristics as possible so that he knows and can specify the nature of the group of patients being examined.

The same comments are applicable to the therapist. Again, as we discussed in Chapter 3, therapists come in many forms. For example, their adherence to a particular school of psychotherapy, their level of experience, the type of training they have had, the values they hold, and their use of certain techniques all play a part in influencing the process and outcome of treatment. Even therapists who belong to the same school and ostensibly obey the same theoretical and practical guidelines may have widely differing clinical styles. The specification of the characteristics of the therapist is clearly an important ingredient of research in psychotherapy.

One main reason for defining types of patient (and sometimes therapist) is to enable the setting up of *control* groups. This applies in particular to the experimental method in which the effectiveness of a specific therapeutic approach is under scrutiny. To be certain that change in the patient is due to the therapy itself, a control group of patients matched on as many variables as possible with the experimental patients, except for the treatment itself, is a basic requirement. The control group can assume several forms. In the no-treatment control design, patients are matched with those receiving therapy, complete the same questionnaires but receive no treatment. There are snags, however, with this approach: serious ethical issues are involved in not offering treatment to someone who may well be in need of it, patients often seek out and receive informal help from relatives and friends, and some have been shown to derive immense benefit from even a single meeting with a researcher.

The commonly used method which partially avoids the ethical hurdle is the 'waiting-list control'. As patients often have to face delay in receiving therapy, it is assumed that this can be done randomly, and those assigned to the waiting-list serve as controls. The limitation here is that the delay cannot be prolonged and the waiting period is commonly much less than the period in which the treatment is given. One obvious exception is crisis intervention which is usually a short-term treatment but here it would be unethical to have patients in crisis waiting for treatment – the crisis might well have resolved by the time the waiting period was over.

The 'attention-placebo' group is useful as a control for non-specific factors such as patients' faith in therapy and their hope for change (see Chapter 1). Patients are seen at a similar frequency to the treated group but not managed with any specific therapeutic procedures. If the treatment under study is indeed superior, this will be reflected in greater improvement rates in patients given the treatment compared to the attention-placebo control patients. Different forms of treatment can be directly compared with one another by using matched groups or similar treatment can be given to two matched groups but with the control group not receiving the entire therapeutic package, that is, one or more key ingredients can be omitted; this enables the researcher to note the differential effects of these ingredients.

Finally, the patient can act as his own control, measures of improvement being made at several points, some of which succeed a period of treatment and others not. For example, after a measure of the patient's state has been taken a waiting period may follow, then a period of active treatment, then a further waiting period. Assessment at each point of change will demonstrate the effect of the treatment given. A number of control groups may be used in the same study and often are. A good illustration of this is the study by Sloane and his colleagues in 1975 (which we shall discuss shortly) who compared psychoanalytically-oriented therapy, behaviour therapy and a waiting list control.

Despite the wide choice open to the researcher in the use of controls he faces major methodological difficulties with each of them. The same is true of the measurement of improvement in the patient. A vast number of measures has been applied in research in psychotherapy ranging from the objective such as rates of rehospitalisation to the subjective such as the patient's assessment of his sense of 'well-being' or level of self-esteem. A wide divergence of views exists among both therapists and researchers on the criteria appropriate in the assessment of change. Much of the divergence stems from basic differences in how psychotherapy's objectives are viewed and conceptualised. The behaviour therapist, for example, who regards the clinical symptom as the chief target of intervention, rates the patient's improvement in terms of how bothersome the symptom is at the end of treatment. The humanist-existential psychotherapist, by contrast, dismisses the symptom as irrelevant and focuses instead on the entire individual; for him, outcome revolves around personal growth, self-awareness and a sense of authenticity. The psychoanalyst prizes his patient's insight into the nature of his symptoms, and sees their disappearance as a primary objective. Thus, therapists from these three schools evaluate their patients' outcome on different criteria.

These differences are compounded by the common finding that the measurements of outcome from various sources – patient, therapist, independent judge, a relative – correlate only moderately with one another. Arguments have been put forward that the patient knows best – after all he is the 'consumer' and the bearer of the problems; alternatively that the independent judge, ostensibly free from any bias because he is not a participant in therapy, is in the best position to make an accurate assessment. The most widely held view regards change as occurring along several, diverse dimensions. The patient changes in a number of areas all of which are pertinent – symptoms, social functioning, sexual adjustment, personal growth, self-awareness, and many others. This accounts in part for the limited agreement in the assessment of change made by different sources. It is not the inadequacy of the measuring instruments or the incompetence of the judges that are responsible. Indeed, different perspectives are all valid and reflect the multi-faceted nature of change. On this premiss the researcher calls on patient, therapist, family and independent judge to assess change and he applies a wide range of measuring instruments. These include rating scales of overall improvement, personality inventories, check-lists of symptoms, and scales of social adjustment.

A criticism of this approach to measurement (referred to as the nomothetic approach) has been expressed in recent years, namely that a patient's unique problems and goals in treatment tend to be ignored. The ideographic approach to assessment maintains that rather than submit a number of common measures to all patients as if they had identical problems, criteria of outcome should be tailored specifically to each patient. Thus, a series of target problems should be mapped out together with the goals to be achieved at the end of therapy. Measuring progress on each of these problems and related goals will establish to what extent a patient has improved. The argument for an ideographic approach is persuasive. For example, one patient may need to achieve a reduction in his anxiety as a central therapeutic goal whereas another should be provoked into feeling anxious in order to work through a conflict which has been denied in the past. In a typical check-list of symptoms anxiety would be rated as an indicator of outcome but in the two cases cited, change would be in diametrically opposite directions.

In 1975 a team of American psychotherapy researchers at the National Institute of Mental Health[4] reported on the selection of a series of methods for measuring outcome. Their work amounts to a compromise between the nomothetic and ideographic positions in that the series of tests involves the use of a check-list of symptoms, target problems specific to the individual patient, and a personality inventory, all completed by the patient; target complaints assessed by the therapist; and measures of a wide range of symptoms and social behaviour completed by an independent judge. Scales of symptoms and social behaviour for administration to a person who knows the patient well, usually a member of the family, are also included. This approach is a reasonable way to assess change but unfortunately it leaves unanswered several basic questions. Should all sources of measurement be accorded the same weighting, should all measures be seen of equal importance, what constitutes a target problem, is one patient's list of target problems equivalent to that of another patient, should various forms of therapy utilise different measures of outcome because their goals differ, can rating scales and questionnaires ever do justice to the complexity and intricacy of human personality and therapeutic change?

For reasons not too difficult to grasp, most research into psychotherapy is defective because an inadequate amount of treatment is provided and the patient's outcome is not assessed at a later point, following the end of treatment. Psychotherapy research is complex and demanding to say the least and frequently compromises have to be made. Thus, duration of therapy is commonly much briefer – four months is the average – than would be the case in clinical practice. The insight-oriented psychotherapist is justified in complaining that his form of treatment is not given an adequate test in such a limited period and that his patient's progress should only be judged after a year or more of therapy. Similarly, assessment is commonly carried out when therapy ends but not afterwards. A proper test of the effectiveness of a therapy entails an examination of outcome one or more years following the end of that therapy, that is, the patient should maintain his improved state for a substantial period independently of the therapist. Only a few research teams, notable among them the Johns Hopkins in Baltimore and the Tavistock in London, have recognised the importance of long-term follow-up.

A final problem in doing psychotherapy research involves the investigator himself. Although he is supposedly neutral and detached and therefore like any other scientist, in practice he is constantly buffeted by his own prejudices and biases. This is not unexpected: it is easier to be neutral when measuring the effects of a chemical reaction than it is the effects of a particular form of psychotherapy. With few exceptions, researchers themselves have a declared preference for one particular school of psychotherapy over others. Even if the latter is denied, the researcher's personal values are apt to influence his attitudes towards various psychotherapeutic theories and styles. A researcher who is fundamentally optimistic and views Man as an ever-developing organism capable of change will be inclined towards the humanist school. A researcher who places a high value on Man's capacity for introspection and self-reflection may prefer therapies in which insight and self-awareness are key features. The whole issue of the influence of personal values has only recently received the recognition it deserves. Even if all the problems in research involving controls, specification of the characteristics of patients and therapists, measures of improvement, and the like, were solved, the subjectivity of the researcher would remain a trap to the unwary.

The effectiveness of psychotherapy

We mentioned earlier Eysenck's critique of psychotherapy's putative effectiveness. His attack ushered in an extremely active period of research on the key question of whether psychotherapy actually does any good. The controversy over Eysenck's handling of the data from which he reached his conclusions is mercifully over but remains an interesting episode in the history of psychotherapy. Several workers, particularly Allen Bergin and David Malan, both notable figures in psychotherapy research, have demonstrated clearly the inadequacy of the studies Eysenck selected (Eysenck is not entirely to blame; the quality of research work on effectiveness done before his report in 1952 was poor in the extreme) and the arbitrary manner in which he designated levels of improvement. For example, Eysenck categorised patients reported as 'slightly improved' to an unchanged group. Their assignment to an improved category yields a radically different picture of psychotherapy's usefulness. Eysenck, it must be said, is a victim of his own prejudice. An ardent proponent of behaviour therapy, it has become patently obvious in his various writings that he is determined to 'prove' that his mode of treatment, the behavioural approach, is superior to any other, in particular to the psychoanalytically-oriented therapies.

Although the battle is still being waged over the Eysenck claim in some quarters,[5] we would be wise to move on to other, more up-to-date, reviews of the research literature to ascertain whether psychotherapy actually works. There are several such reviews. I have focused on three, all of which are thorough and comprehensive. The first is that by Eysenck's chief critic – Allen Bergin.[6] He examined forty-eight studies of psychotherapy regarded as representative of the work published between 1953 and 1969. Although the investigations were to some extent crude and could only shed light on the basic question of whether psychotherapy was effective (rather than what sorts of psychotherapy and how they work), Bergin felt confident in the 'general conclusion that psychotherapy, on the average, has at least modestly positive effects'. The number of studies showing positive results was more than chance and, encouragingly, the better designed studies tended to show positive results more often than inadequate studies.

Meltzoff and Kornreich[7] made a significant contribution to psychotherapy generally in 1970 by reviewing a vast amount of research literature on diverse aspects. With regard to the question of effectiveness, they examined 101 controlled studies of many different forms of treatment given to a wide range of clinical groups, such as neurotics, alcoholics and schizophrenics. Fifty-seven studies were categorised as 'adequate' methodologically, and of these, forty-eight or nearly eighty per cent showed psychotherapy to be effective. In seventy-five per cent of the forty-four 'questionable' studies psychotherapy emerged as beneficial. Again, as in the review by Bergin, we see evidence of more positive outcomes in better designed investigations. Notably, many of the negative findings related to samples of chronic schizophrenics and drug addicts, two clinical groups highly resistant to any mode of psychiatric intervention. Meltzoff and Kornreich concluded that a broad range of psychotherapies aimed at a broad range of clinical conditions produce 'positive changes in adjustment that significantly exceed those that can be accounted for by the passage of time alone'. Indeed, they felt able to claim that the controlled studies had 'been notably successful' in showing a superior response in treated patients compared to untreated controls.

This review, while commendable in its scope and thoroughness, is subject to the criticism, as is Bergin's review, that it lumps together a number of very different treatments – individual therapy, group therapy and hypnosis among them – and a wide array of conditions such as childhood psychiatric conditions, alcoholism and schizophrenia. In some ways the exercise is comparable to reviewing the effects of all sorts of surgery, from renal transplantation to the repair of a simple hernia. Posing the question of whether 'surgery' is effective is nonsense. Yet, there is some justification in a young scientific field, like psychotherapy, to ask some crude questions as a preliminary to asking more specific ones.

Let us consider one other review of this general type before turning to the issue of the effectiveness of different forms of treatment. Smith and Glass,[8] two American psychologists, have tackled the effectiveness question in a novel way, which they refer to as meta-analysis. Briefly, their procedure is to note the level of improvement in treated patients and in untreated controls and to assess the effect of the therapy by computing the mean difference between the two groups. Determining the level of effect entails fairly straightforward statistical methods but we need not concern ourselves with these here. All forms of outcome measurement are included – physiological indices, the patient's assessment of his self-esteem, work or school achievement, and so forth. Smith and Glass argue the reasonableness of mixing various measures of outcomes together on the grounds that they are 'more or less' related to 'well-being' and so, at a general level, are 'comparable'. Their meta-analytic procedure covers 375 outcome studies in which one treatment group is compared to an untreated control group or to another treatment group. The quality of the research is not a criterion for selection. Again, as we noted with previous reviews, a wide range of treatments are studied including 'analogue' therapy, the simulation of actual treatment in laboratory conditions. They regard it as preferable to broaden the 'net' rather than to eliminate arbitrarily a large number of studies and thus to lose potentially valuable information.

What did Smith and Glass find using their meta-analytic approach? 833 levels of effect were computed from the 375 outcome studies (in many studies there was more than one measure of change and/or assessments were done more than once – hence the large number of levels) in which approximately 25,000 experimental and 25,000 control patients were tested. The average patient receiving treatment was better off than seventy-five per cent of the untreated controls which demonstrates the beneficial effects of psychotherapy in general. The authors looked at several other questions in their analysis, including the important one of the comparative effectiveness of different forms of therapy. Against the repeated finding that psychotherapy overall does have a beneficial effect, we can now turn to the interesting issue of comparative effectiveness.

Comparative effectiveness of different forms of psychotherapy

With dozens of 'schools' of psychotherapy available, many claiming their own distinctive style and merit, a salient question is whether any one school is superior to another in producing positive change. The history of psychotherapy has long been typified by assertions of therapists that their brand of treatment is advantageous over all others. Although inter-school rivalry has tended to diminish in recent years as 'facts' from empirical research have emerged, there are practitioners who trenchantly assert the special qualities of their product. We need to remind ourselves how strongly identified and unswervingly loyal therapists can be *vis-à-vis* their school. Any questioning of its value constitutes an enormous threat to their professional integrity. A psychiatrist, informed that a drug he has prescribed customarily is now shown to be relatively ineffective and that a newly developed drug is better, will have little difficulty in abandoning the use of the old drug. The drug is ineffective, not himself. In psychotherapy, by contrast, the professional self is so intimately interwoven with the type of treatment practised, that to face the question of the value of alternative methods, let alone a change to them, is tantamount to self-abnegation. We take up this theme again in the final chapter.

The issue of comparative effectiveness is somewhat more complicated – not only 'schools' of psychotherapy may be compared but also particular procedures such as setting a time-limit on treatment or not, or particular types of therapy, for instance, individual therapy versus group therapy. Moreover, as we shall note later, therapists claiming to belong to a specific school may not necessarily conduct their clinical practice according to the tenets of that school; indeed they may do precisely what the school eschews. For example, the 'true' psychoanalyst should, if he follows classical guidelines, relate to his patients in a neutral, albeit warm fashion and thus allow the possibility of a transference relationship to develop. Yet, some analysts, wittingly or unwittingly, encourage a more intimate relationship with no hint of neutrality whatsoever.

Despite these difficulties there is something to be gained from reviewing the research literature on comparative effectiveness. The most notable review to date is that by Luborsky and his colleagues[9] from the University of Pennsylvania. On the premise that it is not possible to rely on the ultimate, definitive study to settle the question of comparative efficacy because every study has some unique features, the reviewers decided to 'rely on the verdict of a series of at least passably controlled studies'. They therefore included all studies in which one form of psychotherapy was compared with another, and where specified criteria of the quality of research design was satisfied, for example, the treatment of 'real' patients, controlled assignment of patients to treatment, therapy by competent and experienced practitioners, each treatment given in equal and reasonable amounts and adequate size of sample.

The literature on the following comparisons was examined: psychotherapy with a time-limit versus psychotherapy without a time limit; client-centred (the Rogerian School, see Chapter 7) versus other traditional therapies (psychoanalysis and its derivatives); group therapy versus individual therapy; and behaviour therapy (mostly systematic desensitisation) versus psychotherapy. In noting these comparisons we can immediately recognise the vagueness of these groupings. What is meant by 'psychotherapy' in the last comparison? And can we assume that 'other traditional therapies' constitute a single homogeneous group? As in so much psychotherapy research, approximations and compromises are inevitable. We have little choice but to proceed with the comparisons bearing in mind that they are somewhat flawed.

Until the advent of behaviour therapy and crisis intervention, it was assumed that the longer the therapy the more likely it was to produce positive change. In the late 1950s and early 1960s a number of studies were done in which time-limited therapies were compared with ones without a time-limit. Of the eight studies reviewed by Luborsky and his colleagues, only in one was the latter form shown to be superior, whilst in five studies duration was of no significance for outcome: a convincing picture to back the view that it is not justifiable to continue therapy indefinitely, and indeed it may be more efficient to offer a patient a course of treatment with a time-limit specified at the outset.

A widely held belief that individual therapy has better effects than group therapy stems from the assumption that the one-to-one approach is intrinsically more intensive and concentrated. Again, clinical belief must take a tumble in the face of systematic research. In the thirteen comparisons of these two forms of treatment, each was superior to the other in two studies, whilst in the other nine studies there was no significant difference between them. The comparisons between the various therapeutic schools are most revealing: four of the five studies comparing Rogerian and traditional schools show no difference in outcome, and in thirteen of the nineteen comparative studies of behaviour therapy and psychotherapy, neither is more effective than the other. The six studies showing the superiority of behaviour therapy were of poor research quality.

In the sub-title of the Luborsky review the question is posed: 'Is it true that "everyone has won and all must have prizes"?' Our memories of *Alice in Wonderland* will tell us that this was the judgement of the race handed down by the dodo bird. In the psychotherapy stakes, it would appear that everyone has won too – the Rogerian, the behaviour therapist, the group therapist, the individual therapist, and all the other participants. How can we explain this? In Chapter 1 we discussed the concept of 'non-specific factors' and argued that they might be responsible for therapeutic change rather than factors peculiar to particular schools of psychotherapy. The Luborsky review provides us with indirect evidence that this may be so. The schools compared may have similar effects because of the factors they have in common. The non-specific factor notion is perhaps the most significant to have emerged from the theoretical and empirical research of the past twenty-five years.

Although the Luborsky group expressed reservations about obtaining information on comparative effectiveness from any single study, no matter how adequate, let us consider one recent comparison of behaviour therapy and psychoanalytically-oriented psychotherapy conducted by a research team at Temple University.[10] I select this particular study because it is without par in its methodological sophistication. The researchers, in their design and execution, have managed commendably to avoid the manifold pitfalls and deficiencies that typify most studies in this field. By outlining the Temple approach we will be in a position to note its scientific rigour. Ninety-four patients, with neurotic or personality disorders and typical of the population requesting psychotherapy at a university psychiatric outpatient clinic, were matched with respect to sex and severity of symptoms but were otherwise randomly assigned to one of three treatment conditions: short-term psychoanalytically-oriented therapy, behaviour therapy and a minimum treatment waiting-list group.

The six therapists – three analysts and three behaviour therapists – who provided the treatment were highly experienced and enjoyed established reputations. The former used various analytic techniques to promote insight in their patients, whereas the latter applied techniques such as systematic desensitisation and assertiveness training. Analysis of the two groups of therapists confirmed that the approaches they used were different and representative of the schools to which they belonged. The therapy given was of equal amount, usually weekly sessions lasting an hour, over four months. The control group were told that they would receive treatment when vacancies arose and during the next four months they were telephoned periodically by a research assistant and asked how they were getting along.

All patients were assessed four and twelve months after the beginning of therapy on a large number of variables, including inventories of personality, target complaints and social adjustment. Measures of outcome were completed by the patient, his therapist, a relative or friend of the patient's, and by an independent judge. The dodo's verdict applies yet again! After four months both groups of patients which received active treatment had improved, both to a similar extent, and both were significantly better than the control patients. The similar outcome for the two groups which received treatment covered almost all the measures of assessment and held for the twelve-month assessment point too. Only an overall judgement of improvement by the independent assessor at four months showed some superiority for behaviour therapy. (The Temple study is noteworthy for a number of other interesting findings but these are not pertinent to the present discussion. I would recommend the interested reader to turn to the comprehensive report entitled *Short-term Psychoanalytically-oriented Psychotherapy Versus Behaviour Therapy*.[10])

Psychotherapy's harmful effects

Our consideration of psychotherapy's effectiveness so far has assumed that patients either profit from therapy or remain unchanged. Another possibility which only became properly recognised in the early 1960s[11] is psychotherapy's potentially harmful effects. Paradoxically, this 'deterioration' or 'negative' effect, as it is usually called, was introduced into the controversy about whether psychotherapy works or not. Bergin contended that psychotherapy was for better or for worse – 'If therapy has potential for producing beneficial effects, it should also be capable of producing harmful effects'.[2] Since there was evidence that patients could be harmed by treatment as well as benefit from it, this suggested that psychotherapy was potent. For Eysenck, Bergin's argument was defective: there was no way one could assert the efficacy of a treatment by noting its harmful potential.

Whatever the merits of each argument – the concept of the negative effect was born, and has attracted widespread attention since. I am not surprised that it was more than half a century after the founding of systematic psychotherapy that the negative effect came to light. Again, as I have argued before, the possibility of a therapist not acting effectively or worse, acting to his patients' detriment, would inevitably be studiously resisted. Perhaps, a growing sense of confidence in recent years has permitted clinicians to be more realistic about their impact on patients. What exactly is a negative effect, how prevalent is it, and what leads to it?

The definition of the concept is tricky in that at least two issues must be clear: the patient's condition or state is worse following the treatment than before it, and this deterioration is a direct consequence of that treatment. A patient may obviously become worse with treatment, but this may be associated with the patient's intrinsic psychiatric condition, or result from a major event in his life. A negative effect is, therefore, suitably defined as deterioration in a patient directly due to treatment. Although causal links between therapy and deterioration are difficult to prove, a survey of eminent clinicians revealed a firm consensus that genuine negative effects do occur.[12] Moreover, systematic research, scanty as it is, tends to support this clinical impression. Deterioration can assume many different forms. The most obvious is a worsening of the patient's original complaints, for instance, an increase in anxiety or depression or confusion. Treatment may however also result in the development of entirely new symptoms. Other possibilities include a patient's disillusionment with therapy and an associated sense of failure, and his settlement into a role of undue dependency on the therapist, with a constant weakening of his capacity to manage independently.

Because of the difficulties of definition, estimates of the prevalence of negative effects range from rare to extremely common. The type of therapy appears to influence the rate. Encounter group therapies, for example, probably cause worsening in between five to ten per cent of participants while, in the case of marital and family therapy the range is more likely to be in the range of two to six per cent.

The reasons for deterioration in patients are presently a matter of some speculation. Many therapists would point to factors in the patient and assert that poor assessment is a basic cause (we discussed in Chapter 2 the features in the patient that are generally associated with good and poor outcome). Deterioration according to one view is the result of selecting a patient for a treatment for which he is unsuited whether it be because of his limited personal resources, his immersion in an overwhelming crisis, his severe psychiatric condition, and so forth. If this view is correct, refining the assessment process and increasing the clinician's ability to predict response to specific forms of psychotherapy should help to reduce the casualty rate.

Another possible cause of deterioration is obviously the therapist and/or his technique. In Hadley and Strupp's survey the therapist was considered by many to be a common source of negative effects. Inadequate training seems likely to be instrumental here with poor clinical judgement resulting in the inappropriate choice of techniques.

The picture is more complicated however. We noted in Chapter 3 that level of training *per se* may not be the most important determinant of the therapist's effectiveness. It has been repeatedly recognised that some therapists, because of their personalities, are 'naturally' good at their jobs whereas others are hamstrung by certain personal qualities and perform poorly whatever length of training they receive. There is little doubt that the role of therapist does not suit all those who wish to practise psychotherapy.

Incompetence in the therapist, whether due to poor training or undesirable personal traits, may also be related to the style of therapy practised. In a major study of ten different types of encounter groups, seven of the sixteen casualties – defined as 'an enduring, significant, negative outcome which was caused by their participation in the group' – were produced by four leaders, who typically pummelled their group members into immediate self-disclosure and emotional expression. These leaders were authoritarian, confronting, aggressive, intrusive and charismatic. At the same time they showed a caring attitude and revealed much about themselves. They were unaware of their harmful influence on the group, tending to see the members as stubborn and resistant. Interestingly, another leader in the study with a customary aggressive style produced no casualties. He differed, however, in one crucial respect: he recognised that his group contained several vulnerable members and thus refrained from adopting his usual approach. The encounter study illustrates the value of well-conducted research in shedding light on the complex topic of the negative effect. More investigations of this kind will undoubtedly be done to unravel its nature.

Process research

Our discussion so far has centred on outcome research in psychotherapy – examination of whether psychotherapy works, whether one form is superior to another, and whether it causes deterioration. In the second main area of research, commonly referred to as process research, the focus of interest is on the phenomena and processes that actually take place in the therapeutic encounter. Process and outcome are inevitably brought together: if one can identify factors in the therapy that promote or hinder its effectiveness and efficiency, the obvious next step is to manipulate such factors in order to note the result. A simple example illustrates this point. If it is established by process research that patient and therapist tend to have widely differing expectations of how therapy works an additional step could be to test the hypothesis that bridging these differences through preparing the patient for treatment will favourably influence his outcome. And indeed, both these approaches in research have been taken. In the early 1960s, investigators demonstrated that patient and therapist often did have differing expectations about aspects of the therapeutic process.[13] Subsequently, the value of preparing the patient was confirmed in a series of studies on both individual and group psychotherapy.[14]

The advent of recording techniques such as audio and more particularly, video-taping has enabled process research to advance substantially. These direct methods permit the researcher to analyse therapeutic phenomena in the finest detail. Through such close analysis, a wide range of observations of both verbal and non-verbal behaviour in therapist and patient can now be made. A more indirect approach is to obtain perceptions, attitudes, reactions, and the like, from the participants of treatment through the administration of questionnaires and rating scales. One research team in Chicago[15] has painstakingly sought information from patients in this way, with the object of establishing what constitutes the 'good therapy session' – at least from the consumer's point of view. This approach is valuable if one assumes that the patient probably will not benefit from treatment unless he can appreciate the relevance of the therapist's strategies for helping him and the rationale on which they are based.

Yet another approach to the study of process is the measurement of physiological changes that occur in patient and/or therapist. For example, the monitoring of heart rate or sweating permits one to note associations between the level of emotional arousal and aspects such as the intensity of the therapist–patient relationship, or the effect on the patient of particular types of interpretations. The snag with physiological measurement is its obtrusive character, yet it has the advantage of being objective.

We have already alluded to various forms of research in the study of process. The example of emotional arousal typifies the *correlational* approach whereby the investigator seeks to clarify the associations between different phenomena. We can illustrate this further in group therapy research. The cohesiveness of a group is regarded by therapists as a necessary condition for its effective operation. It would therefore be useful to establish what features in the patients and in the relationships between them are associated with cohesiveness. Compatibility between group members has been put forward as a pertinent factor, and indeed, has been shown to be significantly related to cohesiveness. Group therapy might conceivably be more effective if in the selection of members their compatibility was taken into account. A patient would not be placed in a particular group unless he was compatible with at least one of his peers.

Another type of research of process is purely *descriptive* – simply recording as accurately and reliably as possible what occurs in therapy. At first sight this approach appears rather limited, but it can in fact yield valuable information. As we saw in Chapter 1, the non-specific or common factors in psychotherapy are probably more relevant to outcome than the specific ones. Are therapists of various schools, therefore, more similar than different in the things they do with their patients? Here a descriptive study is highly appropriate. By observing systematically what therapists say and do, we can try to answer the question of how distinctive therapeutic schools really are.

The third type of research is *experimental* in which one aspect of the process of therapy is manipulated in some way and the effects on other specified aspects observed. Let us consider the question of a group therapist's effect on patients' expression of anger towards him. In an impressive study by Liberman[16] one therapist was trained to prompt and reinforce his group to ventilate their anger. A second therapist functioned in his usual fashion. In the former case, the therapist influenced his group markedly, and significantly more so than in the control group. Thus it was shown clearly that a particular style of leadership had a potent influence on a specific aspect of patients' behaviour.

It must be obvious by now why research on process is as important as research on outcome. Only with the systematic observation and study of what occurs in treatment can we appreciate its intrinsic nature and the factors which are important both for its effective and efficient operation, and for optimal improvement. Thorough process research provides the foundations for erecting hypotheses about outcome. For instance, comparing the effectiveness of two schools of psychotherapy would be futile unless one had established that the exponents of the two schools actually treated their patients with methods that were distinguishable from one another. Only process research can provide that type of knowledge. The range of questions about phenomena in therapy is unlimited; it is only necessary that the researcher frames the question in a way which has meaning and is amenable to systematic investigation.

Summary

Our look into the subject of psychotherapy research has necessarily been selective and brief. To do it justice would require a book of its own, and a large one too! With the growing interest in the potential contribution of research, the number of investigations done increases year by year. Indeed, it is a major task nowadays to keep abreast of new knowledge. Fortunately, periodic reviews of research on various topics are becoming common and these serve to guide the average therapist as he considers new findings.

With increased quantity has come uneven quality. Some investigations are outstanding in their planning and execution whereas others are so flawed that it is a pity they were conceived in the first place. But, on balance, the quality of research is steadily improving to the point where its contribution to the practice of psychotherapy is becoming of value. Psychotherapy is a science as well as an art and its scientific foundations, therefore, must be made as firm as they possibly can be. Fortunately, progress in achieving such a secure base is steady and sure.

7 An ethical dimension

Consideration of the ethics of psychotherapy is often ignored, even though moral issues surround the therapist. I have limited my discussion to the basic question of the therapist's accountability to patients, colleagues and public.

Contemporary psychotherapy is no stranger to controversy; indeed, they have been constant bed-fellows since psychotherapy's birth. We noted in an earlier chapter the schisms among the ranks of psychoanalysts and the resultant break-away movements. Some observers may wish to lay the blame at Freud's door – his acute sensitivity and obduracy being responsible for dissent; but the many feuds that have occurred long after his death, and feuds not necessarily confined to psychoanalysis, do suggest that the discipline of psychotherapy as a whole is in a continuing state of disarray.

Today, we witness a plethora of staunchly independent schools of psychotherapy each entrenched behind protective barriers. Beyond these barriers, it is as if other potentially useful theories and practices had never – and could never – materialise. Skirmishes between schools are not uncommonly fought in the public gaze, with little appreciation among the participants of the deleterious effects the battle may have on the discipline as a whole. Ultimately, the patient is probably caught in the cross-fire. Therapists can defend themselves behind their barriers and even reinforce their doctrines and become immutably convinced of the value of what they do. They are reasonably safe and may continue to assume that their patients are their beneficiaries; after all, the patient's welfare is the psychotherapist's *raison d'être*. Inter-school warfare is one matter, a global attack on psychotherapy is another. While schools protect themselves, a new development has ensued. This is the call by governmental and other social agencies for greater accountability from psychotherapists. In the United States for example there is growing pressure on psychotherapists to prove the effectiveness and safety of their methods before they receive federal government reimbursement. Similarly, private insurance funders seek evidence of psychotherapy's value and cost-effectiveness. The days of publicly- or privately-funded psychotherapy without comprehensive scrutiny and a resultant increase in cost-effectiveness seem to be numbered.

These developments suggest that the therapist must become more aware of his accountability to his individual patient, to fellow professionals and to the public. It is in this context that I invoke the concept of an ethical dimension to the psychotherapist's work. I do so on the basic premiss that all human conduct occurs within a framework of values: where a person has a choice of one or another course of action, and his activities are not completely prescribed, an inevitable question arises – is the particular action chosen right or wrong, good or bad? The practice of psychotherapy is as much affected by ethical judgements as by scientific or any other judgements. Moreover, these ethical judgements permeate all facets of the therapist's professional work. Let us now consider just some of the important responsibilities borne by a therapist towards his patient, colleagues and society.

The obligations to patients are manifold. The therapist must, *inter alia*, preserve patients' confidences, respect patients and not exploit them in any way, ensure that his methods are safe, and obtain patients' informed consent to treatment in the first place. The last obligation is probably the one least fulfilled. And yet, as Redlich and Mollica[1] point out: 'Informed consent is the basis of all psychiatric intervention and . . . without it no psychiatric intervention can be morally justified'. It is certainly the basis of all medical practice. For example, informed consent is taken as a matter of course before a surgeon will operate (though it should be mentioned that consent is not always fully informed and the method of obtaining it can be perfunctory). What happens in psychotherapy? A patient has been assessed and accepted for, say, long-term therapy. Treatment will be conducted weekly over one to two years requiring a major investment of time, energy and possibly, if carried out privately, money. There is no doubt that this is a most serious undertaking. The argument could be made that informed consent is in this instance unnecessary. The patient presumably knows what he is letting himself in for in that he has come voluntarily. He must have an inkling about what therapy will entail or failing that, he will make it his business to obtain the information he desires.

But in practice, the matter is somewhat complex. The patient is commonly distressed and baffled. The process whereby he seeks and

finally obtains help can be cumbersome: he consults the general practitioner who refers him to the local psychiatric clinic where he is
assessed and then referred for a specialist opinion to the psychotherapist. The route is potentially confusing – as he proceeds the patient is
told different things and although he knows he is in need of some help
he is completely reliant on professionals for guidance.

Apart from the mechanics of referral, the psychotherapist who
ultimately 'takes the patient on' may, as a feature of treatment, not
wish to divulge too much on the assumption that such disclosure will
interfere with the evolution of the therapeutic relationship, and in
particular with the development of transference (see Chapter 4). Alternatively, the therapist may genuinely not know at the outset of treatment what is in store for his patient; assessment at this early stage is
often not entirely successful in clarifying issues such as duration of
treatment and the particular approach that should be followed.

The consequence is a sense of mystification in the patient. The
principle of informed consent provides a means for the psychotherapist to demystify and thus allow the patient to be in a position to know
what he is letting himself in for.

Some psychotherapists go even further in this regard. A particularly
persuasive argument is offered by Carl Goldberg,[2] an American
psychotherapist. Clearly dissatisfied with the system in which a patient
places his trust in the therapist's ability and willingness to make crucial
decisions, Goldberg calls for an alternative approach, namely the
contractual system. In essence, he insists that there be an equal
distribution of power in the relationship during therapy through explicit agreement between therapist and patient on how each will use his
power. In practice, both parties consider the goals of treatment and the
methods whereby they will be reached. Furthermore, both monitor
the effectiveness of treatment. An opportunity is also given for either
patient or therapist to express any dissatisfaction each might have with
the way therapy is proceeding. The contract is not a cut and dry
written formal document but instead a continuing process of negotiation which becomes an intrinsic part of the therapeutic process.

The therapist, as part of the contractual system, has an obligation
to answer a number of questions honestly and unambiguously. Thus
he indicates to his prospective patient: (1) this is what will occur or is
likely to occur (duration of treatment, frequency, the place of meeting,
the fee, the procedure involved); (2) this is my role, these are my tasks,
and these are my responsibilities; (3) this is your role, these are your

tasks, and these are your responsibilities, and (4) this is the possible outcome. The fourth point is probably the most complicated one because predictions of therapeutic outcome are notoriously fallible.

It would seem to me crucial that the therapist should orient his patients realistically, honestly and modestly with a comment along these lines: 'Therapy will, I hope, equip you with new insights about yourself and about the nature of your problems. I cannot predict what the result will be, and I certainly cannot guarantee that you will be transformed into a person totally free of pressure and conflict. None the less, we can have a good try at overcoming your difficulties.'

This honest approach helps to spare the patient who, following a long haul in treatment, departs disillusioned or disappointed. In a notable survey of therapists' views on the effect of deterioration in psychotherapy, by Hadley and Strupp,[3] the authors conclude that a major factor is the therapist who conveys a misleading impression about the goals of therapy and about his own power. The former are construed in over-ambitious terms and with regard to the latter he communicates a sense of omniscience.

As Goldberg suggests, the contract between patient and therapist should involve a continuing process of negotiation throughout treatment. Goals should be repeatedly examined and new ones discussed; progress should be closely monitored and any dissatisfaction with treatment ventilated. By this means, the predominance of the therapist's power is obviated. Freud's comment in this context is highly pertinent: 'the relation between analyst [and the same applies to any type of therapist] and patient is based on a love of truth, that is, on the acknowledgement of reality and that it precludes any kind of sham or deceit'.[4]

The therapist has equally crucial obligations towards his colleagues as part of his membership of a professional discipline. As much as the patient should be informed about what is in store for him when he enters therapy, so should the therapist be familiar with the state of knowledge of his subject – its theoretical advances, its clinical lore, and the information stemming from empirical systematic research. The first clause of article five of the 1980 Principles of Medical Ethics of the American Medical Association is as pertinent to the psychotherapist as it is to the doctor. It reads: 'A physician shall continue to study, apply and advance scientific knowledge.'

This brings us back to the old chestnut of whether psychotherapy is basically an art or a science. If it is an art only, the clause quoted is of little relevance. But, as I hope has become evident from the earlier chapters, there is little doubt (at least in my own mind) that psychotherapy is a blend of art and science and that it is important for the therapist to recognise and optimise both dimensions of his work. The art of psychotherapy is obviously quite dissimilar to scientific knowledge. Here we are concerned with the enhancement of personal qualities in the therapist – his integrity, humanity, compassion, sensitivity, and so forth. The trainee therapist attempts to improve these qualities in himself by imitating his successful, experienced counterpart, receiving good clinical supervision, and increasing his own self-awareness.

The scientific dimension of psychotherapy is relatively more straightforward in the sense that a body of scientific knowledge is available to the therapist and its application can lead to more effective clinical practice. Unfortunately, the bridge between research and practice is slender and there tends to be only minimal impact of scientific knowledge on clinical work. The gulf between researcher and practitioner operates in both directions in that practising psychotherapists are insufficiently curious to explore the research aspects of their work and pose the sort of questions that could profitably be offered to the research investigator. The latter, as a result, may pursue studies of issues that are appealing not because of their clinical relevance but because they are more easily amenable to his scientific methodology.

The psychotherapist, it would seem to me, has an obligation to (1) scrutinise his own clinical practice and its efficacy at all times and (2) remain abreast of, and be able to appraise critically, new research developments and results.

Critical appraisal of the literature on psychotherapy is particularly important in the light of the many new therapies and techniques promulgated. The history of psychiatry is unfortunately riddled with dead therapies; the picture is of a great mass of ditched treatments many of which had a prominent heyday. This is not to argue that therapists should bolt the door against any new developments or methods but that they should evaluate any innovation critically and impartially. The encounter group movement illustrates the point. In the 1960s, arising from the excitement of the human potential movement, the encounter group took off spectacularly. Branded as a solution to all manner of problems, both personal and social, little note was taken of its actual effectiveness or of its potential to cause harm.

It was only with the study conducted at Stanford University in the early 1970s and published as *Encounter Groups: First Facts* (see Chapter 5) that proper scientific knowledge became available. We noted in the previous chapter that a critical finding of this study was the casualty rate. Some nine per cent of the student volunteers who participated were judged to have deteriorated as a result of their experience. Most of these casualties belonged to groups led by charismatic, strong and aggressive leaders who energetically fostered emotional catharsis and self-disclosure. Despite the quality and the scope of the Stanford study, its findings were resisted by some therapists, notably William Schutz, a prominent protagonist of the encounter group. He commented: 'unfortunate is the seriously flawed yet widely publicised study of Yalom, Miles and Lieberman which under the guise of well-controlled research comes up with outrageous findings about 'casualties' of encounter groups, leaving the impression that joining a group is a quick channel to the mental hospital'.[5]

Shifts of attitude among therapists are uncommon and this is perhaps not unexpected. It is understandable, as we mentioned in Chapter 3, that a therapist who identifies closely with his methods and theories will tend to guard them zealously. If he should ascertain that his theoretical foundation is erroneous or that his clinical methods are ineffective, he may feel that he has no choice but to throw the therapy out of the window – a form of professional suicide. We can compare this with the psychiatrist who is accustomed to prescribe a particular drug. When he learns from research that the drug is either useless, dangerous or has been superseded by something better, he is likely to cease using that drug and to prescribe alternative medication. But even here the picture is not straightforward. We need only note how long it has taken for the highly addictive group of barbiturate drugs to be relinquished by some clinicians. Prescribing habits die hard. Similarly, the psychotherapist is reluctant to budge from a position which provides him with a measure of security. He may therefore well deflect any new knowledge which contradicts that position.

In emphasising the therapist's obligation to be aware of and open to scientific developments in his field, I do not advocate an 'empirical revolution'. Foolhardy would be the therapist who relies exclusively on every finding in research that he comes across. Psychotherapy must necessarily rely on theoretical frameworks. Deprived of them, the therapist would rapidly sink into the quagmire that would result. Such frameworks are needed but they should be sufficiently flexible and pliable to accommodate the fruits of new knowledge. Psychotherapy can ill afford dogma. Indeed, dogma, I would contend, is its chief enemy. Moreover, therapists with a blinkered, unswerving allegiance to a particular therapeutic theory and practice who fail to pause and consider how new knowledge may influence their work, are acting unethically.

The therapist's obligations to society include his proper professional conduct. Amid a number of requirements in this regard, let me focus on two. Psychotherapists should relate to one another in a dignified and respectful manner, even in the face of radical differences they may have in their approach to the subject. The most common warring groups are psychoanalysts and behavioural therapists. It is fashionable in some quarters to dub the latter as glorified technicians, brainwashers, people without soul who treat patients as little more than machines. On the other hand, some critics persist in swingeing attacks on psychoanalysis, criticising it for its alleged lack of a scientific base, and its supposed ineffectiveness. But how do they go about this? They distort research data to suit their contention and use almost vitriolic language to make their points. In so doing, they display not only a notably unscientific approach but also a prejudiced view against any therapy with even a whiff of the psychoanalytic in it; meanwhile, their reverence for behaviour therapy remains profound.

If psychotherapy is to be regarded as a professional discipline, its members need to drop their uncompromising and blinkered views and adopt a flexible and open-minded approach. In the absence of such flexibility, it is almost impossible for the profession of psychotherapy to have any credibility.

Credibility is also undermined by the ludicrous way in which some psychotherapists assume an expertise which their more modest counterparts would shy away from. One example will suffice. An American psychoanalyst has written in a book on Richard Nixon that:

Nixon's fascination with potato mashing has psychoanalytic implications. Most children his age release aggression through play, athletics, and peer-group activities. What is unusual in Richard is that he chose to release his energy through potato mashing, which was one way to be close to his mother, to win her love, to be her favourite. The extent and intensity of this activity might suggest that his potato mashing was a form of aggression against an inanimate object which was a substitute for people. Potato mashing allowed this apparently tense and moody child to express his unconscious anger.[6]

At least the author concedes that Nixon was 'apparently' tense and moody as a child because it is clear from the text that the author has never met the ex-President. In the absence of a personal interview, the analyst claims that his book is an attempt to understand the psychodynamics that determine Nixon's make-up and that this attempt rests upon a vast body of scientific knowledge. In my view, there can be little that is scientific about such comments as 'Nixon sought failure', and 'The need to fail stemmed from his guilt feelings which were rooted in his early sexual yearning for his mother'. I should mention that psychohistory is a reasonable pursuit as testified by such work as Erik Erikson's studies of Ghandi and Martin Luther. The issue is the inclination of some psychotherapists to pretend to an expertise which simply does not exist.

In summary, if psychotherapy is to be taken seriously, its practitioners have a responsibility to cease their feuds, be more honest about what they can and cannot do, be more modest about the state of knowledge of the subject, and inform the public intelligently and accurately about the nature of their activities. I leave the last word to Professor Judd Marmor, a distinguished American psychotherapist and past president of the American Psychiatric Association. He comments:

It is probably too much to hope that we shall some day see an end to the passionate and partisan proclamations of the superiority of one technique over all others, but it is to be hoped that the psychotherapies of the future will show increasing flexibility ... and that we will strive towards the goal of a unified science of psychotherapy[7].

I myself remain optimistic that the goal Marmor refers to can be reached. Despite their predilection for a particular school, a growing number of psychotherapists show hints of being prepared to exchange views openly and respectfully with colleagues who have a different orientation. The so-called breed of 'eclectic therapist' – who is ready to make use of concepts and techniques, irrespective of their source – multiplies apace. The voice of responsible consumerism is making itself heard in such a way that psychotherapists (and indeed all the helping professions) have little choice but to attend. Psychotherapy research in recent years has made, and continues to make, a substantial contribution to the subject and is attracting the interest of the average practitioner more than ever before. Finally, psychotherapists are becoming increasingly sensitive to the ethical dimension of their activities and recognising that their treatment of patients always occurs within a context of values. A 'unified science of psychotherapy' is possible.

Chapter references

Preface

1 Corsini, R. J. (ed.) *Handbook of Innovative Psychotherapies*. Wiley, New York, 1981.

2 Garfield, S. L. and Bergin, A. E. (eds.) *Handbook of Psychotherapy and Behaviour Change*. Wiley, New York, 1978.

Chapter 1

1 Bloch, S. (ed.) *An Introduction to the Psychotherapies*. Oxford University Press, Oxford, 1979.

2 We should note that therapists who belong to the behavioural school are a notable exception in this regard as their practices have undergone substantial modification as a result of systematic empirical research.

3 Freud, S. (1913) 'On Beginning the Treatment'. *Standard Edition*, 12, Hogarth Press, London, 1978, p. 123.

4 Klerman, G. L., Dimascio, A., Weissman, M., Prusoff, B. and Paykel, E. S. 'Treatment of Depression by Drugs and Psychotherapy'. *American Journal of Psychiatry*, 1974, 131, 186–191.

5 Beck, A. T. *Cognitive Therapy and the Emotional Disorders*. New American Library, New York, 1979.

6 Strupp, H. H. 'Psychotherapy Research and Practice: An Overview'. In (eds. S. Garfield and A. Bergin) *Handbook of Psychotherapy and Behaviour Change*. Wiley, New York, 1978, p. 3.

7 Noyes, L. C. *Modern Clinical Psychiatry*. Saunders, Philadelphia, 1977, p. 767.

8 Storr, A. *The Art of Psychotherapy*. Secker and Warburg and Heinemann Medical Books, London, 1979, p. vii.

9 Szasz, T. *The Myth of Psychotherapy*. Oxford University Press, Oxford, 1979, p. 3.

10 Lieberman, M., Yalom, I., and Miles, M. *Encounter Groups: First Facts*. Basic Books, New York, 1973.

11   Frank, J. 'Therapeutic Factors in Psychotherapy'. *American Journal of Psychotherapy*, 1971, 25, 350–361.

12   Frank, J. *Persuasion and Healing: A Comparative Study of Psychotherapy.* Johns Hopkins University Press, London, 1973.

13   For a review of the research literature see: Wilkins, W. 'Expectancy of Therapeutic Gain: An Empirical and Conceptual Critique'. *Journal of Consulting and Clinical Psychology*, 1973, 40, 69–77.

14   A brief and clearly written introductory text on crisis intervention is Ewing, C. P. *Crisis Intervention as Psychotherapy.* Oxford University Press, New York, 1978.

15   Erikson, E. H. *Identity, Youth and Crisis.* Norton, New York, 1968.

16   See: Caplan, G. *An Approach to Community Mental Health.* Tavistock, London, 1961 and Caplan, G. *Principles of Preventive Psychiatry*, Basic Books, New York, 1964.

17   See: Bloch, S. 'Supportive Psychotherapy'. In (ed. S. Bloch) *An Introduction to the Psychotherapies.* Oxford University Press, Oxford, 1979, p. 196 for an account of this form of psychotherapy.

18   See: Argyle, M., Bryant, B. and Trower, P. 'Social Skills Training and Psychotherapy'. *Psychological Medicine*, 1974, 4, 435–443.

19   Freud, S. (1937) 'Analysis Terminable and Interminable'. *Standard Edition*, 23, Hogarth Press, London, 1978, p. 250.

20   See: Freud, A. (1936) *The Ego and the Mechanisms of Defence.* Hogarth Press, London, 1976.

Chapter 2

1   Frank, J. D. 'Psychotherapy: The Restoration of Morale'. *American Journal of Psychiatry*, 1974, 131, 271–274.

2   Aronson, H. and Weintraub, W. 'Certain Initial Variables as Predictors of Change with Classical Psychoanalysis. *Journal of Abnormal Psychology*, 1969, 74, 490–497.

3   Siegel, S. M., Rootes, M. and Traub, A. 'Symptom Change and Prognosis in Clinical Psychotherapy'. *Archives of General Psychiatry*, 1977, 34, 321–329.

4   Hoehn-Saric, R., Frank, J. D., Stone, A. R. and Imber, S. D. 'Prognosis in Psychotherapeutic Patients'. *American Journal of Psychotherapy*, 1969, 23, 252–259.

5   Stone, A. R., Frank, J. D., Nash, E. H. and Imber, S. D. 'An Intensive Five-Year Follow-Up Study of Treated Psychiatric Out-Patients'. *Journal of Nervous and Mental Disease*, 1961, 133, 410–422.

6 Psychosomatic disorders are characterised by physical symptoms that are caused or made worse by emotional factors.

7 Kellner, R. 'Psychotherapy in Psychosomatic Disorders. A Survey of Controlled Studies'. *Archives of General Psychiatry*, 1975, 32, 1021–1028.

8 Kantrowitz, J. L., Singer, J. G. and Knapp, P. H. 'Methodology for a Prospective Study of Suitability for Psychoanalysis: the Role of Psychological Tests'. *Psychoanalytic Quarterly*, 1975, 44, 371–391.

9 Frank, J. D. 'The Dynamics of the Psychotherapeutic Relationship: Determinants and Effects of the Therapist's Influence. *Psychiatry*, 1959, 22, 17–39.

10 Bloch, S., Qualls, B., Yalom, I. and Zimmerman, E. 'Patients' Expectations of Therapeutic Improvement and Their Outcomes'. *American Journal of Psychiatry*, 1976, 133, 1457–1460.

11 Garfield, S. L. and Wolpin, M. 'Expectations Regarding Psychotherapy'. *Journal of Nervous and Mental Disease*, 1963, 137, 353–362.

12 Heine, R. W. (ed.) *The Student Physician as Psychotherapist*. Chicago University Press, Chicago, 1962.

13 Hoehn-Saric, R., Frank, J. D., Imber, S. D., Nash, E. H., Stone, A. R. and Battle, C. C. 'Systematic Preparation of Patients for Psychotherapy – 1. Effects on Therapy and Outcome'. *Journal of Psychiatric Research*, 1964, 2, 267–281.

14 Sloane R. B., Cristol, A. H., Pepernik, M. C. and Staples, F. R. 'Role Preparation and Expectation of Improvement in Psychotherapy'. *Journal of Nervous and Mental Disease*, 1970, 150, 18–26.

15 Yalom, I. D., Houts, P. S., Newell, G. and Rand, K. H. 'Preparation of Patients for Group Therapy. A Controlled Study'. *Archives of General Psychiatry*, 167, 17, 416–427.

16 Dewald, P. A. *Psychotherapy: A Dynamic Approach*. Blackwell Scientific, Oxford, 1969.

17 Barron, F. 'An Ego-Strength Scale which Predicts Response to Psychotherapy'. *Journal of Consulting Psychology*, 1953, 17, 327–333.

18 Klopfer, B., Kirkner, F. J., Wisham, W. and Baker, G. 'Rorschach Prognostic Rating Scale'. *Journal of Projective Techniques*, 1951, 15, 425–428.

19 Luborsky, L., Mintz, J., Auerbach, A., Christoph, P. *et al.* 'Predicting the Outcome of Psychotherapy'. *Archives of General Psychiatry*, 1980, 37, 471–481.

20 Auerbach, A. H., Luborsky, L., and Johnson, M. 'Clinicians' Predictions of Outcome of Psychotherapy: A Trial of a Prognostic Index'. *American Journal of Psychiatry*, 1972, 128, 830–835.

Chapter 3

1 Freud, S. (1926). 'The Question of Lay Analysis'. *Standard Edition*, 20, Hogarth Press, London, 1978, p. 179–250.

2 Freud, S. (1912). 'Recommendations to Physicians Practising Psychoanalysis'. *Standard Edition*, 12, Hogarth Press, London, 1978, p. 111–120.

3 Rogers is a prolific writer but the reader can obtain a good understanding of his ideas by referring to two important books: *On Becoming a Person*, Houghton Mifflin, Boston, 1961 and *Client-Centered Therapy*, Constable, London, 1979.

4 Mitchell, K., Bozarth, J., and Krauft, C. 'A Reappraisal of the Therapeutic Effectiveness of Accurate Empathy, Non-possessive Warmth and Genuineness'. In (eds. A. Gurman and A. Razin) *Effective Psychotherapy*. Pergamon Press, Oxford, 1977.

5 Luborsky, L., Chandler, M., Auerbach, A. and Cohen, J. 'Factors Influencing the Outcome of Psychotherapy'. *Psychological Bulletin*, 1971, 75, 145–195.

6 Auerbach, A. H. and Johnson, M. 'Research on the Therapist's Level of Experience'. In (eds. A. Gurman and A. Razin) *Effective Psychotherapy*. Pergamon Press, Oxford, 1977.

7 Luborsky, L., Singer, B. and Luborsky, L. 'Comparative Studies of Psychotherapies: Is it true that everyone has won and all must have prizes?' *Archives of General Psychiatry*, 1975, 32, 995–1008.

8 Sloane, R. B., Staples, F. R., Cristol, A. H., Yorkston, N. J., and Whipple, K. *Psychotherapy Versus Behaviour Therapy*. Harvard University Press, Cambridge: Mass., 1975.

9 Lieberman, M. A., Yalom, I. D. and Miles, M. B. *Encounter Groups: First Facts*. Basic Books, New York, 1973.

10 Freud, S. (1937). 'Analysis Terminable and Interminable'. *Standard Edition*, 23, Hogarth Press, London, 1978, p. 211–253.

11 Strupp, H. H. and Hadley, S. W. 'Specific vs Nonspecific Factors in Psychotherapy. A Controlled Study of Outcome'. *Archives of General Psychiatry*, 1979, 36, 1125–1136.

Chapter 4

1 Freud, S. *The Standard Edition of the Complete Psychological Works*. Hogarth Press and the Institute of Psychoanalysis, London, 1978. (Penguin Books is presently publishing the Pelican Freud Library under the editorship of Angela Richards.)

2 Freud, S. (1910). 'Five Lectures on Psychoanalysis'. *Standard Edition*, 11, Hogarth Press, London, 1978, p. 38.

3 Freud, S. (1900). 'The Interpretation of Dreams'. *Standard Edition*, 4–5. Hogarth Press, London, 1978.

4 Freud, S. (1904). 'The Psychopathology of Everyday Life'. *Standard Edition*, 6, Hogarth Press, London, 1978.

5 Freud, S. (1905). 'Three Essays on Sexuality'. *Standard Edition*, 7, Hogarth Press, London, 1978.

6 Freud, S. (1923). 'The Ego and the Id'. *Standard Edition*, 19, Hogarth Press, London, 1978.

7 Freud, S. (1910). 'Five Lectures on Psychoanalysis'. *Standard Edition*, 11, Hogarth Press, London, p. 33.

8 Freud, S. (1926). 'The Question of Lay Analysis'. *Standard Edition*, 20, Hogarth Press, London, p. 224.

9 There is a growing literature on brief psychoanalytically-oriented psychotherapy. The following texts are recommended: Balint, M., Ornstein, P. H. and Balint, E. *Focal Psychotherapy: An Example of Applied Psychoanalysis*. Tavistock, London, 1972., Davanloo, H. *Basic Principles and Technique in Short-term Dynamic Psychotherapy*. Spectrum, New York, 1978., Malan, D. H. *The Frontier of Brief Psychotherapy*. Plenum Press, New York, 1976., and Sifneos, P. E. *Short-term Psychotherapy and Emotional Crisis*. Harvard University Press, Cambridge: Mass., 1972.

10 Sullivan, H. S. *Conceptions of Modern Psychiatry*. Norton, New York, 1953. Contains a useful critical appraisal of Sullivan's theories by Patrick Mullahy.

11 Fairbairn, W. D. R. *Psychoanalytic Studies of the Personality*. Tavistock, London, 1952.

12 See: Segal, H. *Introduction to the Work of Melanie Klein*. Heinemann Medical Books, London, 1964, for a clear account of Klein's approach. Segal's book on Klein in the Fontana/Collins Modern Masters Series, published in 1979, covers similar ground.

13 Fromm has written extensively; his most influential books include: *Escape from Freedom*. Holt, Rinehart and Winston, New York, 1941; *Man for Himself*. Holt, Rinehart and Winston, New York, 1947., and *The Sane Society*. Holt, Rinehart and Winston, New York, 1955.

14 See: Hall, C. S. and Lindzey, G. *Theories of Personality*. (Chapter 9), Wiley, New York, 1978 for an excellent account of the ideas of these therapists; and for a comprehensive bibliography of their works.

15 See: Laing, R. D. *The Divided Self*. Penguin, Harmondsworth, 1965 and *Self and Others*. Penguin, Harmondsworth, 1971.

16 May, R., Angel, E. and Ellenberger, H. F. (eds.) *Existence*. Basic Books, New York, 1958.

17   See: Maslow, A. *The Farther Reaches of Human Nature*. Viking Press, New York, 1971 and *Towards a Psychology of Being*. Van Nostrand, Princeton, 1968., Rogers, C. *On Becoming a Person*. Houghton-Mifflin, Boston, 1961 and *Client-Centred Therapy*. Constable, London, 1979., and Allport, G. W. *Pattern and Growth in Personality*. Holt, Rinehart and Winston, New York, 1961.

18   For a sound discussion of existentialism see: Macquarrie, J. *Existentialism*. Penguin, Harmondsworth, 1977.

19   Yalom, I. D. *Existential Psychotherapy*. Basic Books, New York, 1980.

20   For Rogers, see ref. 17.
      Useful introductory accounts on Gestalt therapy are: Perls, F., Hefferline, R. F. and Goodman, P. *Gestalt Therapy*. Julian Press, 1958 and Fagan, J. and Shepherd, I. L. *Gestalt Therapy Now*. Science and Behaviour Books, Palo Alto: Calif., 1970. Frankl, V. *Man's Search for Meaning. An Introduction to Logotherapy*. Pocket Books, New York, 1972 is an eminently readable summary of Frankl's approach.

21   Bugental, J. F. T. *The Search for Authenticity: An Existential-Analytic Approach to Psychotherapy*. Holt, Rinehart and Winston, New York, 1965.

22   Frankl, V. *Man's Search for Meaning. An Introduction to Logotherapy*. Pocket Books, New York, 1972, pp. 206–207.

23   Wolpe, J. *Psychotherapy by Reciprocal Inhibition*. Stanford University Press, Stanford: Calif., 1958.

24   Helpful introductory texts to behavioural therapy are Rimm, D. C. and Masters, J. C. *Behaviour Therapy: Techniques and Empirical Findings*. Academic Press, New York, 1974 and Marks, I. M. *Cure and Care of Neuroses. Theory and Practice of Behavioural Psychotherapy*. Wiley, New York, 1981.

25   Beck, A. T. *Cognitive Therapy and the Emotional Disorders*. International Universities Press, New York, 1976.

26   Ellis, A. *Reason and Emotion in Psychotherapy*. Lyle Stuart, New York, 1962. Also see his chapter in (ed. R. Corsini) *Current Psychotherapies*. Peacock, Itasca: Ill., 1973, pp. 167–206.

27   See: Watson, J. B. *Behaviourism*. University of Chicago Press, Chicago, 1963 and Watson, J. B. and Rayner, R. 'Conditioned Emotional Reactions'. *Journal of Experiential Psychology*, 1920, 3, 1–14.

28   Marks, I. M. 'Cure and Care of Neurosis'. *Psychological Medicine*, 1979, 9, 629–660.

29   Skinner, B. F. *Science and Human Behaviour*. Macmillan, New York, 1953.

30   See: Kazdin, A. E. *The Token Economy: A Review and Evaluation*. Plenum Press, New York, 1977.

31 Bandura, A. *Principles of Behaviour Modification*. Holt, Rinehart and Winston, New York, 1969.

Chapter 5

1 Rosenbaum, M. and Berger, M. (eds.) *Group Psychotherapy and Group Function*. Basic Books, New York, 1974 contains several interesting chapters relevant to the history of group psychotherapy.

2 Freud, S. (1921). 'Group Psychology and the Analysis of the Ego'. *Standard Edition*, 18, Hogarth Press, London, 1978.

3 See: Yalom, I. D. *The Theory and Practice of Group Psychotherapy*. Basic Books, New York, 1975 for what is certainly the best account of this approach to group therapy.

4 Bion, W. R. *Experiences in Groups*. Tavistock, London, 1961.

5 See the following for other applications of the group approach:
– Two helpful books on Gestalt therapy are Perls, F., Hefferline, R. F. and Goodman, P. *Gestalt Therapy*. Julian Press, New York, 1958 and Fagan, J. and Shepherd, I. L. *Gestalt Therapy Now*. Science and Behaviour Books, Palo Alto: Calif., 1970.

– Berne, E. *Principles of Group Treatment*. Oxford University Press, Oxford, 1966 is an account of the application of transactional analysis to groups.

– Jones, M. *Social Psychiatry in Practice: The Idea of the Therapeutic Community*. Penguin, Harmondsworth, 1968, and Hinshelwood, R. D. and Manning, N. (eds.) *Therapeutic Communities: Reflections and Progress*. Routledge and Kegan Paul, London, 1979, read in conjunction are useful texts.

– Blatner, H. A. *Acting-In. Practical Applications of Psychodramatic Methods*. Springer, New York, 1973 is a clear, brief introduction to psychodrama and contains a good bibliography.

6 Bateson, G., Jackson, D., Haley, J. and Weakland, J. 'Towards a Theory of Schizophrenia'. *Behavioural Science*, 1956, 1, 251–264.

7 Lidz, T. *The Origin and Treatment of Schizophrenic Disorders*. Basic Books, New York, 1973.

8 Ackerman, N. W. *The Psychodynamics of Family Life*. Basic Books, New York, 1958.

9 Speck, R. V. and Attneave, C. 'Network Therapy'. In (ed. J. Haley) *Changing Families*. Grune and Stratton, New York, 1971.

10 Beels, C. C. and Ferber, A. 'Family Therapy. A Review'. *Family Process*, 1969, 8, 280–318.

11   Satir, V. *Peoplemaking*. Souvenir Press, London, 1978, p. 197.
      Also see her *Conjoint Family Therapy. A Guide to Theory and Technique*.
      Science and Behaviour Books, Palo Alto: Calif., 1964.

12   Minuchin, S. *Families and Family Therapy*. Tavistock, London, 1974.

13   Haley, J. and Hoffman, L. *Techniques of Family Therapy*. Basic Books,
      New York, 1967.

14   Paul, N. 'The role of Mourning and Empathy in Conjoint Marital
      Therapy'. In (eds. G. Zuk and I. Boszormenyi-Nagy) *Family Therapy and
      Disturbed Families*. Science and Behaviour Books, Palo Alto, 1967.

15   MacGregor, R., Ritchie, A. M., Serrano, A. C., Schuster, F. P.,
      MacDonald, E. C. and Goolishian, H. A. *Multiple Impact Therapy with
      Families*. McGraw-Hill, New York, 1964.

16   Dominian, J. 'Marital Therapy.' In (ed. S. Bloch) *An Introduction to the
      Psychotherapies*. Oxford University Press, Oxford, 1979.

17   See: Masters, W. H. and Johnson, V. E. *Human Sexual Inadequacy*.
      Churchill, London, 1970 and Kaplan, H. S. *The New Sex Therapy*.
      Baillière, Tindall, London, 1975 (also in Penguin, Harmondsworth,
      1978).

18   Dicks, H. V. *Marital Tensions*. Routledge and Kegan Paul, London,
      1967. (Chapters 4–7 are especially valuable as an introduction to the
      psychoanalytic approach.)

19   Stuart, R. B. 'Operant-Interpersonal Treatment for Marital Discord'.
      Journal of Consulting and Clinical Psychology, 1969, 33, 675–682.

20   Gurman, A. S. and Kniskern, D. P. 'Research on Marital and Family
      Therapy: Progress, Perspectives and Prospect'. In (eds. S. Garfield and
      A. Bergin) *Handbook of Psychotherapy and Behaviour Change*. Wiley,
      New York, 1978.

21   Rogers, C. Interpersonal Relationships: Year 2000. *Journal of Applied
      Behavioural Science*, 1968, 4, 265–280.

22   *Psychology Today*, 1975, No. 2, p. 31.

23   Lieberman, M. A. and Gardner, J. R. 'Institutional Alternatives to
      Psychotherapy'. *Archives of General Psychiatry*, 1976, 33, 157–162.

24   Parloff, M. 'Assessing the Effects of Head-Shrinking and Mind-
      Expanding'. *International Journal of Group Psychotherapy*, 1970, 20,
      14–24.

25   Meador, B. D. and Rogers, C. R. 'Client-Centered Therapy'. In (ed. R.
      Corsini) *Current Psychotherapies*. Peacock, Itasca: Ill., 1977.

26   Rogers, C. 'What Happens in an Encounter Group?' *Psychology Today*,
      1975, 2, 21–26.
      Also see his *On Encounter Groups*. Penguin, Harmondsworth, 1973.

27 Lieberman, M. A., Yalom, I. D. and Miles, M. B. *Encounter Groups: First Facts*. Basic Books, New York, 1973.

28 See for example: Lieberman, M. A. and Borman, L. D. *Self-Help Groups for Coping with Crisis*. Jossey-Bass, San Francisco, 1979 and Robinson, D. and Henry, S. *Self-Help and Health: Mutual Aid for Modern Problems*. Martin Robertson, London, 1977.

29 Killilea, M. 'Mutual Help Organizations: Interpretations in the Literature'. In (eds. Caplan, G. and Killilea, M.) *Support Systems and Mutual Help: Multidisciplinary Explorations*. Grune and Stratton, New York, 1976.

Chapter 6

1 Eysenck, H. J. 'The Effects of Psychotherapy: An Evaluation'. *Journal of Consulting Psychology*, 1952, 16, 319–324.

2 See: Bergin, A. E. and Lambert, M. J. 'The Evaluation of Therapeutic Outcomes'. In (eds. S. L. Garfield and A. E. Bergin) *Handbook of Psychotherapy and Behaviour Change*. Wiley, New York, 1978.

3 See for example: Garfield, S. L. and Bergin, A. E. (eds.) *Handbook of Psychotherapy and Behaviour Change*. Wiley, New York, 1978; Gurman, A. S. and Razin, A. M. *Effective Psychotherapy: A Handbook of Research*. Pergamon Press, New York, 1977 and Meltzoff, J. and Kornreich, M. *Research in Psychotherapy*. Atherton Press, New York, 1970.

4 Waskow, I. E. and Parloff, M. B. (eds.) *Psychotherapy Change Measures*. DHEW, Washington D.C., 1975.

5 See for example: Rachman, S. J. and Wilson, G. T. *The Effects of Psychological Therapy*. Pergamon Press, Oxford, 1980.

6 Bergin, A. E. 'The Evaluation of Therapeutic Outcomes'. In (eds. A. E. Bergin and S. L. Garfield) *Handbook of Psychotherapy and Behaviour Change*. Wiley, New York, 1971. See also reference 2.

7 Meltzoff, J. and Kornreich, M. *Research in Psychotherapy*. Atherton Press, New York, 1970.

8 Smith, M. L. and Glass, C. V. 'Meta-Analysis of Psychotherapy Outcome Studies'. *American Psychologist*, 1977, 32, 752–760.

9 Luborsky, L., Singer, B. and Luborsky, L. 'Comparative Studies of Psychotherapies: Is it true that everyone has won and all must have prizes? *Archives of General Psychiatry*, 1975, 32, 995–1008.

10 Sloane, R. B., Staples, F. R., Cristol, A. H., Yorkston, N. J. and Whipple, K. *Short-term Analytically Oriented Psychotherapy versus Behaviour Therapy*. Harvard University Press, Cambridge: Mass., 1975.

11 Interestingly, Abraham Kardiner writes in his *My Analysis With Freud* (Norton, New York, 1977) that: 'Freud was always infuriated whenever I would say to him that you could not do harm with psychoanalysis. He said: "When you say that, you also say it cannot do any good. Because if you cannot do any harm, how can you do good?"'

12 Hadley, S. W. and Strupp, H. H. 'Contemporary Views of Negative Effects in Psychotherapy'. *Archives of General Psychiatry*, 1976, 33, 1291–1302.

13 Garfield, S. L. 'Research on Client Variables in Psychotherapy'. In (eds. S. L. Garfield and A. E. Bergin) *Handbook of Psychotherapy and Behaviour Change*. Wiley, New York, 1978.

14 See for example: Sloane, R. B., Cristol, A. H., Pepernik, M. C. and Staples, F. R. 'Role Preparation and Expectation of Improvement in Psychotherapy'. *Journal of Nervous and Mental Disease*, 1970, 150, 18–26.

15 Orlinsky, D. E. and Howard, K. I. 'The Relation of Process to Outcome in Psychotherapy'. In (eds. S. L. Garfield and A. E. Bergin) *Handbook of Psychotherapy and Behaviour Change*. Wiley, New York, 1978.

16 Liberman, R. 'A Behavioural Approach to Group Dynamics. II Reinforcing and Prompting Hostility to the Therapist in Group Therapy'. *Behaviour Therapy*, 1970, 1, 312–327.

Chapter 7

1 Redlich, F. and Mollica, R. F. 'Overview: Ethical Issues in Contemporary Psychiatry'. *American Journal of Psychiatry*, 1976, 133, 125–136.

2 Goldberg, C. *Therapeutic Partnership: Ethical Concerns in Psychotherapy*. Springer, New York, 1977.

3 Hadley, S. W. and Strupp, H. H. 'Contemporary Views of Negative Effects in Psychotherapy: An Integrated Account'. *Archives of General Psychiatry*, 1976, 33, 1291–1302.

4 Freud, S. (1937) 'Analysis Terminable and Interminable'. *Standard Edition*, 23, Hogarth Press, London, 1978.

5 Schutz, W. C. 'Encounter'. In (ed. R. Corsini) *Current Psychotherapies*. Peacock, Itasca: Ill., 1977, p. 432.

6 Abrahamson, D. *Nixon vs Nixon: An Emotional Tragedy*. Farrar Straus, Giroux, New York, 1977.

7 Marmor, J. 'Recent trends in psychotherapy'. *American Journal of Psychiatry*, 1980, 137, 409–416.

Suggestions for further reading

The list below should be used in conjunction with the references that follow each chapter. Some references mentioned there are repeated because they are especially important. The list is only a selection of the vast number of books available, but it should be helpful for the reader who wishes to pursue some of the topics discussed in this book.

Historical

Ellenberger, H. *The Discovery of the Unconscious*. Basic Books, New York, 1970.

A major, scholarly history of dynamic psychotherapy which covers such figures as Janet, Freud, Jung and Adler.

Roazen, P. *Freud and his Followers*. Penguin, Harmondsworth, 1979.

An eminently readable account of the history of psychoanalysis.

Szasz, T. *The Myth of Psychotherapy*. Oxford University Press, Oxford, 1979.

A highly thought-provoking view of psychotherapy, presented in an historical context.

General texts

Bloch, S. (ed.) *An Introduction to the Psychotherapies*. Oxford University Press, Oxford, 1979.

The first chapter by Jerome Frank answers the question 'What is Psychotherapy?' Other chapters are on individual long-term psychotherapy, group therapy, sex therapy, marital therapy, family therapy, crisis intervention, supportive therapy and behaviour therapy.

Brown, D. and Pedder, J. *Introduction to Psychotherapy: An Outline of Psychodynamic Principles and Practice*. Tavistock, London, 1979.

The first section of the book is concerned with psychodynamic theory; the second with its application in various forms of psychotherapy including family and marital therapy, individual therapy, group therapy and social therapy.

Frank, J. D. *Persuasion and Healing*. Johns Hopkins University Press, London, 1973.

A classic by a pioneer of psychotherapy research, the book examines the basic principles on which all forms of psychological healing are based.

Storr, A. *The Art of Psychotherapy*. Secker and Warburg and Heinemann Medical Books, London, 1979.

    A clear introduction to the practice of individual psychotherapy based on psychoanalytic principles.

Wolberg, L. R. *The Technique of Psychotherapy*. Grune and Stratton, New York, 1977.

    Encyclopaedic volume which covers virtually the entire field of psychotherapy.

Schools of psychotherapy

The literature here is voluminous. I have made my selection – a combination of primary and secondary sources – on the basis of what I believe will be the most helpful first step for the reader to take in pursuing a particular interest.

The Psychoanalytic Approach

Dewald, P. A. *Psychotherapy: A Dynamic Approach*. Basic Books, New York, 1969.

Freud, S. 'Introductory Lectures on Psychoanalysis'. *Standard Edition*, vols. 15 and 16, Hogarth Press, London, 1978.

Laplanche, J. and Pontalis, J. B. *The Language of Psychoanalysis*. Hogarth Press, London, 1973.

Rycroft, C. *A Critical Dictionary of Psychoanalysis*. Penguin, Harmondsworth, 1972.

Sandler, J., Dare, C. and Holder, A. *The Patient and the Analyst. The Basis of the Psychoanalytic Process*. Allen and Unwin, London, 1973.

Variations of the psychoanalytic approach
Alfred Alder

Adler, A. *Practice and Theory of Individual Psychology*. Harcourt, Brace, Jovanovich, New York, 1927.

Way, L. *Alfred Adler*. Penguin, Harmondsworth, 1956.

Karen Horney

Horney, K. *The Neurotic Personality of Our Time*. Norton, New York, 1937.

Horney, K. *New Ways in Psychoanalysis*. Norton, New York, 1939.

C. J. Jung

Fordham, F. *An Introduction to Jung's Psychology*. Penguin, Harmondsworth, 1966.

Storr, A. *Jung*. Fontana (Modern Masters), London, 1972.

Melanie Klein

Segal, H. *Introduction to the Work of Melanie Klein*. Heinemann Medical Books, London, 1964.

Segal, H. *Klein*. Fontana (Modern Masters), London, 1979.

David Malan

Malan, D. H. *The Frontier of Brief Psychotherapy*. Plenum Press, New York, 1976.

Malan, D. H. *Individual Psychotherapy and the Science of Psychodynamics*. Butterworth, London, 1979.

H. S. Sullivan

Sullivan, H. S. *Conceptions of Modern Psychiatry*. Norton, New York, 1953.

Sullivan, H. S. *The Interpersonal Theory of Psychiatry*. Norton, New York, 1953.

The humanist-existential approach

Frankl, V. *Man's Search for Meaning: An Introduction to Logotherapy*. Pocket Books, New York, 1972.

Laing, R. D. *The Divided Self*. Penguin, Harmondsworth, 1965.

May, R., Angel, E. and Ellenberger, H. F. (eds.) *Existence*. Basic Books, New York, 1958.

Perls, D., Hefferline, R. F. and Goodman, P. *Gestalt Therapy*. Julian Press, New York, 1958.

Rogers, C. R. *On Becoming a Person*. Houghton-Mifflin, Boston, 1961.

Yalom, I. D. *Existential Psychotherapy*. Basic Books, New York, 1980.

The behavioural approach

Bandura, A. *Principles of Behaviour Modification*. Holt, Rinehart and Winston, New York, 1969.

Marks, I. M. *The Cure and Care of Neuroses. Theory and Practice of Behavioural Psychotherapy*. Wiley, New York, 1981.

Rimm, D. C. and Masters, J. C. *Behaviour Therapy: Techniques and Empirical Findings*. Academic Press, New York, 1974.

Wolpe, J. *The Practice of Behaviour Therapy*. Pergamon, New York, 1973.

Yates, A. J. *Theory and Practice in Behaviour Therapy*. Wiley, New York, 1975.

The cognitive approach

Beck, A. T. *Cognitive Therapy and the Emotional Disorders*. International Universities Press, New York, 1976.

Ellis, A. *Reason and Emotion in Psychotherapy*. Lyle Stuart, New York, 1962.

Meichenbaum, D. *Cognitive Behaviour Modification*. Plenum Press, New York, 1977.

The group approach

Group therapy

Bion, W. R. *Experiences in Groups*. Tavistock, London, 1961.
 An account of Bion's theories on group process, which became central to the Tavistock model of group therapy.

Foulkes, S. N. and Anthony, E. J. *Group Psychotherapy. The Psychoanalytic Approach*. Penguin, Harmondsworth, 1965.

    A good introduction to the Foulkes approach which has been an important influence on British group therapists.

Whiteley, J. S. and Gordon, J. *Group Approaches in Psychiatry*. Routledge and Kegan Paul, London, 1979.

    A clearly written introduction to the use of the group approach in psychiatry generally, for instance therapeutic community, large and small groups, mental hospital as a small society.

Yalom, I. D. *The Theory and Practice of Group Psychotherapy*. Basic Books, New York, 1975.

    An excellent account of small group therapy which pays particular attention to the application of research findings to treatment.

Family therapy

Haley, J. and Hoffman, L. *Techniques of Family Therapy*. Basic Books, New York, 1967.

    An interesting presentation of the work of leading American therapists with detailed clinical illustrations.

Minuchin, S. *Families and Family Therapy*. Tavistock, London, 1974.

    A clear account of the structural approach; includes transcripts of therapy sessions.

Satir, V. M. *Conjoint Family Therapy*. Science and Behaviour Books, Palo Alto: Calif., 1964.

    Describes an approach whose focus is strongly on patterns of communication in families.

Skynner, A. C. R. *One Flesh, Separate Persons. Principles of Family and Marital Psychotherapy*. Constable, London, 1976.

    A comprehensive account of a popular British model of family (and marital) therapy.

Marital therapy

Dicks, H. V. *Marital Tensions*. Routledge and Kegan Paul, London, 1967.

    An introduction to the psychoanalytic approach to marital therapy.

Dominian, J. *Marital Breakdown*. Penguin, Harmondsworth, 1968.

    A useful brief text on marriage and its problems.

Skynner, A. R. C. See under *Family Therapy*.

Encounter groups

Lieberman, M. A., Yalom, I. D. and Miles, M. B. *Encounter Groups: First Facts*. Basic Books, New York, 1973.

    A thorough report on the most comprehensive research study on encounter groups to date.

Rogers, C. R. *On Encounter Groups*. Penguin, Harmondsworth, 1973.
  Brief but clear description of the processes that occur in the typical encounter group.

Self-help groups

Caplan, G. and Killilea, M. (eds.) *Support Systems and Mutual Help: Multi-Disciplinary Explorations*. Grune and Stratton, New York, 1976.
  The chapter by Killilea, a review of the literature on self-help groups, is especially valuable.

Lieberman, M. A. and Borman, L. D. *Self-help Groups for Coping with Crisis*. Jossey-Bass, San Francisco, 1979.
  A report of a series of research projects into various aspects of self-help groups.

Robinson, D. and Henry, S. *Self-help and Health: Mutual Aid for Modern Problems*. Martin Robertson, London, 1977.
  Useful introduction to the self-help concept.

Sex therapy

Kaplan, H. S. *The New Sex Therapy*. Baillière, Tindall, London, 1975.
  A masterful account of the treatment of sexual dysfunctions with clinical illustrations.

Masters, W. H. and Johnson, V. E. *Human Sexual Inadequacy*. Churchill, London, 1970.
  A classic in which the authors, pioneers in the field, describe their approach to sex therapy.

Research

Fisher, S. and Greenberg, R. P. *The Scientific Credibility of Freud's Theories and Therapy*. Basic Books, New York, 1977.
  A thorough survey of the scientific research literature on various aspects of psychoanalytic theory.

Garfield, S. L. and Bergin, A. E. (eds.) *Handbook of Psychotherapy and Behaviour Change*. Wiley, New York, 1978.
  The primary source book of research in psychotherapy; exceptionally comprehensive and detailed coverage.

Meltzoff, J. and Kornreich, M. *Research in Psychotherapy*. Atherton, New York, 1970.
  Similar to Garfield and Bergin but less comprehensive and somewhat out of date.

Index

143; key figure in rise of behavioural therapy, 85

Fairbairn, W. R. D. 63, 72, 122–3
family therapy, 16, 54, 106–19, 122; assessment of suitability, 108–9, 112; categorisation of disorders, 109–10; frequency of sessions, 112–13; growth of, 97; historical background, 107–8; multiple impact, 118–19; number of sessions, 113; as panacea for all ills, 108; practice of, 111–19; structural, 115–17; variations in approach, 112, 113–119
Ferber, A., 113–14
follow-up, importance of, 150
Foulkes, Michael, 98
Frank, Jerome, 6; on demoralisation, 26–7; factors common to all forms of therapy, 6–13, 15
Frankl, Viktor, 77, 81, 82, 84
Free association, 68, 72
Freud, Sigmund: on age limit for treatment, 37; on aims of psychoanalysis, 21; on analysis of therapists, 55; behavioural studies, 77; concepts and guidelines, 143–4; on distinguishing neuroses, 67; on dreams, 64–5, 69; early patients, 25; *The Ego and the Id*, 66; *Group Psychology and the Analysis of the Ego*, 98; on group therapy, 97–8; on human behaviour, 72; on hypnosis, 47–68; instinct theory, 123; *The Interpretation of Dreams*, 64; Jung's disagreement with, 72–4; on origins of neurosis, 77; *Psychopathology of Everyday Life*, 64, 65; on psychotherapy, 2; recommendation for assessment, 42; on relationship between therapist and patient, 166; on resistance, 71; responsibility for dissent, 163; school of psychotherapy, 16, 63; *Standard Edition of the Complete Psychological Works*, 64; on suitability of patients, 29; on therapists, 56; *Three Essays on Sexual Theory*, 65; on transference, 71

Fromm, Erich, 48, 75, 80; contribution to practice of psychotherapy, 77

Galveston, Texas, 118–19
Gamblers Anonymous, 136
Gay Movement, 136
General Medical Council, 57
Genuineness: of therapist, 49
Gestalt: school of psychotherapy, 16, 52, 63, 82, 83–4, 106
Glass, C.V.: effectiveness of treatment by meta-analysis, 152–3
Goldberg, Carl: contractual system, 165–6
group therapy, 16, 54, 97–142; founding of, 97; growth of, 97; main features of, 100–1; Second World War spur to development, 98; typical meeting, summary of, 103–5; *and see* encounter groups; family therapy; marital therapy; self help groups *and* small group therapy
guidance, 19
guilt, 80–1

Hadley, S. W., 166; survey of therapists, 158–9
Haley, Jay, 107; therapy approach, 117–18
head-shrinking, 128–9
Heidegger, Martin, 79, 80
homosexuality, 135–6, 139
Horney, Karen, 72; school of psychotherapy, 63, 75–7
Human Potential Movement, 26, 99
humanist-existential movement: roots of, 77; school of psychotherapy, 23, 48, 63, 77–85, 148
humanistic psychology, 78; mounting interest in, 99
Husserl, Edmund, 79
hypnosis, 47, 63, 68
hypochondria: importance in assessment, 32

id, 66, 67
illness: factors relating to for assessment, 30–2

OPUS

The Standing of Psychoanalysis

B. A. Farrell

Psychoanalysis is a notoriously controversial and confusing subject. What are we to make of it? In this book B. A. Farrell addresses the two central problems psychoanalysis raises. How believable is it as a doctrine? And how effective is it as a therapy?

He examines the credibility of the doctrine by asking whether it can be validated or invalidated by reference to fact. It is widely accepted that its chief support comes from the case material; and so he explores the character and strength of this support, especially in the light of some transcripts of an actual analysis. He also looks into the validity of psychoanalytic method as a tool of enquiry, and surveys the scientific studies that have been made of psychoanalytic generalisations and concepts. And he investigates the current debate about the therapeutic effectiveness of psychoanalysis.

Mr. Farrell's book offers a view of what Freud's 'discoveries' amount to, and what psychoanalysis has achieved. It places the subject on our contemporary map of knowledge and belief by showing where it stands in relation to science, history, psychiatry, objective psychology, and common sense. And by clarifying the controversy which surrounds the subject, it dispels some of the confusions which perplex experts and laymen alike.

A complete list of Oxford Paperbacks, including books in
the World's Classics, Past Masters, and OPUS series, can
be obtained from the General Publicity Department,
Oxford University Press, Walton Street, Oxford OX2 6DP.